Prentice Hall Advanced Reference Series

Physical and Life Sciences

Poisonous and Medicinal Plants

WILL H. BLACKWELL

Department of Botany
Miami University

illustrations by THOMAS J. COBBE

chapter 5 written by MARTHA J. POWELL

PRENTICE HALL
Englewood Cliffs, New Jersey 07632

Library of Congress Cataloging-in-Publication Data

Blackwell, Will H.
   Poisonous and medicinal plants / Will H. Blackwell ; illustrated by Thomas J. Cobbe ;
chapter 5 by Martha J. Powell.
     p.   cm. -- (Prentice Hall advanced reference series. Physical and life sciences)
    Includes indexes.
    ISBN 0-13-684127-9
    1. Poisonous plants. 2. Medicinal plants. 3. Poisonous plants—Toxicology.
4. Poisonous plants—United States. 5. Poisonous plants—United States. I. Title.
II. Series.
QK100.A1B57 1990
581.6′9—dc19
                                                     89-3771
                                                     CIP

Editorial/production supervision
  and interior design: GERTRUDE SZYFERBLATT
Cover design: WANDA LUBELSKA DESIGN
Manufacturing buyer: MARY ANN GLORIANDE
Page make-up: JUNE SANNS

Published by Prentice-Hall, Inc.
A Division of Simon & Schuster
Englewood Cliffs, New Jersey 07632

The publisher offers discounts on this book when ordered
in bulk quantities. For more information, write:
      Special Sales/College Marketing
      Prentice-Hall, Inc.
      College Technical and Reference Division
      Englewood Cliffs, NJ 07632

Printed in the United States of America

10 9 8 7 6 5 4 3 2 1

ISBN   0-13-684127-9

PRENTICE-HALL INTERNATIONAL (UK) LIMITED, *London*
PRENTICE-HALL OF AUSTRALIA PTY. LIMITED, *Sydney*
PRENTICE-HALL CANADA INC., *Toronto*
PRENTICE-HALL HISPANOAMERICANA, S.A., *Mexico*
PRENTICE-HALL OF INDIA PRIVATE LIMITED, *New Delhi*
PRENTICE-HALL OF JAPAN, INC., *Tokyo*
SIMON & SCHUSTER ASIA PTE. LTD., *Singapore*
EDITORA PRENTICE-HALL DO BRAZIL, LTDA., *Rio de Janeiro*

Contents

Foreword

The economic importance of plants to humans during our long history is immense. Prehistorically, the detection of plants as sources of food and for construction, fuel, fabric, and medicine attested to human's curiosity driven in large part by a quest to survive and flourish. Early searches for edible plants, for example, must have turned up those that besides being nonedible were also toxic, and between these extremes a large number of interesting plants that relieved pain or fought symptoms of disease when used in small amounts. From these early findings, refined and extended as they were passed from generation to generation, sprang industries and technologies based on products isolated from these plants and required by the developing needs of the civilized world. The use of these products and their analogs and semisynthetics reached a zenith in the late nineteenth century during a period of unprecedented growth and diversity of industrial phytochemistry, only to recede under competition from synthetic organic chemistry during the twentieth century. In many ways, humans nurtured in the European culture had become antithetic to their prehistory by becoming increasingly independent of plants in everyday life, and, as a consequence, they found little need to study them in any serious and rigorous way.

Only in recent years has this trend, certainly as it pertains to medicine, been forestalled. In the 1960s appeared *Green Medicine* by Margaret Kreig (Rand McNally & Company, Chicago, 1964), and in 1977 alone, three books were published that focused on plants in relation to human health: Lonnelle Aikman, *Nature's Healing Arts: From Folk Medicine to Modern Drugs* (National Geographic Society, Special Publications Division, Washington DC, 1977); Walter H. Lewis and Memory P.F. Elvin-Lewis, *Medical Botany: Plants Affecting Man's Health* (Wiley-Interscience, New York, 1977); and Julia F. Morton, *Major Medicinal Plants: Botany, Culture and*

Uses (Charles C. Thomas, Springfield, Illinois, 1977). These works were responding to a rekindled interest in the use of natural plant products for improved health, particularly among laymen. Their impact among professionals was more gradual, but even here there has been a renewed consideration of natural products in teaching and research about medicine and health in the final decades of the twentieth century, in essence reversing the neglect of the past 100 years.

No better indication can be found of this renewed concern than in Dr. Will H. Blackwell's account, *Poisonous and Medicinal Plants*. This timely and well-conceived text tells about plant poisons and medicines in a way that can be understood and appreciated by all readers, regardless of background. A major and important audience he has defined, however, is the undergraduate student whose appreciation of plants will be stimulated by this introductory but up-to-date coverage. Such students will not only learn the value of plants in health, but they will also understand how great a natural resource remains untapped for future development. Their interest, and that of others as well, will help propel a rejuvenated awareness of plant biology in our daily lives as we enter the twenty-first century, and *Poisonous and Medicinal Plants* will share in this event.

Walter H. Lewis
Washington University
St. Louis, Missouri

Preface

The objectives of this book may be stated straightforwardly. One is to provide, without falling into an abyss of tedious detail, a comprehensive and up-to-date coverage of the fields of poisonous plants and medicinal plants. A second objective is to merge and meld these fields into a coherent whole. A fundamental belief held throughout this book is that the best interests of the two fields will not be served by their continued separation and that they are both enhanced in combination, in a kind of ultimate synergism. After all, and as one will continue to note at various points in the book, the difference between the consideration of a plant as poisonous versus medicinal is often only one of dose. As an example, we may cite the case of chemicals from plants known to have caused internal bleeding in cattle and subsequently used as rodenticides, which have also found a use in human medicine (see "One Man's Poison," by John M. Kingsbury, *BioScience*, March 1980, concerning molded sweet clover and dicoumarol).

Another goal of the book is inclusiveness, both of topic and audience. This writer is not of the opinion that there must necessarily be, as is frequently the case, two categories of books (with different purposes) on a topic such as this, one type of book being scholarly and technical and aimed for the academic classroom and the other made simple (perhaps too much so) and "fun" for the layperson—and never the twain shall meet! It is my view that in one book both objectives can pertain in a way and with a result perhaps exceeding that of either disparate approach (that is, strictly popular versus strictly scientific). If excessive detail is not indulged, then I consider it feasible to develop comprehensive and scientifically meaningful coverage and presentation of poisonous and medicinal plants, and yet with high readability and even high entertainment; and that both lay and professional audiences may be satisfied in their reading. I believe that I have reached this composite goal; but you, the reader, will pass the final judgment.

If it is not the case already, I hope that this book will stimulate in you an awareness of the resurgence of interest and belief in the possibilities of the natural medicines of our green earth—and also an awareness of the inherent dangers contained therein (after all, a large number of plants are indeed not harmless if consumed or, in some cases, touched). Perhaps surprising is the fact that even in the midst of the present, overwhelming synthetic drug market, approximately 25 percent of all prescription drugs still contain natural plant materials as active ingredients (Dr. Norman R. Farnsworth, Research Professor of Pharmacognosy, College of Pharmacy, University of Illinois at Chicago, public communication). And yet these prescriptions are filled from the utilization of a mere 90-odd species of plants. Of the approximately 300,000 species of plants estimated to exist on earth, wouldn't you think that it might be possible to utilize more than 90 some species in medicine? As is often the case, we may take a lesson from history. If we turn the clock back only to the early mid-nineteeth century, and even without invoking such a vast source of drug plants as the tropical rain forests of the world, we find more than 150 plant species (many native to eastern North America) employed in the medical practice of one Dr. Wooster Beach, the progenitor of the eclectic medical movement so prominent in the eastern and central United States even into the early twentieth century. Hence, might we not thumb through the pages of a number of past works on medicinal and poisonous plants and attempt to discover if old wonders (perhaps still present in our midst) do not await our discovery or, better stated, our rediscovery? Might not one, or many more, of these plants find a place in modern medicine, along with the approximately 90 that are now utilized? I think the answer is yes! Perhaps you, the new or, as the case may be, experienced student of this topic, could uncover such a lost treasure from the rich history of botanical medicine. And who knows but what your discovery might eventually prove of benefit to humankind.

This book is intended for use by college students, high-school students, doctors, paramedics, nurses, lawyers, plumbers, housewives or househusbands, historians, farmers, foresters, horticulturalists, gardeners, radio announcers, teachers, secretaries, meterologists, talk-show hosts, professional and amateur naturalists, girl and boy scouts (of all ages), and anyone else who might read it and gain pleasure and benefit from its pages. It is suitable for use as a complement to a general botany or an economic/ethnobotany course, or more especially for a course in medical botany or a coverage of poisonous plants; it might supplement a course in pharmacognosy, herbology, public health, natural history, local flora, or even outdoor recreation and/or survival techniques. Regardless, as you scan the pages and the many illustrations provided for the book, I hope that I am able to impart to you the great significance of this field of study to the past, present, and most especially to the future. After all, plants, in addition to their esthetic value, constitute the major natural source of the food we eat, the air we breathe, and the medicine to cure our many ills (a major focus of this book). What topic thus could be more meaningful to our life on earth? Hence, I urge you to read on and to discover (or perhaps to rediscover) the importance, potential, and excitement of this most fundamental field of study, as I have.

This book may be read in various sequences, and the table of contents will serve as a guide for your reading selection. Before beginning your reading, perhaps you will wish to scan various chapters to examine some of the handcrafted illustrations, as well as to determine if a particular chapter might be of special interest to you. If the chapters are taken in numerical order, they attempt to build historical, chemical, and biological background leading toward the ultimate presentation of poisonous and medicinal plants. Throughout the preparation of this book, this writer has tried to take into account the variation that exists in individual backgrounds, and has not assumed or taken for granted, at any point, prior knowledge and expertise on the part of the reader. I have attempted to explain each topic fully and from the beginning; but so as not to bore the experienced reader, I have not dallied too very long on a topic's very beginning. My wish for you is good reading and, most importantly, continued education, especially in the marvelous topics of botany, medicine, and natural history.

ACKNOWLEDGMENTS

I would like to take this opportunity to acknowledge, with all gratitude possible, the staff of the Lloyd Library, Cincinnati, Ohio, most especially Rebecca Perry, Judith Curran, and Anne Abate, for their most able assistance in my search for and through sources dealing with many aspects of poisonous plants, medicinal botany, and pharmacognosy. I am most sincerely appreciative of the availability of the marvelous holdings and facilities of the Lloyd Library during the course of preparation of this manuscript. I am grateful to Dr. Martha J. Powell, not only for her preparation and provision of Chapter 5 (dealing with poisonous and medicinal fungi), but for assisting me with the proofreading of the manuscript at various stages. I am grateful to Dr. Jerry W. McClure for his astute reading of Chapter 3 (on toxic chemicals) and to Dr. John R. Stevenson for providing helpful information on immunology. I also wish to express gratitude to Dr. Thomas J. Cobbe for his labor of love in the preparation of illustrations for this book. Herbal-style illustrations at various points in the book, such as those presented in Chapters 2 and 11, are broadly patterned after the sixteenth-century herbals of Pier Mattioli, Otto Brunfels, Rembert Dodoens, and Charles de l'Ecluse. Additionally, some of the drawings in Chapters 9 and 10 are in the style of illustrations appearing in certain older seed catalogs, such as McCullough's catalogs of the latter nineteenth and very early twentieth centuries. Again, I thank the librarians of the Lloyd Library for making these materials so readily available.

Will H. Blackwell
Oxford, Ohio

Caution

FROM THE AUTHOR AND PUBLISHER:

The reader should be cautioned with regard to several points. Medications should not be concocted and especially not tried (ingested, injected, and the like) based on information presented in this book. This is by no means to be regarded as a book of medicine; rather it is a book providing interesting information about poisonous and medicinal plants. In general, self-medication, botanical or otherwise, is unwise; only licensed physicians should be the prescribers of your medications. An additional caution is that a given plant that you might encounter should not be assumed to be non poisonous simply because mention of it does not occur within these pages. Due to the great size of the topic, the treatment of poisonous plants in this book focuses on the eastern United States. Even in the eastern United States, it is quite possible to encounter toxic plants introduced from other parts of the world that are not covered in this text. Also, poisonous plants of tropical Florida, per se, are not necessarily covered in this volume. A final point is that knowledge of toxic plants is incomplete; and it is feasible that, in a few cases at least, plant species now assumed to be harmless may in actual fact not be so (or not in all instances). To summarize, one should not consume any plant material without full knowledge of its beneficial, or at least harmless, nature, and the possibility of individual allergic reactions.

*Alphabetical List of Illustrations**

The figure number in parentheses, as in *"Achillea.* Woundwort (2-7)," indicates the chapter (2) and the illustration sequence (seventh) within that chapter.

*Drawings made to scale from specimens (as those in Chapters 12 and 13 and a few elsewhere) are indicated by a (usually double) scale line; the shorter (or single) line equals 1 inch of actual size, and the longer line, 2 inches. All drawings are by Thomas J. Cobbe.

Introduction

The topic of poisonous and medicinal plants can be viewed as a very specific topic or, considering all ramifications, one as broad as medicine itself, especially in historical context. The twentieth century has witnessed a tremendous boom in the synthetic drug industry. In our "pill happy" culture, natural (plant) medicines have for decades seemed to take a distant back seat to the numerous synthetic drugs available. This is surely in contrast to the many preceding centuries in which natural drugs and medicines dominated formal medical practice and, of course, folk medicine as well. It is perhaps hard for us to realize now that natural product drugs were the mainstay of medicine even in the early part of this century. What has happened in the course of the twentieth century is that a dichotomy of sorts has developed between "crude" drugs from natural products (usually extracted or prepared directly from plants) and the bewildering array of often complicated synthetics sitting on the druggist's shelf (although examination of some of these would reveal active plant ingredients). In all, plant remedies or "green cures" would probably be considered to have "slipped back" to the provenance of the herbalist or "herb doctor," and in a sense this is undeniable; however, a careful perusal of the shelves of the modern-day pharmacist may yield some surprises. A number of more or less direct natural products from plants are still available from the druggist and going strong as ever. Interestingly, it is on the pharamacist's shelf that the present apparent dichotomy of the nature of drugs (synthetic versus natural product) is perhaps most stridently underscored.

Two simple examples, from a number possible, should make this dichotomy clear; these examples should also illustrate that the seemingly disparate nature of natural product versus synthetic drugs may be in some cases more apparent than real. The first example selected is that of witch-hazel. Witch-hazel (known to botanists as

Hamamelis virginiana) is a fall-flowering shrub or small tree native to woodlands of the eastern United States; its fragrant flowers are characterized by four unusual, yellowish, straplike (linear) petals. The leaves of witch-hazel bear some resemblance to those of alder, and hence the common names striped alder and spotted alder, although the plant is clearly not an alder. (The potential confusion in common names of plants will be addressed later; see Chapter 7.) The name witch in this context probably stems from the Anglo-Saxon *wice*, that is, "weak," in reference to the flexible branches, once used in divining for water (dowsing or water witching). A small amount of digging into the history of witch-hazel and many other plants thus reveals a rich lore in relation to humankind; such sleuthing into the history and names of plants often pays dividends to the interested reader.

Over time, witch-hazel has found a variety of medicinal uses. Extracts from the leaves and/or the bark (often prepared simply by boiling the plant material in water) have been valued for their astringent properties and used to soothe and draw up skin irritations and vesications. Witch-hazel teas have found use as sedatives, as counteractants to diarrhea, and as gargles to relieve sore throat. Witch-hazel "water" has also been used as a douche in cases of vaginitis. A witch-hazel poultice has been employed to relieve eye inflammation as well as the irritation of hemorrhoids.

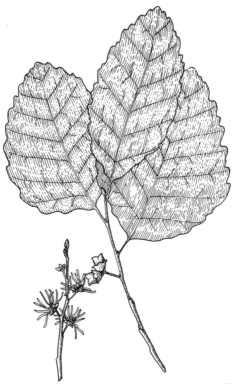

Figure 1–1 *Hamamelis virginiana.*
Witch-hazel

Witch-hazel extract would seem to be in the category of medicines or tinctures that would these days be relegated to the herbal trade (herb or health stores) or perhaps even to the traveling "snake oil" salesman, right? Wrong! Witch-hazel (water or alcoholic) extract, or aqua hamamelis, is a very common resident of the modern pharmacy shelf. It is probably valuable in the relief of skin irritations and, presumably, external use is what is recommended. Although available in the contemporary pharmacy, witch-hazel water is a crude drug (crude extract from the plant), very much a natural product, of which we have (or are provided) very little idea as to its specific contents. No listing of chemical constituents or ingredients appeared on the label of the bottle of witch-hazel "water" recently seen by this writer (although a peek in the *Merck Index* indicates the presence of astringent tannin, probably accounting for its effectiveness in relieving skin inflammation). In spite of its relatively inscrutable content, witch-hazel extract is offered to us, in its designated place on the shelf, by very reputable manufacturing companies. To reemphasize, the main point here is that some natural remedies from plants are still to be found among the menagerie of over-the-counter, packaged products available in the contemporary drugstore.

To begin our second selected example, we ask the question, what is the most successful (at least in a monetary sense) synthetic drug on the market today? Any takers? The answer is, resoundingly, aspirin! Between 40 and 50 million tablets a day are estimated to pass the lips of Americans. Aspirin is entirely synthetic. However, knowledge of the pain-relieving agent we now know as aspirin has a long history, traceable to the use of willow bark by the ancient Greeks to alleviate pain. From the willow (*Salix*), salicylic acid was eventually isolated. Salicylic acid, or else methyl salicylate (oil of wintergreen), was isolated as well from various other plants, including wintergreen, sweet birch, poplars, and spiraea. Salicylic acid (or more technically, *o*-hydroxybenzoic acid), a relatively simple organic acid, was made synthetically in the 1850s. Around the turn of the century, the Bayer company adopted acetylsalicylic acid (simply the synthetic acetyl derivative in which two molecules of salicylic acid are joined) for marketing as an analgesic and antirheumatic pill. The basis for the derivation of the name aspirin is a-, from acetyl, and -spirin, from spiraea (one of the sources of salicylic acid). You know the rest of the success story.

A main point here is that, although commercial aspirin is an entirely synthetic drug, the prototype of this drug was a natural chemical (product) from plants. Perception of the potential medical and market value of aspirin came about through knowledge gained from historical experiences with plants and their use in folk medicine. Indeed, a great many drugs, considered entirely synthetic, are somehow, somewhere rooted in botanical history—in the "old-time" use of some sort of crude plant drug. In digging deeply, thus, and this is an essential point, the difference between natural product medications and synthetic drugs may in some cases prove to be a matter of only minor chemical alterations or manipulations. Building on this point, we might well ask the question, how many more drugs, whether they be analgesics, anticarcinogens, liver agents, heart medicines, or simple skin balms, await our attention in the standing chemical factories we call plants? In the tropical rain forests especially, if not under our very noses, is there not yet a great potential for the discovery of many natural chemicals, perhaps serving as models for future synthetic drugs, of possible immeasurable benefit to humanity? This writer indeed believes so.

So, what does the future hold? Will synthetic drugs (whether based or not on prototypic chemicals from plants) continue to proliferate, while natural plant drugs decline or remain static? There might seem some basis for pessimism regarding the outlook for natural product drugs. In the foreword to Jonathan Hartwell's compilation of plants used against cancer (1982; see selected references), James Duke, chief of the Germplasm Resources Laboratory of the USDA, alludes to the unfortunate demise (in 1981) of the program within the American National Cancer Institute to develop antitumor agents from plants. Varro Tyler of the School of Pharmacy and Pharmacal Sciences at Purdue University, in two recent articles (respectively published in 1986 and 1988), "Plant Drugs in the Twenty-first Century" and "Medicinal Plant Research: 1953–1987" (see references), echoes Duke's regrets over the outcome of this governmental plant (anticancer activity) testing program, and discusses the general lack of practical results from this program, as well as (in the 1988 article) possible reasons for its failure (such as the fact that broader physiological testing of many plant extracts did not occur). Both Duke (1982) and Tyler (1986 article) allude to the general lack

Figure 1–2 *Salix*. Willow

of interest in screening plants for drugs by private pharmaceutical companies in the United States; reasons for this apparent disinterest include high costs, the very limited practical progress over the last 35 years in producing new marketable drugs from plants, the need for more suitable bioassays, the imposition of strict federal regulations, and the lack of effective research cooperation among scientists in various fields. However, as Tyler (1988) points out, there is nevertheless much reason for optimism; that is, there is reason to believe that the most significant time for plant research in all probability awaits us in the future. In effect, through increased knowledge of basic technology (including methods of analysis and the production of plant materials through tissue culture techniques) and improved knowledge of plant metabolism, the stage is set for the potential discovery of important new drugs from plants in the relatively near future. Tyler (1986), harkening to the substantial (and financially impressive) herb trade in American health-food stores, believes that a "green wave" of interest and demand from an increasingly health conscious laity will eventually prevail (perhaps in the early years of the twenty-first century) against the rigid federal regulatory atmosphere currently holding sway in the United States, an atmosphere that has rendered the investigation and refinement of new plant drug products frequently unprofitable. Tyler cites the recent discovery and marketing of a number of new, exciting, and promising plant drugs (such as silymarin from milk thistle, used in "hepatoprotection" against viral hepatitis and alcoholism) in the German Federal Republic (West Germany), in which a "more favorable regulatory climate" prevails. It does seem likely that the United States will eventually, of necessity, follow suit, simply because the need for such drugs is definitely on the horizon, if not here already. One cannot doubt the lay interest in medicinal plants, as attested by the various popular books and publications dealing with the topic. A growing scientific interest in medical botany is evident in the recent increase in university programs offering training in pharmacognosy (natural product drugs) and related topics. A rebirth of plant medicine is thus apparently no more than just around the corner. It may well prove to be true, considering the sweep of human history, that in only a portion of the twentieth century was medicine predominantly something other than botanical medicine.

And what of this book? Certainly it is one of those works signaling a possible renaissance of green medicine and interest in same. This book, however, attempts to serve two masters, or, seemingly, two major topics. A major objective of the book is a survey of poisonous plants and topics providing background to this survey; another objective is to provide information on medicinal plants. Too much for one book? This writer believes not, simply because it is often impossible to separate the topic of poisonous plants from that of medicinal plants. Although only one of many, an example may help to clarify this point. *Digitalis* (foxglove), once used in the treatment of dropsy (congestive heart failure), has found a highly significant place in American heart medicine. Hundreds of thousands of patients are treated yearly with the cardiotonic substances isolated from one of two species of foxglove. These cardioactive chemicals have never been adequately replaced synthetically. As any cardiologist knows, the difference between a medically valuable dose of compounds from digitalis and a toxic dose may be measured in tenths of milligrams. Digitalis poisoning or "intoxication" is indeed a problem in chronic heart patients, one serious enough to have led to the development of an antidote to counteract the toxic effect of digitalis. The story of digitalis is accorded more appropriate treatment at other points in this book. The point here is that it is often (perhaps usually) not possible to isolate consideration of the medical value of a truly significant medicinal plant from that of its toxic nature. Another reason for including a strong coverage of poisonous plants in a book dealing with medical botany is that it is probably true that most physicians of the present day, unlike their counterparts of the past, have scant knowledge of botany. How many contemporary physicians, often highly specialized, would be able to identify a large number of plants, recognize which species are poisonous, know offhand their toxic substances and effects, and be able to offer other than the most general treatment for a plant-induced toxic condition? I leave the answer to you.

I urge you, the reader, to peruse the remaining chapters in this volume, to examine the illustrations provided, and to speculate as to the need for each chapter and its relation to the book as a whole. I ask you to appreciate at least the attempt to bring a wide variety of potentially related subjects to bear, between the covers of one book, so that the reader may find the basic, necessary information in one place. I challenge you to become stimulated by this vital field of science and discovery, now on the verge of being reborn—perhaps to a level exceeding that of its historical heyday. I urge you to read further on various topics, guided perhaps by the selected readings provided at the end of each chapter, and to get in on the groundwork of the renaissance of medical botany. It is my wish that you, the reader, will become as thrilled about the history, the facts, and the future of the field of poisonous and medicinal plants as I have been in writing for you about it. Happy reading, and best wishes for success in your personal investigation of this area of knowledge, simultaneously both old and revered and now new and exciting. Welcome aboard!

SELECTED REFERENCES

HARTWELL, JONATHAN L. 1982. *Plants Used Against Cancer*. Quarterman Publications, Inc., Lawrence, Mass. This book is an extensive and scholarly listing of plants utilized at one time or another through history against alleged cancers or cancerlike diseases of various sorts; the reader is directed to Hartwell's Introduction, and especially to the Foreword by James A. Duke.

KREIG, MARGARET B. 1964. *Green Medicine*. Rand McNally & Company, Chicago. An entertaining account of the major contributions of plants to medicine, in historical context; must reading as a lively introduction to the topic.

TYLER, VARRO E. 1986. Plant Drugs in the Twenty-first Century. *Economic Botany* 40(3): 279–288. This and the following article basically foretell the great future promise of medically important drug discoveries from plants.

―――. 1988. Medicinal Plant Research: 1953–1987. *Planta Medica* 54: 95–100. I cannot encourage the reader too strongly to read this and the preceding article for an understanding of the possible significance of natural product drugs in the years to come.

Medicinal and Poisonous Plants in History

The relevance of examining the topic of medicinal and poisonous plants in historical context is simply this: many ancient plant remedies for disease have turned out in one way or another to have significant value for modern medicine; how many more remedies of potential value to medicine might be uncovered if the folk medicines of past peoples and cultures are studied with an open mind? In the case of medicinal plants, we may definitely, as the adage goes, learn something from history. It is a reasonable assertion that herb medicine, or "natural" medicine, is (other than perhaps prayer) the main method by which human beings have tried to cure themselves of ills through the centuries. Herb medicine is certainly one of the oldest arts, dating well into prehistory. In historical time, the significance of medicinal botany is evident in all major civilizations of antiquity.

ANTIQUITY

Egypt. Knowledge of medicinal plants employed by the ancient Egyptians is substantial because of their practice of recording information on papyrus, a scroll-like paper made from the pith of the papyrus plant (a type of river sedge, *Cyperus papyrus*). Two famous surviving Egyptian papyri are the Hearst papyrus and the Ebers papyrus, written circa 1500 B.C., perhaps by physician/priests. Plants mentioned medicinally in these papyri include barley, beans, cedar, crocus, dates, garlic, grapes, lotus, myrrh, olives, onions, pomegranate, sycamore fig, tamarisk, and wheat. The Ebers papyrus alone contains approximately 800 prescriptions; more than 20 of these mention garlic (*Allium sativum*) as an effective agent against a variety of disorders, including

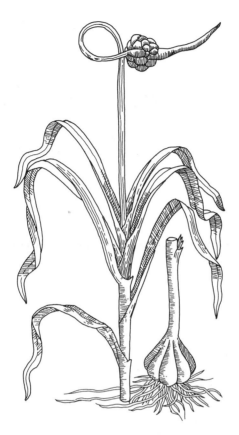

Figure 2–1 *Allium sativum.* Garlic

headaches, worms, and heart or circulatory difficulties. Statements on garlic are particularly significant because recent interest has developed in garlic and onions for alleviation of circulatory problems. Odoriferous compounds in garlic and onions have recently been found to have a significant anticoagulant and antithrombotic action on the blood, underscoring the point of the potential value of centuries-old folk remedies for modern medicine (see Eric Block, "The Chemistry of Garlic and Onions," Scientific American, March 1985, pages 114–119; also see E. Block in R. P. Steiner, editor, cited under selected references). There is some evidence that the ancient Egyptians used autumn crocus (*Colchicum autumnale*) in the treatment of gout or what we might term gouty arthritis; this is intriguing because an extract of autumn crocus (colchicine) is used in the present day for this purpose. Other Egyptian remedies, including the use of the astringent fruit of the pomegranate, *Punica granatum*, as a vermifuge (worm medicine), although not leading to formal modern medicinal use, could well bear reinvestigation.

The ancient Egyptians gave much attention to plants in association with death and the afterlife (passage through the netherworld). More than 20 different kinds of plants have been identified in funeral wreaths found in tombs, sometimes almost perfectly preserved; grapes (*Vitis vinifera*), the leaves, branches, and raisins, are among the plants often found in tombs. Tomb paintings (paintings on the inner walls of crypts or temples) are commonly of plants; pomegranate and lotus (a water lily)

Figure 2–2 *Punica granatum.*
Pomegranate

are frequently represented. Plants were the major source of substances or ingredients used in mummification. In the long process of preparing (preserving) a mummy, palm wine was used to clean out the body cavity, following evisceration, and aromatic wood (perhaps cedar of Lebanon) and spices (such as myrrh) were added to fill the cavity. Cedar oil was used to cleanse the bowel, and mastic (resin from *Pistacia vera*) was spread on the skin as a preservative. Onions, considered sacred by the Egyptians, were often used to fill the eye sockets and were common as burial offerings to the dead. Linen was most commonly used to wrap a mummy; however, grape leaves were occasionally a substitute wrapping. Various plant species might be placed in or around the mummy wrappings. At least 30 different kinds of plants are known to have been used in mummification, a number being identified directly from remains inside coffins (sarcophagi).

Mesopotamia.   The ancient civilization of Mesopotamia (Assyria) was located in the valley of the Tigris and Euphrates rivers at the north end of the Persian Gulf. Knowledge of Assyrian medical botany is not as great as that of Egypt. However, written

Figure 2–3　*Vitis vinifera*. Wine grape

records were left, not on papyrus, but as engravings on large clay tablets that hardened like stone. In this form, an Assyrian herbal of the seventh century B.C. does provide some information. It is clear that the date palm, the major tree of the area, found a use in almost everything (food, medicine, and building materials). It is known that the Assyrians cultivated wheat and barley and made beer. Hops (*Humulus lupulus*) were used as a bitters in beer, much as today. Beer containing hops was considered to be useful in preventing the development of leprosy (a claim that could bear substantiation). Thyme in beer or oil, or simply "sniffed," was considered beneficial to the lungs or generally for difficulties in breathing. The use of thyme to improve breathing is perfectly logical, since various mint oils have been employed over the centuries to treat the symptoms of coughs and colds. It is interesting that some of the names that the Assyrians gave to their plants have persisted as English names. Apricot, cherry, almond, and poppy are names ultimately derived from the Assyrian language.

China. Knowledge of medicinal plants in ancient China is largely attributed to the Emperor Shen-nung (Chin-nung), who is China's legendary father of both agriculture and medicine. At some time prior to 2500 B.C. (probably between 3000 and 2500 B.C.), Shen-nung allegedly wrote the first pharmacopoeia (the *Pun-tsao*), not actually published until nearly 1600 A.D. (by Li-Shi-Chin). Medicinal plants men-

Figure 2–4 *Humulus lupulus.* Hops

tioned in the *Pun-tsao* include Indian hemp, aconite, opium poppy, and croton. A number of poisons and antidotes are also given.

Oral tradition has been the primary medium responsible for communication of knowledge of Chinese folk (botanical) medicine over the centuries. However, one should not minimize the potential value of centuries-old, oral communication. The unusual looking gymnospermous plant, *Ephedra*, was used by the ancient Chinese to treat bronchial asthma. The drug ephedrine (an alkaloid isolated from *Ephedra*) is valued for its antihistamine properties and has found a place in modern, over-the-counter nasal sprays and decongestants. Knowledge of the "medicinal value" of ginseng also comes from Chinese folk medicine. The fact that the root may sometimes be said to resemble a human form probably contributed to the quasi-mystical belief in the attributes of ginseng in relieving human disease and distress. Ginseng is one of those plants considered to be a panacea (cure-all). It has been considered of value in relieving respiratory disease (of various sorts), digestive upset (nausea, diarrhea, and indigestion), diabetes, rheumatism, and even external sores. Ginseng has been especially valued as a remedy for difficulties in "love-making," that is, as an aphrodisiac. Asiatic and American species of ginseng (respectively, *Panax ginseng* and *P. quinquefolius*) exist; both are valued by herb doctors and root diggers. However, ginseng presently holds a much more esteemed place in formal Chinese and Soviet medicine than in the current medical establishment of the United States. In the United States, ginseng is considered to have value primarily as a stimulant or tonic and is largely relegated to the shelves of herb stores or health food stores, where it is sold as a tea. Nonetheless, considerable research on ginseng is in progress (see *Economic and Medicinal Plant Research*, Vol. 1, H. Wagner and others, editors, Academic Press, 1985). At present, however, ginseng, medically speaking, must be said to remain an enigma, with little proven, substantial medical benefit (see "Ginseng: A Medical Enigma," by Walter H. Lewis, Chapter 15 in Nina L. Etkin, editor, *Plants in Indigenous Medicine & Diet: Biobehavioral Approaches*, 1986).

India. In a similar vein to Chinese folk medicine, information on medicinal plants from ancient India has also largely been passed down by oral tradition. Knowledge of medicinal plants (and medicine in general) in India was traditionally tied in with Hindu scriptures or Vedas. Over the years, this traditional Indian medicine has become rather well codified in a holistically oriented practice or system of health care known as Ayurvedic medicine; Ayurveda means "knowledge of life" (see N. G. Patel in R. P. Steiner, selected references). To make the point again, this type of knowledge, based

Figure 2–5 *Panax quinquefolius.*
American ginseng

as it often is in both legend and fact, may contain components of great value indeed. For centuries in India, the plant called snakeroot (*Rauwolfia serpentina*) was used to treat a condition the name of which is interpretable as "moon disease," or, as we might put it, lunacy. In spite of centuries of successful use in treating forms of mental illness in India, snakeroot (or, more properly, its extracts) were not adopted by the *U.S. Pharmacopoeia* until the early 1950s. Since this time, a variety of useful compounds, especially reserpine, has been isolated (see Chapter 13). The reserpine alkaloids have found great use not only in treating particular forms of mental illness, but also in treating the ever-growing American problem of hypertension (high blood pressure). It is somewhat of a shame that earlier advantage was not taken of the ancient knowledge, available all along, of snakeroot and its medicinal properties.

Greece.   Coming forward somewhat in time (to roughly 450 to 300 B.C.), we can take a brief look at botany during the Golden Age of Greek civilization. Much of modern science and philosophy traces its origins to Greece during this time interval. Rightly called the father of medicine is Hippocrates of the Island of Cos, whose oath is still recited by graduates of medical school. Hippocrates' school of medicine was founded on the belief that disease had natural rather than supernatural causes, and that health was a matter not for the whims of the gods but of proper adjustment of four basic body fluids (humors): blood, phlegm, yellow bile, and black bile. The two basic avenues to proper fluid adjustment were (1) bleeding practices (phlebotomy), and (2) herbal medicine. Hippocrates mentioned more than 200 plants, without botanical description, in connection with drugs and medicine. Hippocrates did not gather his herb remedies. However, spurred on by the demand for plant drugs based on Hippocrates' prescriptions, a cult of root diggers (*rhizotomoi*) developed, as did a group of drug merchants (*pharmacopuloi*). It takes little extrapolation to realize that these same "guilds" persist in present-day society. Many Hippocratean drugs are still included, one way or another, in modern guides to botanical medicine.

In spite of the rational approach of Hippocrates, to study Greek civilization is to realize that the supernatural (deities) played a large role in many lives. As a case in point to botany, Nichomachus (the father of Aristotle) was a physician belonging to a society that believed that medicine was a gift of the Greek god of medicine, Aesculapius (Asclepias). This guild of the Asclepiads did not transmit their knowledge beyond their own membership, but rather practiced the art of healing through knowledge of secret herb remedies imparted to them by Asclepias. The name *Asclepias* is now that of a genus of milkweeds; whether or not milkweeds were used medicinally by the guild is unknown.

In Greece, plants were used not only for healing, but as a means of inducing death, either through suicide or execution. The case of Socrates is well known. Upon falling from political favor, he was allowed the privilege of dying by partaking of poison hemlock prepared in a special cup. Many facts or events are fuzzy when viewed through time's looking glass. However, there is no doubt that Socrates was put to death specifically with poison hemlock (*Conium maculatum*), because of the survival of a detailed account of the event in the writings of Plato (specifically, in

Figure 2–6   *Conium maculatum.* Poison hemlock

the biographical dialog known as the *Phaedo*), including some description of symptoms of the poisoning.

Aristotle was a zoologist, and his writings contain only passing references to plants. Although famous as a natural historian, Aristotle is also noteworthy as a teacher, having both Alexander the Great and Theophrastus as students, among many others, in the Lyceum at Athens. Aristotle bequeathed his library and garden to Theophrastus. Alexander the Great supplied Theophrastus with plants from various parts of the known world. Thus Theophrastus was the botanist and is considered by many to be the father of botany. From his two surviving botanical works, it is clear that Theophrastus first observed or, more accurately, deduced many technical features of plants. Theophrastus accurately noted the parts of a flower, the ovary as an immature fruit, differences in ovary position in different types of flowers, fused versus free petals, the mode of development of the inflorescence, a thistle head as a composition of many small flowers (that is, as an inflorescence and not a single flower), and differences in the life span and ecology of plants. The works of Theophrastus, Aristotle, and others highlight the point that the best of Greek science and philosophy was a pure science approach, that is, a pursuit of knowledge for the sake of knowledge, to understand more fully the world and the universe.

After the golden age of Greek civilization, the center of Greek intellectual activity was transplanted to Alexandria in Egypt, with its great library. This Hellenistic Greek society is notable for its achievements in mathematics and physical sciences through the ingenuity of men such as Euclid and Archimedes. Achievements in botany or biology are less compelling. Nicander, a priest living between 185 and 135 B.C., wrote a treatise on poisons in which 125 plants are mentioned either as poisons or antidotes. For some reason, there was considerable interest in poisons and antidotes during the Alexandrian age, and Mithridates, the last King of Pontus, sought an apparently universal antidote against all poisons. Although his concoction (of many ingredients) was of little worth, if one checks in an unabridged dictionary, the word mithridate is found to be synonymous with antidote.

Rome.   Next we turn to the first century A.D. and the peak of the Roman Empire and Roman domination of the known world. We find during this time the efforts of one of the most prolific encyclopedists of antiquity, Caius Plinius Secundus, or Pliny the Elder. His surviving work, *Historia Naturalis*, is an attempt to compile all knowledge on natural history available at that time. Of the 37 books comprising his natural history, 16 deal with plants. More than 1000 plants are mentioned, and some information on medical use is given. However, Pliny's work is considered to be error laden, and precise scholarship seems often to have been lacking.

Of much greater interest to medical botany is the work of Pedanios Dioscorides, a virtual contemporary of Pliny. Dioscorides, by birth a Sicilian Greek, was a military physician under the Emperor Nero of Rome. Although Nero and various other Roman luminaries were known to have used poisons on or commissioned the poisoning of their adversaries, Dioscorides' mission was to heal. As military physician, Dioscorides traveled widely with the Roman legions, gathering much information on medicinal plants. He recorded this information in his work, *De Materia Medica*, an account of more than 600 species of plants of presumed medical value. Dioscorides used Greek vernacular names for the plants in his book, some of which survive as modern generic names (for example, *Anemone* and *Aloe* survive unchanged). The book is of great interest because descriptions, although sometimes skimpy, are provided (often all parts of the plant, even the roots, are described), along with illustrations (although the source of the illustrations remains unclear). Importantly, medicinal preparations of the plants are given, along with expected beneficial effects and even possible toxic side effects; in pioneering drug preparation from plants, Dioscorides is to be regarded as the founder of pharmacognosy. Regardless of shortcomings, *De Materia Medica* is by far the most important and original work on medical botany coming to us from antiquity. This book remained the ultimate reference source on medicinal plants for nearly 1500 years. Dioscorides' goal was to solve the problems of the day; for example, he might well have used an ointment of woundwort (*Achillea*) as a styptic to stop the bleeding of a Roman soldier wounded in battle. Interesting is his recommendation for the use of autumn

Figure 2–7 *Achillea.* Woundwort   **Figure 2–8** *Colchicum autumnale.* Autumn crocus

crocus (*Colchicum autumnale*) for what was apparently cancer, especially in the light of modern-day attempts (although largely unsuccessful) at a similar use for extracts of this plant. Dioscorides was certainly one of the earliest writers in history to write on the possible use of plant materials (for example, juniper berries and hawthorn root) as topical or oral contraceptives. The work of Dioscorides epitomizes the practical or applied approach that is in general characteristic of Roman scholarship.

Further exemplifying the pragmatic bent of learned men of the Roman Empire are the efforts of Galen (second century A.D.), a one-time physician to the gladiators. Galen systematically began studying medicine at an early age in preparation for a career that would make him perhaps the most famous physician of his day. Galen adopted the outdated Hippocratic medical practice of adjusting the four body humours (and thus is said by some to have set medical practice back for centuries). However, Galen added the dimension of experimentation upon animals. Also, he developed methods of obtaining plant extracts for use in experimentation that are still mentioned today (as galenical or galenical products).

Botany and the Bible.   The time of the height of the Roman Empire also corresponds to what might be called biblical time, in terms of the life of Christ and the years immediately following. But, of course, it is virtually impossible to define the limits of biblical time, as it could be (and is by many) considered to span many centuries prior to the birth of Christ (and to continue today). Regardless of definitions or viewpoints, the Bible is a relatively rich source of allusions to plants. Although many references to plants in the Bible constitute generalities, for example, "bitter herbs," "thorns and thistles," "seed," "grain," "bush," and the like, scarcely a book in the Bible fails to mention plants in some context. In all, well more than 100 "kinds" of plants are included. Although a number of plants mentioned are known to have medicinal value, only a small handful of Bible citations make direct reference to medicinal use. In the very select group referred to directly in medical context is the fig (*Ficus carica*). Figs are the first plants mentioned in the Bible,

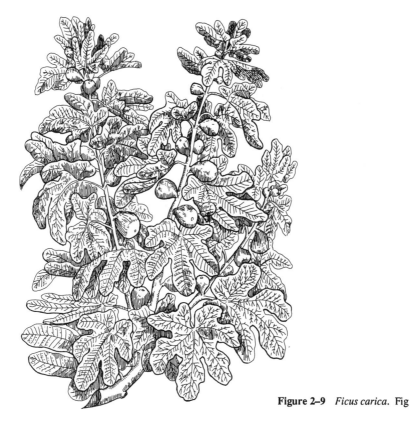

Figure 2–9 *Ficus carica.* Fig

the fig leaf being considered a symbol of fertility (Book of Genesis, Adam and Eve in the Garden of Eden). In the book of Second Kings, reference is made to the use of the fig in the treatment of boils. This is consistent with the long and widespread folk use of the latex of a green fig (fruit) or of fig leaves to treat eruptions of the skin, ranging from pimples to skin cancer. As an aside, the "sycamore" that Zacchaeus climbed to see Jesus pass is actually a type of fig (*Ficus sycomorus*, the sycamore fig). One other plant mentioned directly in medical context is the mandrake (*Mandragora officinarum*). The Song of Solomon alludes to the fragrance of mandrake in reference to its supposed aphrodisiacal properties. This reference to mandrake actually has its origins in the book of Genesis (the story of Leah and Rachel, both vying for the affection of Jacob). Except for a very few direct references, most discussion of medicinal plants of the Bible must be by the extrapolation of possibilities from presently known properties of the plants (see Duke, 1983). Certainly, one of the most famous allusions to plants in the bible, the parable of the grain of mustard seed in Matthew 13, for example, has no medical context. However, the medicinal uses (as plasters and gargles) of mustards (*Brassica*) through the centuries are well known and doubtless existed in biblical time as well.

Figure 2–10 *Mandragora officinarum.* Mandrake

MIDDLE AGES AND THE RENAISSANCE

Medieval botany.   Accompanying the decline of the Roman Empire was the rise of the Christian church (and Christendom). From the period of about 500 to 1400 A.D., a time interval often referred to as the Middle Ages, the church greatly expanded its empire and clearly was the dominant institution in all walks of life and fields of endeavor. In a very real sense, the church controlled scholarship. During the Middle Ages of Europe, what passed for scholarship was primarily hand-copying of valued, ancient Greek and Roman manuscripts. Hand-copied more than any book other than the Bible was Dioscorides' *De Materia Medica*. Of the many different hand copies ("editions") of Dioscorides herbal, the most famous (and valuable for its beauty and accuracy) is the *Anician Codex*, prepared in honor of Princess Juliana Anicia, the Christian daughter of the Roman Emperor Flavius Anicius Olybrius. An early sixth-century manuscript, the *Anician Codex* (preserved at Vienna) is botanically an important link between the ancient world, the early Middle Ages, and all the centuries that followed. Certain other copies of Dioscorides' work are less admired, with errors (and Christian teachings) creeping into the pages over time; in some copies, illustrations of the leaves of the strawberry (*Fragaria vesca*) became altered to show five rather than three leaflets (although the strawberry plant in the garden continued to have but three leaflets per leaf). Regardless of variations in copies, the herbal of Dioscorides was accorded blind acceptance as the authoritative source on medical plants for virtually the entire 1000-year interval of the Dark Ages.

Since scholarly activities consisted mainly of hand-copying old manuscripts, little botanical (and, in general, scientific) progress occurred. However, originality was not at a total standstill, especially in northern Europe. The *Leech Book of Bald* (Leech means physician, and Bald was the man who either prepared or commissioned the book), written in Anglo-Saxon England (in the British vernacular) during the early tenth century, stands somewhat apart in that it was not entirely copied or translated from early Greek or Roman sources. Although loaded with superstition, it contains information on ancient British plant lore and as such is a valuable resource. It is to the Anglo-Saxons that we owe the commonly used botanical term *wort*, implying generally some sort of small, herbaceous plant (as in liverwort).

One specialized area of "progress" or knowledge during the Middle Ages (and continuing through Renaissance times) was in the art of poisoning, a much more common practice than today. In Italy, several families (for example, the Borgia and Baglioni families) made their living as "professional poisoners." Many ingenious methods for poisoning were devised, including the application of poison as lipstick and its transmission through kissing. Poison rings were very popular in medieval times; typically, a decorative face (lid) concealed the chamber below containing the poisonous powder. At the appropriate moment, the ring's contents could be emptied into the beverage of the unwitting and unlucky victim. Such "succession powders" were commonly sold as a quick means of ascendency up the rungs of life. Substances utilized as poisons included (in various mixtures) mineral toxins such as arsenic or copper, poison from venomous toads, and toxic plant materials such as monkshood (aconite), yew, and nux vomica (strychnine). Animals

Figure 2–11 *Fragaria vesca.* Strawberry

Figure 2–12 *Aconitum.* Monkshood, wolfsbane

were poisoned as well as people; monkshood (*Aconitum*) was employed to poison wolves, and hence its second common name, "wolfsbane." *Aconitum* eventually became associated with werewolf legends, as did garlic (*Allium sativum*). A highly entertaining account of poisoning through the ages is presented in the work of C. J. S. Thompson (see selected references; see also the reference by Stary).

Poisoning for purposes other than simply inducing death was also common in the Middle Ages in Europe, as in the practice of witchcraft and sorcery. In these dark arts, medieval knowledge and expertise was certainly greater than in the present day. Although we do not know many of the details associated with the practice of medieval witchcraft, some facts are known. Henbane (*Hyoscyamus niger*) was a mainstay of the witches brew, a concoction doubtless composed of a variety of ingredients (some functional and some not). Other somewhat similar plants of the nightshade family that were also often employed included deadly nightshade or "witch's berry" (*Atropa belladonna*) and mandrake (*Mandragora officinarum*). Mandrake was also known as "gallows man" because of the belief that it would grow beneath a gallows, stimulated by the urine or semen of a hanged man. Mandrake occurring near a gallows was considered to have greater power than if found growing elsewhere. All three of these "hexing herbs" contain similar psychoactive compounds and were employed by witches in rituals of the sabbat (witches' celebration or ceremony) to induce the desired hallucinogenic state in themselves and their disciples and to cast spells (see reference by Schultes and Hofmann, 1979). Salve prepared from one or more of these nightshades, applied to the upper thighs or genitals, could induce the sensation of rising into the air or flying (on a broom). Jimson weed (*Datura stramonium*), yet another nightshade, apparently also found its way to the witch's cauldron. Foxglove or "witch's bells" (*Digitalis purpurea*) is known to have been used as a witch's poison.

During the Middle Ages, a perhaps greater level of intellectual activity took place in the Arab world than in Europe. Although accomplishments in Arabian mathematics and astronomy are most notable, some progress in botany and medicine also occurred. Standing out is the name of Avicenna (Ibn Sina), a Persian who in the early eleventh century wrote a *Canon of Medicine*, a voluminous book that became a medical text in both the Christian and Moslem worlds. Although the majority of Avicenna's work was based on ancient authorities, parts are original, including information on herb medicine. During the eleventh and twelfth centuries, much knowledge gained in Islam was transmitted back to Christian Europe during a sequence of bellicose pilgrimages known as the Crusades.

Figure 2–13 *Hyoscyamus niger.*
Henbane

Figure 2–14   After Frontispiece of the Herbal of Otto Brunfels (1532)

Botany in the Renaissance.   Although scholasticism took a turn for the better in Europe during the thirteenth and fourteenth centuries, we must move on to the fifteenth and sixteenth centuries, that is, to the Renaissance, before we see significant progress in various areas of intellectual endeavor.   One cannot minimize the invention, circa 1440, of the printing press with movable type as a means for disseminating information (making books available to everyone) and as a stimulus for the reawakening of intellect associated with the Renaissance.   In botany, this rebirth of progress is manifest in a movement known as herbalism.   Herbalism embodied a significant renewal of interest in searching for plants of medical value; it represented partly a continued admiration of Dioscorides and partly (and importantly) a return to nature in the search for additional herb remedies.   The objective of herbalism became to gather as much information on medicinal plants as possible, both written and "available from the field."   Renaissance herbals consequently came to be, quite literally, bigger and better books on plants of actual or presumed medical worth.   Herbalism was a movement occurring simultaneously in several countries, each having its noteworthy herbalists.   During the sixteenth century, the "four German fathers of botany," Otto Brunfels, Jerome Bock, Leonhart Fuchs, and Valerius Cordus, all produced significant herbals.   Particularly interesting is the herbal of Bock, a person gifted at field observation who wrote vivid descriptions of the plants he saw; because of a patriotic bent, Bock's descriptions were not written in Latin as were those of a number of the herbalists, but rather were composed in his native German tongue.   Herbals comparably good to those of the German fathers were written in Holland (by Charles de l'Ecluse, Mathias de l'Obel, and Rembert Dodoens, writing respectively under the latin pen names of Clusius, Lobelius, and Dodonaeus) and in Italy (by Mattioli, an incurable fan of Dioscorides).   Several herbals were also produced in England (for example, those by Gerard and Turner).   The herbal of John Gerard is among the most famous in the present day; however, it is considered inferior in content to some other herbals (perhaps being largely "translated" from the Dutch herbal of Rembert Dodoens) and is laced with myth and superstition.   Gerard's herbal contains, for example, the legend of the "goose tree," the fruits of which upon falling into the water may change into geese or barnacles.   Although written earlier, of much greater scientific worth is William Turner's herbal, which included, among many other plants, more than 200 species native to England.

Except for the herbal of Cordus (and the first edition of Bock's *Herbal*), Renaissance herbals were copiously and often ornately illustrated, typically not by the herbalists themselves but by commissioned artists.   It is probably true that the often magnificent woodcut illustrations or illuminations, especially of the German and Dutch herbals, impart the greatest present-day value to these Renaissance works on medical plants.   But let us not minimize the value of herb remedies ("botanicals" or "simples") to the average person living during Renaissance time, perhaps cut off from any but simple, self-administerable medications available at no expense in woods or fields.   The arrangement of presentation of plants in herbals was generally by medicinal use.   However, certain botanical families (mints, umbellifers, crucifers, and composites, among others) were frequently grouped together.   Regardless of present judgments as to botanical value, herbalism, admittedly both medieval and

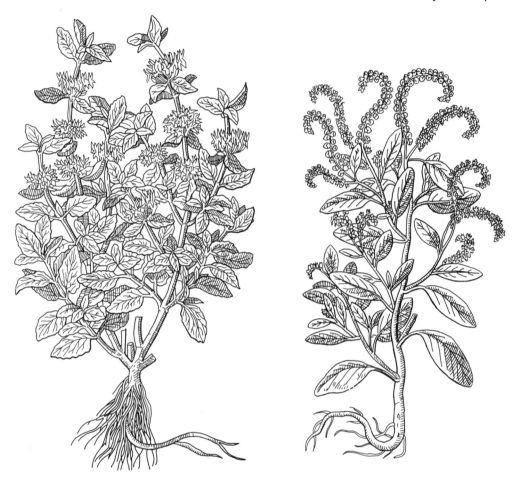

Figure 2–15 Mint, herbal-style illustration   **Figure 2–16** Heliotrope or Borage, stylized
                                                            herbal illustration

modern in its character, represented an important breakthrough in the knowledge, description, and illustration of medicinal plants. Although botany and medicine remained joined as one and deference was still accorded Dioscorides, the mental straightjacket that had enshrouded the study of plants for 1500 years (that is, since the first century A.D.) was finally broken.

An aberrant form of herbalism is known as the doctrine of signatures. The doctrine of signatures is a very old belief that the Creator had put a sign or signature on certain valuable plants to enable people to perceive their worth. Put simply, it might be possible to tell what a plant might be used for, that is, might cure, by merely looking at it. For example, herbs with red juice or yellow juice would respectively be good for the blood or for urinary difficulties. Plants with coiled inflorescences (for example, borages) might be good for snakebite or for the sting of a scorpion. The convoluted surface of a walnut would imply that the brain might be affected (that is, walnuts might help relieve

Figure 2–17 *Hepatica nobilis.* Liverleaf

headaches). The nature of the leaf lobing of certain plants, for example, the liverleaf, *Hepatica nobilis* (= *H. triloba* of some authors), suggested a remedy for bilious (liver) ailments; in fact, the common name of an entire group of plants, the liverworts, is loosely tied into the doctrine of signatures. The Swiss Renaissance herbalist Paracelsus (whose real name was Theophrastus Bombastus von Hohenheim), although certainly not originating this doctrine, was both credited and discredited for espousing its tenants. It should be noted that the most reputable among the herbalists of the Renaissance denounced the doctrine of signatures.

SEVENTEENTH CENTURY TO PRESENT

Seventeenth century.   Herbalism is synonymous with botany of the Renaissance. Many botanists of the present day consider herbalism as merely a phase through which botany passed during the Renaissance, en route to becoming a very different discipline, finally quite distinct from medicine. In the seventeenth century, the divergence of botany and medicine began, but the change was far from immediate. Interest in herbalism continued through much of the century, as evidenced by the production of, perhaps text-wise, the "greatest herbal of them all," John Parkinson's *Theatrum Botanicum* (Theatre of Plants) in the mid-1600s. In the *Theatrum*, more than 3800 plants are discussed, including 33 British medicinal plants "overlooked" by previous herbalists. Adding much knowledge of his own, Parkinson draws richly as well from herbalists who preceded him. Parkinson's monumental herbal is thus a kind of final compilation in which one can sense and sample the sweep and richness of all of herbalism. It might be mentioned in passing that the doctrine of signatures clearly persisted into the seventeenth century in the writings of another Englishman, William Cole. In fact, in Cole's *The Art of Simpling* (1656) this doctrine may be viewed in perhaps its most extreme form.

Regardless of the persistence of herbalism, as the seventeenth century wore on, botany found itself en route to becoming more self-defined and more of a pure science discipline. This transformation in botany was not unique to that field, but was a part of larger movements known as natural philosophy, scientific deism, and the scientific revolution. Interest in experimentation, observation, and rational explanation increased greatly during the seventeenth century, ushering in a new intellectual age (in outlook not unlike that of Greece in the Golden Age). Actually, botany lagged behind the physical sciences in development as a discipline. The mid-century botanical–philosophical writings of the great German botanist Joachim Jung gave a new, nonmedical emphasis and impetus to botany. Jung wrote extensively on the true morphological nature of plants. No doubt stimulated by Jung's great thinking, significant advances were seen in botany (as a self-contained discipline) by the end of the seventeenth century. Advances made in plant morphology, anatomy, physiology, and taxonomy indicate that several of the main subfields of botany also emerged in the late seventeenth century. The writings of the Englishman, John Ray, in the field of taxonomy placed emphasis on the classification of plants by their own inherent natural relationships, rather than by their medical (herbal) uses. The pure science approach of the botanist Ray provides a striking contrast to the applied approach of herbalists of the previous century.

Eighteenth century. Scientific investigations characteristic of the seventeenth century come into full bloom in the Age of Enlightenment, an interval in history corresponding rather well to the eighteenth century. It is almost enough to mention the name Linnaeus to appreciate progress made in eighteenth-century botany. This great Swedish physician classified the plants "of the world" in a two-volume work known as *Species Plantarum* (published in 1753). This work is highly significant for the following reasons, among others: (1) Although in an unusual way (that is, by writing a "trivial epithet" in the margins), Linnaeus consistently used the binomial method of naming plants, the system used today. (2) The book embodied a review by Linnaeus of the plethora of past names of many plants (and the works of various authors), bringing order out of chaos and incorporating a wealth of references. (3) A great many species new to science were described (specimens being supplied to Linnaeus from various regions by collectors, even in North America). (4) A handy, readily understandable system of classification was used as an underlying framework (actually first introduced by Linnaeus in another publication in 1735). (5) The book served to popularize botany as a discipline. Of significance is the fact that Linnaeus (his real name was Carl von Linné), although a highly respected physician in his time (he was personal physician to the Queen of Sweden), wrote *Species Plantarum* exclusive of reference to the medicinal uses of plants. Linnaeus's work, although doubtless of use to physicians seeking plant identification, was nonetheless pure botany.

In the eighteenth century, a clear distinction had developed between "regular" physicians and herbal healers. To some eighteenth-century physicians, however, herbal medicine and formal medicine could still be intertwined for great benefit. Most notable in his ability to meld botany and medicine was William Withering, an M.D. from Edinburgh University, who practiced medicine in Stafford and later Birmingham, England. Withering became famous for his ability to treat certain disorders, especially dropsy, a disease characterized by a fluid buildup in the extremities (and lungs), a weak pulse, and shortness of breath. Dropsy was later to become known as congestive heart failure. Prior to Withering, treatment of dropsy often consisted literally of puncturing patients to drain fluid from swollen tissues. Withering learned to treat these patients, often successfully, with foxglove (*Digitalis purpurea*). Withering initially gained knowledge of digitalis from a midwife and herbal healer from Shropshire. Her knowledge was in all likelihood traceable, directly or indirectly, back to the use of foxglove as a poison by witches during the Middle Ages. From the midwife's concoction, Withering was able to conclude that digitalis was the agent effective against dropsy. For 10 years (1775–1785), Withering did extensive clinical experiments on carefully measured dosages of powdered digitalis leaf (extract). His thorough, controlled experimentation not only gave the world a major heart medicine (capable of slowing and strengthening the heartbeat, improving circulation, and moving out excess fluid), but

Figure 2–18 *Digitalis purpurea.*
Foxglove

served as a model to put pharmacognosy (the science of natural product drugs) back on its feet. Through the efforts of Withering, pharmacognosy regained an impetus given to it by Dioscorides more than 1700 years earlier.

Nineteenth century.   Nineteenth-century medicine and pharmacy is a strange mishmash indeed. So many lines of endeavor or schools of thought emerge that it is difficult to weave a common thread. It is clear though that in some circles the efforts of men like William Withering in perfecting crude plant drugs had their impact. A logical extension of the level of pharmacognosy practiced by Withering would be that of isolating and purifying the active ingredients of the cruder (raw) plant product drugs. Such work was undertaken very successfully by Justus von Liebeg of Germany, considered to be the father of physiological chemistry (or more appropriately, perhaps, pharmacology). In the first two-thirds of the nineteenth century, von Liebeg, following up on the work of Friedrich Sertürner (who had isolated morphine from the opium poppy, *Papaver somniferum*), refined practices of drug isolation and purification that still have their impact today. The middle of the nineteenth century also saw the initial production of simple synthetic drugs; for example, salicylic acid (the active ingredient in aspirin), a natural product obtainable from several different plants, was made synthetically in 1853.

Figure 2–19 *Papaver somniferum.*
Opium poppy

On the other hand, the formally educated physicians of the nineteenth century quite often practiced a brand of medicine seemingly having little to do with the sophistication of achievement of men like von Liebeg. Often as not, these regular, or allopathic, doctors used methods and technology that now seem almost barbaric. Dating back centuries to a one time belief in the "invading-spirit theory of disease," the allopaths (although one cannot tar them all with the same brush) frequently used harsh techniques to treat their patients, including practices of blistering, phlebotomy (bleeding), and administration of strong emetics and even mineral poisons (such as mercury and arsenic). Surgery was often performed without sufficient (or any) anesthetic. The use of courses of bleeding, blistering, and poisoning was known as "heroic" medication, the idea being that it would take a strong (heroic) dose or method of medication to cure a serious illness. It is no wonder that patients feared their doctors and that alternative approaches were sought. However, any physician bucking the standard practice of the medical establishment was branded "irregular," and change was hard-wrought and not necessarily rapid.

An early nineteenth-century crusader against heroic medicine was New England-born Samuel Thomson, whose influence was eventually felt over much of the eastern United States. Thomson, lacking a formal education, was a self-proclaimed healer. He believed in the unity of disease and that if, in fact, disease had ultimately a single basis, then a panacea or universal medication could be found. Based, among other things, on knowledge of Indian uses of medicinal herbs and on "curative" properties suited to his self-generated theory of disease, Thomson selected *Lobelia inflata* (Indian tobacco) as the panacea. Eventually known as the "emetic herb," lobelia was combined with various other ingredients (for example, cayenne pepper), in connection with steam baths, in a sequence of treatment steps or courses basically designed to purge and to heat up the digestive tract, and through the digestive tract to provide benefit to other parts of the body. Thomson amassed quite a following, in some cases handing out certificates or "patent rights" to the enlightened (bestowing the privilege of practicing his brand of medicine). Because (as we know today) of lobelia's content of physiologically active alkaloids, there was doubtless on occasion some merit to Thomsonian medication; however, these alkaloids are toxic (with an action similar to nicotine), and illness and even death allegedly resulted from his treatment. At one time, Thomson was involved in litigation for his treatment of a patient.

Regardless of the merit of Thomsonian medicine per se, the Thomsonian movement offered an alternative to regular medicine. Also, it provided impetus to subsequent alternative movements or schools. Particularly influenced were the homeopaths. Although originating prior to Thomsonian medicine, homeopathic medicine began to flourish as Thomsonianism wanned. The northeast-central United States (particularly Ohio and Pennsylvania) became a center for homeopathic medicine in the mid- and late nineteenth century. The homeopaths, similar to the Thomsonians, emphasized plant remedies. However, smaller doses and more diverse medications were advocated. The underlying principle of homeopathy may be stated as follows: a small dose of a drug might alleviate symptoms or disease similar to those induced (in a healthy person) by larger doses of the same drug. For example, dogbane (*Apocynum*), a favorite of the

Figure 2–20 *Lobelia inflata.* Indian tobacco

homeopaths, containing as it does digitalislike substances, causes (in larger doses) irregularities in the heartbeat of healthy individuals. However, a smaller dose may well help to stabilize a weak, irregular heart. Hence, the basic tenant of homeopathy, "let similars be treated by similars," is not without merit, although, of course, it is difficult to generalize or extrapolate to all cases. Doses administered by homeopaths were often so small as to be ineffectual; however, it was rare that any harm came to the patient. The ultimate impact of the ideas and knowledge of the homeopaths and the homeopathic movement was beneficial.

In the late nineteenth century, the Thomsonians, the homeopaths (at least in part), and other sectorial medical groups not mentioned became more or less melded into a compromise school of medicine (which still stood in opposition to the regular medical establishment, that is, to the allopaths). This eclectic school, as it was called, sought not to espouse one particular dogma or belief, but to select the best drugs, methods, and treatments from the wide array available. It is very clear from the extensive literature of eclectic medicine that the overwhelming emphasis was on a variety of plant drugs (but not to the exclusion of drugs from sources other than plants). A leader in the eclectic medical movement in the late nineteenth and early twentieth centuries was John Uri

Figure 2–21 *Apocynum.* Dogbane

Lloyd of Cincinnati. Lloyd spoke out vehemently against the allopathic practices as "cruelty piled on top of torture." A voluminous publisher and inventor of laboratory apparatus, Lloyd was very influential in making drugs "more specific," that is, in perfecting techniques of drug isolation and purification (particularly in regard to drugs listed in the *U.S. Pharmacopoeia*). Lloyd and his brothers owned their own pharmacy and founded their own library, the now famous Lloyd Library of Cincinnati (a great historical resource of pharmacy, botany, and eclectic medicine). Although associated with the Eclectic Medical Institute (College) of Cincinnati and the Cincinnati College of Pharmacy, Lloyd did a great deal of hands-on research on plant drug purification in his own laboratory. In terms of achievement in pharmacognosy, it seems that the nineteenth century closed in Lloyd's laboratory, much in the tradition of former efforts in von Liebeg's laboratory. Although refined, medicines were still largely of natural product (botanical) origin.

Twentieth century.   In the early years of the twentieth century, distinctions between allopaths and eclectics disappeared, and medicine became for a time perhaps more truly eclectic. However, the recent decades of the twentieth century have been dominated by the boom in synthetic drugs. By many it was doubtless assumed that the days of herbal medicine and natural product drugs were numbered for the final time. However, certain major drugs, such as the heart medicine digitalis and the molecules (from Mexican yams) employed as starting points by the steroid industry, have never been adequately replaced synthetically. More cogently, perhaps partly in realization of the shrinkage of the tropical rain forests of the world (and their rich natural warehouses of potentially valuable, unknown, and even unthought-of chemicals), a resurgence in pharmacognosy and herbal medicine in general is occurring. Several American universities now specifically offer graduate degree instruction in pharmacognosy. And let us not forget the many synthetic drugs of today that were based initially on knowledge of naturally occurring chemicals. The question is, how many more natural chemicals of possible aid in combatting pain and disease, the twin companions of the human condition, still await discovery? The answer is, in all likelihood, many!

SELECTED REFERENCES

ANDERSON, FRANK J. 1977. *An Illustrated History of the Herbals.* Columbia University Press, New York. An excellent overview of the renaissance phenomenon of herbalism, tracing its historical roots.

DUKE, JAMES A. 1983. *Medicinal Plants of the Bible.* Trado-Medic Books, New York. At a minimum, be sure to read Duke's highly entertaining introduction.

ETKIN, NINA L. (editor). 1986. *Plants in Indigenous Medicine and Diet: Biobehavioral Approaches*, Redgrave Publishing Co., Bedford Hills, N.Y. See Chapter 15, "Ginseng: A Medical Enigma," by Walter H. Lewis, for a balanced account of the medicinal value of ginseng.

LE STRANGE, RICHARD. 1977. *A History of Herbal Plants.* Angus and Robertson, London. Presents herbal history on a plant-by-plant basis.

READER'S DIGEST (staff). 1986. *Magic and Medicine of Plants.* Reader's Digest Association, Pleasantville, N.Y. Pages 9–23, "Plants in Myth and Magic," and pages 49-73, "Plants, People, and Medicine," constitute particularly interesting reading.

REED, HOWARD S. 1942. *A Short History of the Plant Sciences.* Chronica Botanica, Waltham, Mass. A standard reference on botanical history, from Ancient Egypt forward.

RIDDLE, JOHN M. 1985. *Dioscorides on Pharmacy and Medicine.* University of Texas Press, Austin. Riddle's scholarship renders Dioscorides' monumental work and place in Roman medicine, and more broadly in history, understandable and meaningful to the reader.

SCARBOROUGH, JOHN (editor). 1987. *Folklore and Folk Medicines.* American Institute of the History of Pharmacy, Madison, Wisc. The article by John M. Riddle, "Folk Tradition and Folk Medicine: Recognition of Drugs in Classical Antiquity," is especially enlightening, with specific reference to Hippocratic medications from plants and Greco-Roman medicine in general.

SCHULTES, RICHARD EVANS, AND ALBERT HOFMANN. 1979. *Plants of the Gods.* McGraw-Hill Book Co., New York. "The Hexing Herbs," pages 86–91, deals with plants employed in witchcraft during the Middle Ages.

STARY, FRANTISEK. 1983. *Hamlyn Coulour Guides—Poisonous Plants.* Hamlyn Publishing Group Ltd., London. The Introduction, pages 6–14, contains interesting information on historical poisoning practices.

STEINER, RICHARD P. (editor). 1986. *Folk Medicine—The Art and the Science.* American Chemical Society, Washington, D.C. See especially, Chapter 3, "Ayurveda: The Traditional Medicine of India," by N. G. Patel, and Chapter 8, "Antithrombotic Agent of Garlic: A Lesson from 5000 Years of Folk Medicine," by Eric Block.

STUART, MALCOM (editor). 1979. *The Encyclopedia of Herbs and Herbalism.* Grosset & Dunlap, New York. "The History of Herbalism," pages 13–27, by Kay Sanecki and Christopher Pick, and "The Medicinal Uses of Plants," pages 47–69, by Peter Hylands and Malcolm Stuart, are chapters particularly pertinent to the topic of medicinal plants in history.

THOMPSON, C. J. S. 1931. *Poisons and Poisoners.* Macmillan Company, New York. An interesting account of poisoning and substances employed as poisons through various historical episodes.

THOMSON, WILLIAM A. R. (editor). *Medicines from the Earth.* McGraw-Hill Book Co., New York. See pages 137–149, "The Heritage of Folk Medicine," by Richard Evans Schultes, for an improved understanding of "the contribution of folk healers to the modern science of ethnopharmacology."

VAN DER ZEE, BARBARA GRIGGS. 1981. *Green Pharmacy—A History of Herbal Medicine.* Viking Press, New York. Good coverage of botanical–medical movements, such as those in nineteenth-century America.

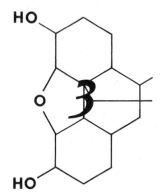

Toxic Plant Substances: The Chemistry of Poisonous and Medicinal Plants

A given plant is literally a warehouse of thousands of kinds of chemicals. Most of these compounds are harmless. Indeed, many chemicals of plants are of great value, and a number are essential to the sustenance of life on earth, both plant and animal life. Life as we know it is carbon based, and the simple sugar molecules (for example, glucose) generated in the interaction of sunlight with cells of green plants in photosynthesis fuel the fire for virtually all the food chains in nature. From these simple sugars, other critical molecules, such as the amino acids, may be generated through often complex biochemical pathways. Amino acids are the building blocks of proteins, which in turn constitute the basic framework of protoplasm (the living substance); some 20 amino acids are essential in sustaining life and its attendant biochemical processes (metabolism). The pathways of metabolism that are essential to life are as termed primary metabolism, and the compounds directly involved in these pathways (such as glucose or essential amino acids) are referred to as primary compounds or primary metabolites. However, a host of other types of compounds are produced by plants in secondary pathways, and even primary metabolites such as glucose may occur secondarily (for example, as components of types of glucosides). The functions of these secondary compounds, (alkaloids, glucosides, or more broadly glycosides, phenolic compounds, and so on) are less clear, and often they do not appear to be obligatorily related to the maintenance of life. It is this broad and rather ill-defined group of secondary compounds to which most toxic plant substances belong; in a sense, plant toxins may be viewed as a sort of subcategory of secondary compounds from plants (that is, those secondary compounds that are toxic). Many, certainly not all, of these toxic compounds seem without apparent function in the plant, except as one could argue their potential value as survival adaptations (defense mechanisms)—in certain instances a strong argument indeed! Whether some among these compounds arose simply as "evolutionary noise," doing no particular good nor harm in the plant, is still a matter of debate. Regardless, toxic plant substances belong mostly to a relatively few broad categories of compounds. The major groupings of potentially toxic substances are listed next. The order given will be followed in the ensuing discussion. All but the last category (minerals) are organic compounds (compounds of carbon).

> Alkaloids
> Glycosides
> Proteinaceous compounds
> Organic acids
> Alcohols
> Resins and resinoids (including phenolics)
> Mineral toxins (nonorganic compounds)

ALKALOIDS

Of premier importance among potentially toxic plant compounds are the alkaloids. Several thousand individual kinds of molecules belong to the general and heterogeneous category of chemical known as alkaloid. As a group, alkaloids defy definition, and more precision of classification may well arise in the future. The word alkaloid means alkalilike, and indeed the majority of these usually bitter tasting molecules are mildly alkaline in chemical reaction; but some clearly are not! Alkaloids vary greatly in their chemical structure, and there is no uniform model for an alkaloid molecule. Alkaloid molecules generally have a ringlike configuration (single or multiple rings) and contain nitrogen. But these features do not distinguish alkaloids from all other types of compounds.

Alkaloids are reasonably common molecules in certain groups of plants; it is estimated that alkaloids occur in perhaps 20 percent of higher plant families. The production of this type of molecule by animals is considerably more rare. In plants, alkaloids have in the past commonly been interpreted to be nothing more than waste products or by-products of metabolism and to be for the most part apparently functionless. It was considered that they may play some role in plant tissues in binding up potentially reactive ionic nitrogen (but then, what of plants that do not produce alkaloids?). There is now strong support for the idea that the bitter alkaloids may play a highly significant role in chemical defense, that is, in controlling animal (including insect) predation of plants. In animals (especially mammals), the effect of many alkaloids, even in minute quantities, can be profound indeed. The most universal effect of alkaloids in animals is on the nervous system; however, other organ systems are often affected as well in one way or another.

Regarding the effects of alkaloids on animals or humans, it is sometimes assumed that alkaloids are psychoactive; however, this is true for only a small minority of these compounds. Clear examples of psychoactive alkaloids are the following: Morphine is the principal alkaloid extracted from opium, which is the crude, milky latex that exudes from the cut surface of the unripe opium poppy capsule (fruit of *Papaver somniferum*). Morphine and derivatives such as heroin have a strong sedative or narcotic effect on the central nervous system. Cocaine, an alkaloid of the belladonna type (see the following listing) obtained from leaves of *Erythroxylum coca*, has a stimulating effect on the nervous system, resulting in euphoria. Hyoscyamine and scopolamine (atropinelike alkaloids) are tropane alkaloids found in henbane (*Hyoscyamus niger*) and belladonna (*Atropa belladonna*). More specifically than simply being psychoactive, the alkaloids of henbane and belladonna are truly hallucinogenic (see Chapter 13 under *Atropa belladonna*). Henbane and belladonna were among species of plants used in the practice of sorcery during the Middle Ages. Henbane (more accurately its tropane alkaloid content) is known to be capable of producing a state of permanent insanity. Mescaline, the main alkaloid from the small and spineless peyote cactus (*Lophophora williamsii*) of central Mexico, causes profound, kaleidoscopic hallucinations involving a progression of rich colors. Peyote has been used for centuries for divination in religious ceremony by various Mexican Indians (including, formerly, Aztecs in pre-Columbian Mexico). LSD (lysergic acid diethylamide), an alkaloidal substance isolated from the ergot fungus (*Claviceps purpurea*), produces visual and tactile hallucinations; ergot has been implicated in the Salem, Massachusetts witchcraft trials in the 1690s. Employed in religious ritual by the Mazatec Indians of central Mexico, *Psilocybe* (the magic mushroom) contains psilocybin or psilocin, an intensely hallucinogenic alkaloid chemically similar to LSD. Understanding of the action of hallucinogenic alkaloids in the brain is incomplete; however, it is now known that alterations of the essential neurotransmitter chemical serotonin (itself similar in chemical makeup to LSD) are involved (see B. L. Jacobs, selected references).

One type of alkaloid of concern in regard to psychoactive responses in animals (for example, cattle) is the peculiar indolizidine alkaloids found in locoweeds of western rangelands (one species of locoweed involved being spotted locoweed, *Astragalus lentiginosus*). Cattle suffering locoweed intoxication (locoism) literally act as if they are crazy; they may walk into obstructions, leap imaginary objects, and move suddenly backward for no apparent reason. Strangely, affected animals will continue to seek out locoweed for consumption. Over time, actual structural changes in certain cells (vacuolation of Purkinje cells) of the central nervous system of the animals will take place. Emaciation and eventually death may occur (see Molyneux and James, selected references).

Although most typically affecting the nervous system, the vast majority of alkaloids are not psychoactive (and certainly not hallucinogenic); however, many are toxic to one extent or another. Some significant and perhaps familiar alkaloids are the following: caffeine, in coffee; theobromine, in chocolate; ephedrine, in some nasal sprays; nicotine in tobacco; lobeline, from Indian tobacco (once in stop-smoking aids); coniine, present in poison hemlock (coniine was the first alkaloid produced synthetically); quinine, effective in treatment of malaria; strychnine, a powerful convulsant poison; the curare alkaloids, useful in relaxing muscles during surgery; and solanine, extractable from the green parts of tomato and potato.

The following diagrammatic sketches show the major types (configurations) of alkaloids of significance in considerations of plant toxicity.

BELLADONNA TYPE (TROPANE OR ATROPINE ALKALOIDS)

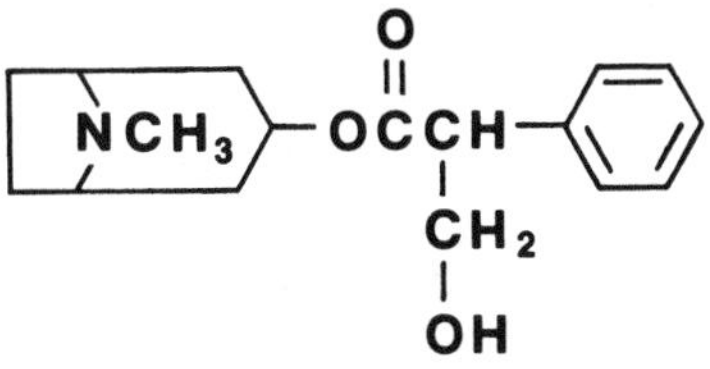

Belladonna (*Atropa*)
Jimson weed (*Datura*)
Henbane (*Hyoscyamus*)
Mandrake (*Mandragora*)
Coca tree (*Erythroxylum*)

Figure 3–1 Atropine

GROUNDSEL TYPE (PYRROLIZIDINE ALKALOIDS)

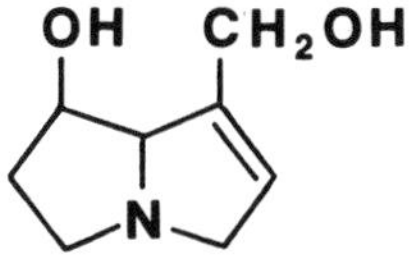

Groundsel (*Senecio*)
Blue devil (*Echium*)
Heliotrope (*Heliotropium*)

Figure 3–2 Retronecine

HEMLOCK TYPE (PYRIDINE OR PIPERIDINE ALKALOIDS)

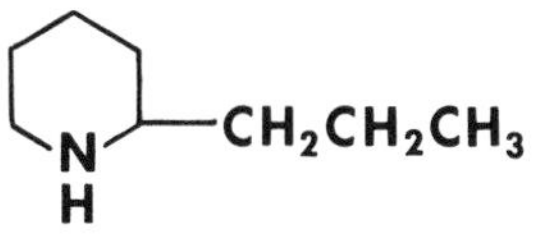

Poison hemlock (*Conium*)
Indian tobacco (*Lobelia*)

Figure 3–3 Coniine

NICOTINE OR TOBACCO TYPE (PYRROLIDINE–PYRIDINE ALKALOIDS)

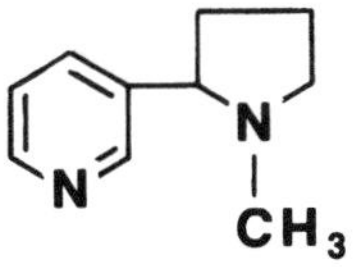

Tobacco (*Nicotiana*)
Horsetail (*Equisetum*)

Figure 3–4 Nicotine

COFFEE OR CAFFEINE TYPE (PURINE ALKALOIDS)

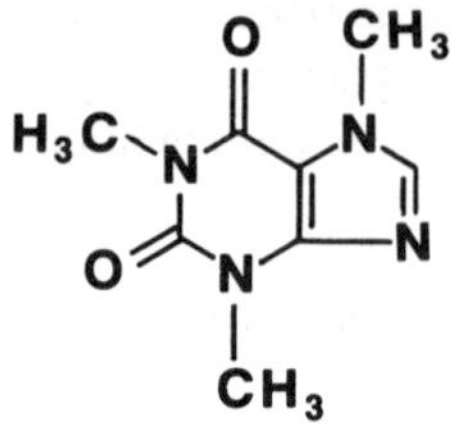

Coffee (*Coffea*)
Chocolate, "cola"
Cocoa (*Theobroma*)
Tea (*Camellia*)

Figure 3–5   Caffeine

QUININE TYPE (QUINOLINE ALKALOIDS)

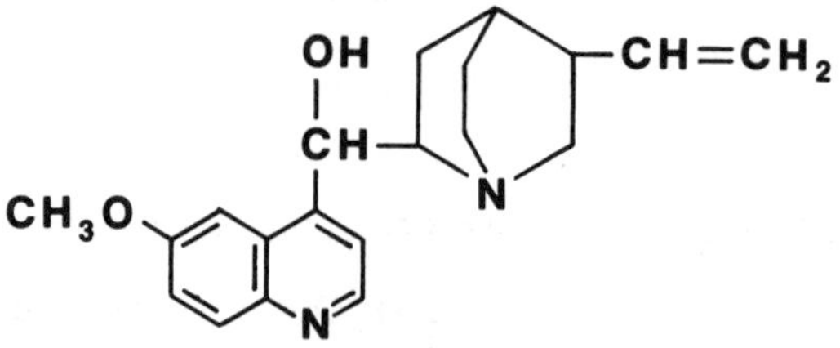

Quinine tree (*Cinchona*)
Globe thistle (*Echninops*)

Figure 3–6   Quinine

OPIUM OR MORPHINE TYPE (ISOQUINOLINE ALKALOIDS)

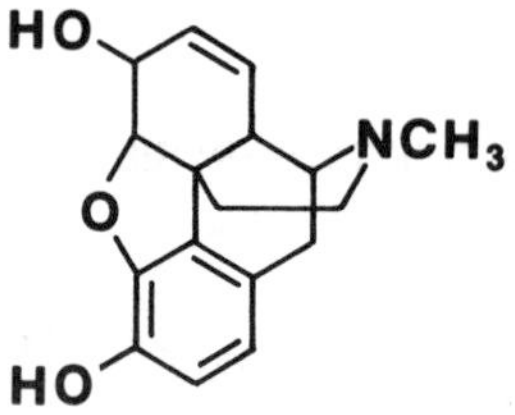

Opium poppy (*Papaver*)
Bloodroot (*Sanguinaria*)
Dutchman's britches,
Squirrel corn (*Dicentra*)
Golden seal (*Hydrastis*)
Fumatory (*Corydalis*)

Figure 3–7   Morphine

ERGOT TYPE (INDOLE OR INDOLIZIDINE ALKALOIDS)

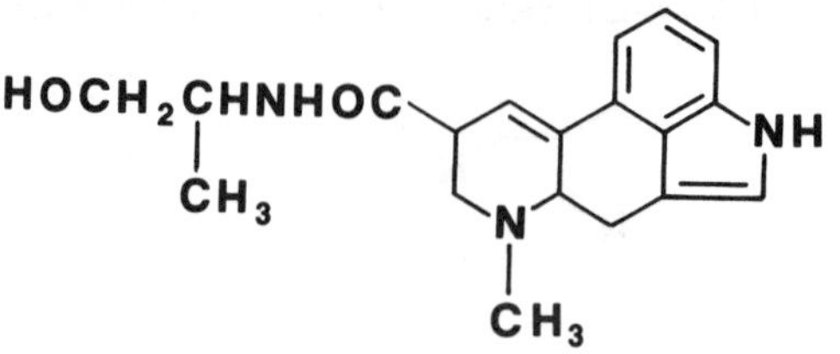

Ergot (*Claviceps*)
Magic mushroom (*Psilocybe*)
Locoweed (*Astragalus*)
Carolina jessamine (*Gelsemium*)
Strychnine (*Strychnos*)

Figure 3–8   Ergonovine

LUPINE TYPE (QUINOLIZIDINE ALKALOIDS, THAT IS, CYTISINE TYPE)

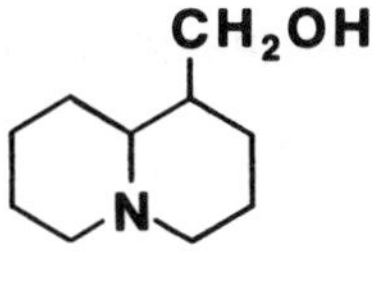

Lupines (*Lupinus*)
Golden chain (*Laburnum*)
False indigo (*Baptisia*)
Scotch broom (*Cytisus*)
Kentucky coffee tree (*Gymnocladus*)

Figure 3–9   Lupinine

TOMATO OR SOLANINE TYPE (STEROIDAL, GLYCOALKALOIDS)

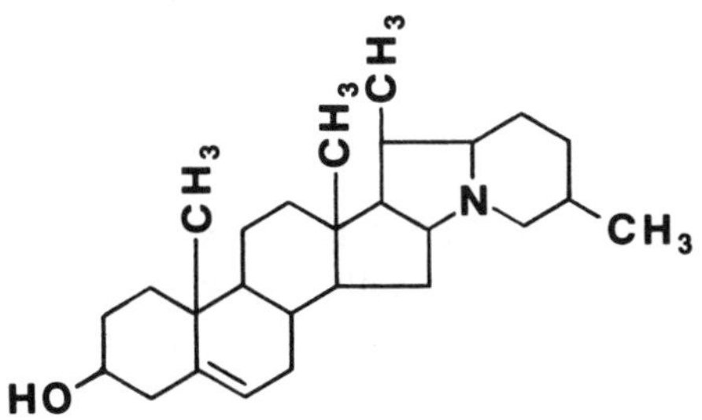

Tomato (*Lycopersicon*)
Irish potato (*Solanum*)
Nightshades (*Solanum*)

Figure 3–10   Solanidine

VERATRUM TYPE (STEROID ALKALOIDS)

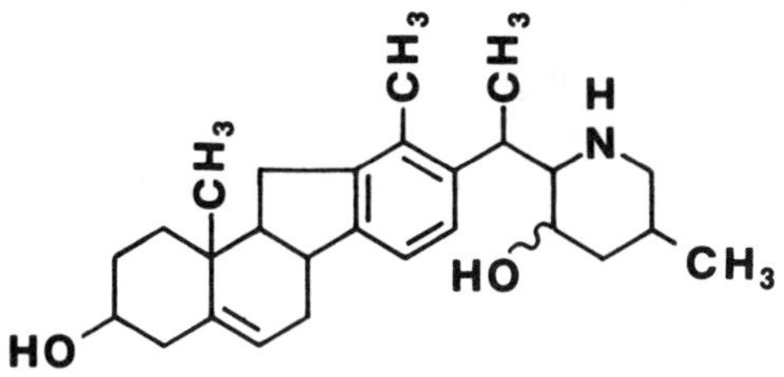

False hellebore (*Veratrum*)
Death camus (*Zigadenus*)

Figure 3–11   Veratramine

LARKSPUR TYPE (DITERPENOID ALKALOIDS)

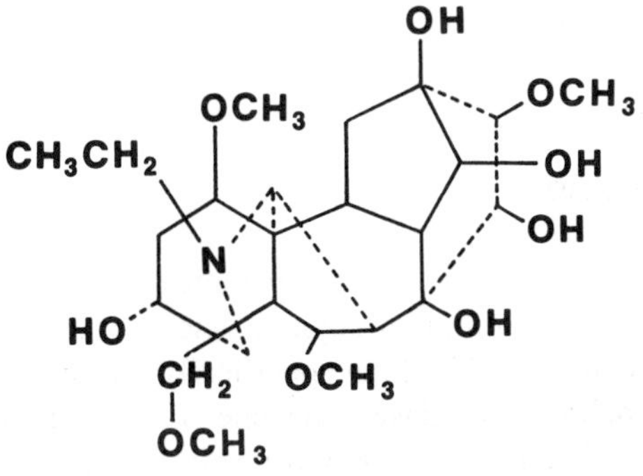

Larkspur (*Delphinium*)
Monkshood (*Aconitum*)

Figure 3–12   Aconitine

MESCALINE TYPE (PHENYLAMINE ALKALOIDS)

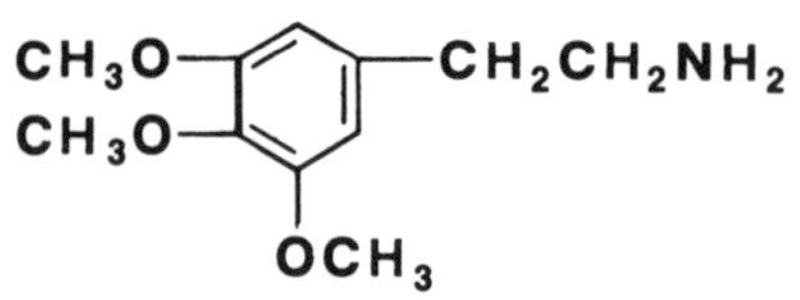

$$CH_3O\text{—}\underset{OCH_3}{\overset{}{\bigcirc}}\text{—}CH_2CH_2NH_2$$

Peyote (*Lophophora*)
Ephedra (*Ephedra*)

Figure 3–13 Mescaline

GLYCOSIDES

Second in importance only to the alkaloids as toxic plant substances is the broad category of glycosides. Glycosides vary greatly in structure. However, all glycosides are, at least, two-part molecules: (1) a simple sugar (like glucose, but definitely not restricted to glucose) joined to (2) something that is not a sugar. The nonsugar portion of a glycoside molecule is known as the aglycone (or genin). Glycosides often are relatively inert when the two parts of the molecule are connected; however, when separated from the sugar moiety, the aglycone may show more activity (that is, toxicity). Separation of the aglycone is to be expected as a consequence of hydrolysis of the oxygen bond (between sugar and aglycone) during animal digestion. At least in regard to toxic plant substances, the major categories of glycosides are recognized by the type of aglycone present (that is, generated as a result of hydrolysis of the molecule). Major categories of potentially toxic glycosides occurring naturally in plants are listed next, and discussion of each follows this outline.

1. Cyanogenic (cyanogenetic) glycosides
2. Steroid glycosides
   a. Cardiac glycosides (cardenolides)
   b. Saponins (sapogenic glycosides)
3. Coumarin glycosides
4. Anthraquinone glycosides
5. Mustard oil (and related) glycosides

Cyanogenic Glycosides

In cyanogenic glycosides, the aglycone is cyanide or, more appropriately, hydrocyanic acid (HCN); in older literature, hydrocyanic acid is often referred to as prussic acid. Cyanide (HCN) is cytotoxic, blocking specifically the activity of one of the enzymes of respiration (cytochrome oxidase), the one directly involved in oxygen uptake. Consequently, cyanosis and asphyxia will result from cyanide poisoning. A number of plants (or at least portions of them), for example, hydrangea (*Hydrangea*), flax (*Linum*), elderberry (*Sambucus*), and wild cherry (*Prunus*), are cyanophoric (that is, contain cyanide-releasing substances). Best known of these substances is the cyanogenic glycoside (amygdalin) found in seeds or pits of certain members of the rose family, such as wild cherry, peach, apricot, apple, and almond. Amygdalin is actually a three-part molecule, on hydrolysis yielding sugar + cyanide + benzaldehyde. Benzaldehyde is the "fragrance of almond" and may be perceived on the breath of persons poisoned with amygdalin. Amygdalin, prepared commercially from ground up apricot pits, is also known as laetrile. Laetrile is a highly controversial substance used in cancer chemotherapy (mostly illegally in the United States). Studies by the National Cancer Institute proved inconclusive, but the majority of evidence as to the value of laetrile is on the negative side. The Federal Drug Administration opposes laetrile because (1) it may be of little ultimate value in chemotherapy, and hence its use gives cancer patients false hope and wastes valuable time (when they could be obtaining more truly effective treatment), and (2) the cyanide released is not specific for cancer (tumor) cells and is systemically cytotoxic.

Steroid Glycosides

In steroid glycosides, the sugar is joined to a steroid molecule (steroid nucleus). In the cardiac glycosides (cardenolides or cardenolide glycosides), a major category of steroid glycoside, an additional side ring (the lactone ring) is connected to the fundamental four-ringed steroid nucleus. The presence of this lactone ring imparts the cardioactive properties to these molecules. Cardiac glycosides, in medicinal dose, increase the contractility of heart muscle and consequently the force of (at the same time slowing) the heartbeat. Cardiac output is thereby regulated in patients suffering congestive heart failure. Toxic doses (often not greatly different in quantity from medicinal doses) may cause arrhythmias or even cardiac arrest. Digoxin (or digitoxin) from foxglove (see Chapter 13 under *Digitalis*), convallarin from lily-of-the-valley (*Convallaria*), and ouabain from *Strophanthus* (Chapter 13) have been perhaps the principal cardiac glycosides employed in formal medicine (use of extracts of lily-of-the-valley is basically restricted to the Soviet Union). Other plants containing cardiac glycosides include dogbane (*Apocynum*), various species of milkweed (*Asclepias*), and oleander (*Nerium*). In particular, the cardiac glycosides of oleander are much too toxic for medicinal use. Various glycosides extracted from *Asclepias* species (milkweeds) have received considerable study (for example, Seiber and others *in* Keeler and Tu, 1983, selected references), following up on the initial classic work on the role of milkweed glycosides in biochemical ecology by Brower (selected references). These glycosides are toxic to vertebrate animals and are accumulated by various species of insects (to which there is no apparent harm) feeding on certain milkweeds for protection against vertebrate predation. It appears that at least the majority of species of milkweeds may contain cardenolides, although the concentrations and exact nature of the compounds may vary greatly from one species to another.

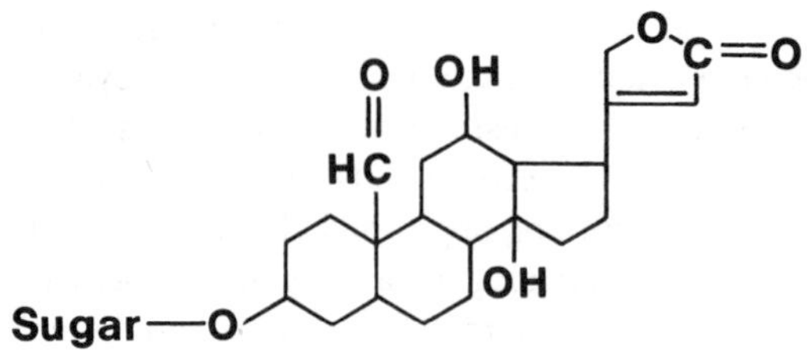

Figure 3–14 Calotoxin (glycoside from milkweed)

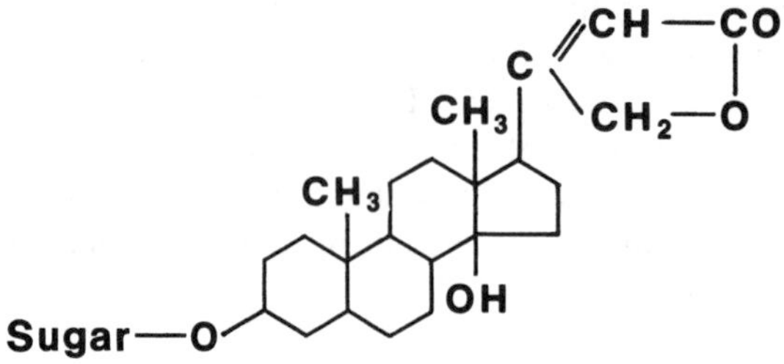

Figure 3–15 Digitoxin (glycoside from foxglove)

The second category of steroid glycosides is that of the saponin (sapogenic) glycosides. The steroid skeleton of a saponin is not connected to a lactone ring as it is in the cardiac glycosides. Saponins are not especially cardioactive and are of much less significance in medicine than cardiac glycosides. However, typically, saponins are toxic. Taken internally, they will often cause severe gastric irritation (perhaps injuring the lining of the digestive tract). Although not readily absorbed into the bloodstream, their sapogenins (aglycones) are hemolytic; that is, they will cause rupturing or lysis of red blood cells (erythrocytes)by reacting with cholesterol in the cell membrane. Plants containing intestinally corrosive saponins include corn cockle (*Agrostemma*), tungnut (*Aleurites*), pokeweed (*Phytolacca*), English ivy (*Hedera*), and soapwort or bouncing Bet (*Saponaria*). Saponins in soapwort account for the frothing or soaplike action of the minced plant when mixed with water; soapwort was at one time actually employed as a soap substitute.

Coumarin Glycosides

In coumarin glycosides the aglycone to which sugar is connected is a peculiar, oxidized, phenolic type of molecule (a coumarin). Coumarins are found scattered throughout the plant kingdom. Seeds of Ohio buckeye (*Aesculus glabra*) contain a coumarin that is a mild toxin of the nervous system. Both yellow and white sweet clover (*Melilotus* spp.) contain coumarins, which account for the characteristic smell of freshly cut hay. These particular coumarins are harmless except under certain moldy conditions, when the combination of sweet clover coumarin, moisture, and fungal activity results in the formation of double coumarin molecules, or dicoumarins. Molded sweet clover was responsible for "bleeding disease" in cattle, appearing during 1921–1922 in the upper Midwest and Canada. Dicoumarins are powerful anticoagulants, and the affected cattle literally bled to death by internal hemorrhage (visible externally only by swollen or bruised areas on parts of the body). In some cases herds were virtually decimated.

However, as is sometimes true, benefit may eventually grow out of hardship. Knowledge gained (of the anticoagulant dicoumarins) was eventually put to use in human medicine, in medications designed to control clotting, or "thin" the blood. As peripheral and seemingly unlikely as connections can be, knowledge of dicoumarol substances has found significant application in rat control. Dicoumarol is the main ingredient (trade name of Warfarin) in major rodenticides used today, such as Decon. Rats consuming this type of rat poison simply go off and die by bleeding to death inside—no muss, no fuss.

Compounds (sometimes toxic) related to coumarins, the furans, occur in various plants (for example, moldy or "stressed" sweet potatoes, *Ipomoea*). Furans may be combined with coumarins (furanocoumarins or furocoumarins), as in the potentially photoallergenic substance (psoralen) found in wild parsnip (*Pastinaca*). The black mold *Aspergillus flavus* produces furanocoumarin substances (known as aflatoxins), often associated with spoiled grain, which may be carcinogenic to liver cells, among other effects.

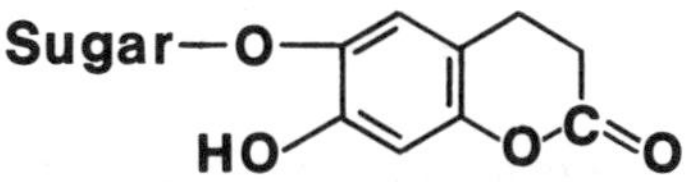

Figure 3–16 Esculin (aesculin), coumarin glycoside from buckeye

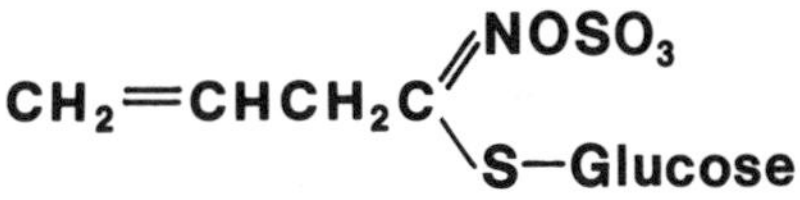

Figure 3–17 Sinigrin (glucosinolate from black mustard)

Anthraquinone and Mustard Oil Glycosides

To wrap up other types of glycosides expeditiously, the aglycones (anthraquinones) of anthraquinone glycosides are typically cathartic substances. Anthraquinones of senna (*Cassia fistulosa*) and of *Aloe* spp. have been ingredients of commercial cathartics. Mustard oils (of mustard-oil glycosides or glucosinolates) are rather simple, sulfur-containing compounds found in a number of members of the mustard family (for example, black mustard, *Brassica nigra*). Mustard oils (technically, thiocyanates or isothiocyantes) are irritants of the digestive tract, usually causing no more than mild gastric distress; more serious problems, however, are occasionally encountered in cattle consuming wild mustard in quantity (especially mustard seed accidentally mixed in feed). Closely related to mustard oil glyclosides are goitrogenic (goiter-inducing) glycosides, also found in certain members of the mustard family (for example, cabbage). These may cause the development of goiter in iodine-deficient diets by blocking iodine uptake and hormone production in the thyroid gland, resulting in an enlarged thyroid (goiter).

PROTEINACEOUS COMPOUNDS

Proteinaceous compounds constitute a vast assemblage of molecules. Many are involved directly in the structure and chemical machinery of the cell, and hence the sustenance of life. Proteins are a generally harmless and often beneficial group of substances. The number of actually harmful or toxic proteinaceous substances occurring naturally in plants is small; however, this limited group of poisonous compounds is nonetheless quite significant in terms of toxicity. Whether beneficial or toxic, proteinaceous substances are nitrogenous compounds of carbon and may often contain sulfur as well. In terms of structure, nature may often be viewed as being ordered into subunits or subsets; this is true of the living substance (protoplasm) and especially of proteins. Just as proteins (or proteinaceous materials) are considered to be the building blocks of protoplasm, amino acids are considered to be the building blocks of proteins. Amino acids are indeed the subunits of which proteins are built. Since it is essentially impossible to have a meaningful discussion of proteins without consideration of amino acids, the structure of a typical amino acid is presented in Figure 3–18.

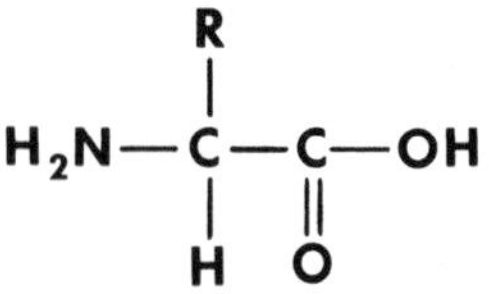

$$H_2N-\overset{\overset{\displaystyle R}{|}}{\underset{\underset{\displaystyle H}{|}}{C}}-\overset{\displaystyle C}{\underset{\underset{\displaystyle O}{\|}}{}}-OH$$

Figure 3–18 Amino acid (generalized structure)

As the name indicates, amino acids are (organic) acid molecules on one end of the molecule and are basic (amino, that is, ammonia) on the other end. This molecular polarity enables amino acids to join together (acid end to base end), often in long chains, by peptide (carbon to nitrogen) bonds. Isolated or noncombined amino acids exist (nonprotein amino acids, such as canavanine from jack bean in the legume family), and these may be toxic because of their tendency to substitute into protein structure in place of more standard amino acids. However, as indicated, most proteinaceous compounds (or more specifically, toxic proteinaceous compounds) in plants are various combinations (or derivatives) of amino acids. The categories of proteinaceous compounds, determined in part by the number of amino acids per molecule, are as follows:

1. *Proteins:* Hundreds to thousands of amino acids joined together per molecule (macromolecules).
2. *Polypeptides:* Smaller; usually between five and ten amino acids per molecule.
3. *Amines:* Smallest; derivatives of single amino acids.

Proteins

Toxic substances that are true proteins, in older literature referred to as phytotoxins or toxalbumins, are known from relatively few plants. However, some of these are quite significant in terms of their toxicity and potential use in medicine. Noteworthy examples of specific, poisonous, plant macromolecules (proteins) are abrin, found in seeds of the rosary pea or precatory bean (*Abrus precatorius*), and ricin, occurring in castor bean (*Ricinus communis*) seeds. Abrin and ricin have somewhat similar effects and are among the most potent toxins known (certainly among flowering plants). Both are significantly more toxic if injected directly. The minimal lethal dose of pure ricin is 0.00000001 percent of the animals weight by injection. Taken orally, a few seeds at most of either *Abrus* or *Ricinus* are likely to prove fatal if masticated. Abrin and ricin are interesting compounds in that, chemically, they are similar to bacterial toxins, such as those of cholera, tetanus, and diphtheria, as well as to certain snake venoms; however, they are somewhat more readily absorbed through the lining of the digestive tract. Both abrin and ricin can ulcerate the digestive tract, thereby increasing the possibility of absorption into the bloodstream. In addition to intense abdominal pain and bloody diarrhea, when distributed systemically by the circulatory system, cell damage to various organs or systems (for example, liver, kidneys, nervous system) may occur.

Abrin and ricin are potent cytotoxins, acting as proteolytic enzymes, and acting on the cell's ribosomes (where amino acids are joined together to form enzymes and other proteins) to prevent necessary protein synthesis; the result is cell destruction and degeneration. Probably because of their peculiar binding potential, abrin and ricin are selectively transported (suicide transport) by nerve cells (neurons), a fact that has clinical application in neurology (in the intentional denervation of specific portions of the nervous system; see Wiley, Blessing, and Reis, selected references). Abrin, in particular, is known to cause the agglutination (clumping) of red blood cells (forming small clots or thrombi). Abrin binds to surface glycoproteins of the erythrocytes, forming bridges between cells. Such plant seed proteins, which agglutinate blood cells, are most generally known as lectins.

In *Abrus* seeds there is a virtually identical toxin (technically, abrin) and a lectin, both of which are capable of hemagglutination. Some lectins, such as that from *Abrus*, are capable of stimulating other types of blood cells (lymphocytes) to divide (and mature). Plant lectins stimulating mitosis in white blood cells are known more specifically as mitogens. Most significant among plant mitogens are proteins (glycoproteins) from pokeweed (*Phytolacca americana*). Division of both T and B lymphocytes is stimulated by pokeweed mitogens. Since these types of lymphocytes are critical to immunity, pokeweed mitogens have assumed an important role as a tool used to study the onset of the immune response and the immune responsiveness of the body under pathological states (such as Hodgkin's disease). Initial discovery of plant mitogens came from postmortem examination of the blood of a child who died from pokeweed poisoning, and whose immune system, it was discovered, had been triggered. Plant mitogens are now considered powerful clinical and research tools and are receiving great interest, with those from pokeweed foremost on the list. Other, perhaps less significant, mitogenic lectins have been isolated from black locust (*Robinia pseudo-acacia*) and the sandbox tree (*Hura crepitans*).

Polypeptides

Toxic polypeptides are to be found in several species of fungi belonging to the genus (*Amanita*), including *A. phalloides* (the death cap) and its close relatives. These polypeptides (amatoxins, phallotoxins, and phalloidin) are composed variously of seven or eight amino acids and are cyclic (circular) in their molecular architecture (that is, they are cyclopeptides). Among other effects, and not unlike the toxic protein from rosary pea, the toxic cyclic polypeptides from *Amanita* interfere with the genetic message of the cell, specifically with RNA-polymerase, inhibiting the synthesis of new and necessary proteins. Cell destruction or degeneration in the intestine, liver, kidney, and even the heart wall is typical of poisoning by *Amanita*. *Amanita* is the genus of mushrooms most often reportedly involved in fatal human mushroom poisoning. Cyclic polypeptides, causing digestive upset and liver damage, are also to be found in certain blue-green algae (cyanobacteria), which become common in farm ponds in late summer. Livestock are rather commonly victims of blue-green algal poisoning.

Amines

Toxic amines are known in the genus *Lathyrus* (vetchlings, sweet peas), specifically a variant of aminopropionitrile (the amine and nitrile groups of the molecule both contributing to the toxicity). As discussed in Chapter 11, the amines (in the seeds) of *Lathyrus* cause degeneration in motor tracts of the spinal cord, perhaps resulting in paralysis (or even death), in a condition known as lathyrism. The berries of mistletoe, *Phoradendron* spp., likewise contain toxic amines (in this case tyramine and a variant of phenylethylamine). Symptoms include acute gastroenteritis and a drastic lowering of blood pressure(and perhaps cardiovascular collapse). Mistletoe extract was for a time employed in France in the treatment of high blood pressure.

ORGANIC ACIDS

Organic acids (carbon-based acids not containing nitrogen, that is, nonamino acids) that occur naturally in plants and that are actually toxic to animals are restricted to a very few types. The only common example is oxalic acid, a simple organic acid composed of only two carbon atoms. Oxalic acid and its soluble salts (for example, sodium oxalate and potassium acid oxalate) are toxic; however, only a limited number of plants contain soluble oxalate in sufficient quantity to cause serious toxicity. A dry weight oxalate content of approximately 10 percent is usually requisite to the consideration of a plant as dangerous in terms of oxalate poisoning (if consumed in average quantity). Such levels of oxalate are occasionally seen in beet tops and more commonly in rhubarb (the leaf blades, not the leaf stalks). Perhaps most significant among plants causing oxalate poisoning is *Halogeton glomeratus*, an accidentally introduced weed that has become locally common in cold desert regions of certain western states (for example, Nevada, Utah, Idaho). Native to steppe areas of southern Russia, *Halogeton* was apparently introduced by imported sheep and spread along sheep trails during the early part of this century. In the 1940s, major poisonings of sheep feeding on *Halogeton* occurred in western Nevada and even more dramatically in southern Idaho, where thousands of head were lost, and entire ranches were abandoned as a consequence. Better agricultural education and range practices have now reduced cases of poisoning by *Halogeton*. Although variable, the dry-weight oxalate content of *Halogeton* has been found to exceed 30 percent. Ingestion of as little as 9 ounces of potent *Halogeton* has the potential to kill a mature sheep within 10 hours. Soluble oxalate, readily absorbed from the digestive tract (especially in connection with a low-calcium diet), reacts with blood calcium (to form calcium oxalate), causing ionic imbalance and decreasing the coagulatory properties of the blood; internal hemorrhage is sometimes a result. Perhaps of more immediate significance in causing death, however, is the damage to the kidneys (nephritis and renal failure), which occurs as a consequence of the rather rapid accumulation of insoluble (calcium oxalate) crystals in the kidney tubules.

Plant species containing low to moderate levels of soluble oxalate (for example, dock, *Rumex* spp.; sorrel, *Oxalis* spp.; and spinach, *Spinacia oleracea*) typically cause little trouble in terms of toxicity. Likewise, plants in which oxalate is present in the tissues in solid form (calcium oxalate) are of relatively little concern. In representatives of the aroid family (for example, jack-in-the-pulpit, dumbcane, and caladium), oxalate occurs as sharp, needlelike crystals of calcim oxalate (raphides). If plant parts are chewed, these crystals may become lodged in the mucous lining of the mouth and throat, causing burning, irritation, and swelling. However, this is typically not serious, and symptoms disappear in a few days at most. Ingestion of solid oxalate (calcium oxalate) represents no danger to the blood and kidneys, because insoluble oxalate is not absorbed through the wall of the digestive tract.

Figure 3–19   Oxalic acid and its soluble salts

ALCOHOLS

Although it can be argued that all alcohols are at least somewhat toxic, and alcohols are common compounds, examples of naturally occurring, truly poisonous alcohol substances in plants are few. Although few in number, toxic plant alcohols constitute a significant topic, if for no other reason than the example of water hemlock (*Cicuta maculata* and related species), found in moist habitats throughout North America. Water hemlock has been responsible for many deaths of humans and animals. It looks much like wild carrot, but sectioning of the underground portion of the stem (at the vicinity of the point of origin of the fascicled, tuberous roots) reveals chambers (diaphragms) and a yellowish, oily exudate (neither feature found in wild carrot). The toxic compound, isolated from the yellow fluid, is a long (about 17 carbon atoms), straight-chain, unsaturated alcohol molecule, cicutoxin. Water hemlock is commonly mistaken (by people and animals) for a wild edible plant (for example, wild carrot or wild parsnip) and, unfortunately, eaten. Cicutoxin is a powerful and rapidly acting central nervous system convulsant. Convulsions are extremely violent, and symptoms are among the most fearsome that might be encountered (including, in some cases, biting the tongue to shreds, followed by convulsive closure of the mouth, preventing adequate vomiting; bloating and uncontrolled urination may be observed). Death may occur within a few hours or a relatively few minutes after the onset of symptoms.

A somewhat similar alcohol is found in white snakeroot (*Eupatorium rugosum*), common along the borders of woods in the fall in the eastern United States. This toxic alcohol (tremetol), while not necessarily a convulsant, affects the nervous system, and in cattle produces a disease known as trembles. Tremetol (being fat soluble) may become concentrated in the milk or butterfat of cows. In this way, the compound is passed on to suckling animals or to human beings drinking the milk. In human beings the disease (characterized by trembling, weakness, nausea, and prostration) is known as milk sickness. During the first half of the nineteenth century, milk sickness was responsible for great loss of human life in local areas of the eastern United States because of lack of knowledge of the source of the disorder. The localization of milk sickness was of course due to cattle in a particular location

$$HOCH_2CH_2CH_2C \equiv C - C \equiv C(CH = CH)_3 \overset{\overset{\displaystyle OH}{\displaystyle |}}{C}HCH_2CH_2CH_3$$

Figure 3–20   Cicutoxin (alcohol from water hemlock)

feeding heavily on white snakeroot. Milk sickness is a historical disease, only rarely seen at the present time. Its decline is due largely to the practice of pooling of milk from diverse areas in large vats for pasteurization and homogenization, greatly diluting any tremetol that might be present.

RESINS AND RESINOIDS

Resinous substances constitute the group of plant toxins perhaps most difficult to categorize in chemical terms. This is because chemically diverse and sometimes unrelated molecules have been placed under this heading. However, at least some of the noteworthy toxic "resins" from plants are actually phenolic compounds, which themselves constitute a diversified group of compounds. Phenolic compounds could be considered to be aromatic alcohols, in that alcohol (hydroxyl) groups are connected to aromatic (benzene or phenyl) rings in the fundamental composition of the molecule.

Important, naturally occurring phenolic resins in plants are tetrahydrocannabinol (THC) and related compounds from marijuana or hemp (*Cannabis sativa*). Considered a mild euphoric and narcotic drug, the basic structure of THC, illustrated in Figure 3–21, consists of three phenyl rings joined together. Marijuana was initially introduced into the United States as a fiber plant. Although the last factory making rope from hemp fibers closed in the mid 1950s, *Cannabis sativa* became naturalized and rather widespread in the Mississippi, Missouri, and Ohio river valleys and adjacent territory. Variants of marijuana naturalized in the United States typically have a relatively low THC content (having been selected initially for fiber, not drug, yield); however, leaves from plants naturalized in the United States are nonetheless smoked (illegally) to achieve a "high." Much more potent biotypes of *Cannabis* are grown in tropical American countries and, as is well known, illegally imported into the United States. Grades of marijuana cultivated in the Arab world are often high in potency (THC content); resin from the female flowers of Arabian *Cannabis* is known specifically as hashish and is probably the most potent form of marijuana. In the United States, marijuana has been legalized in several states for medical use (only!). The cannabinol drugs (especially THC and synthetic derivatives or analogs) have found some efficacious use in the treatment of glaucoma (blocking adrenaline, and hence pressure buildup in the eyeball) and in combating the nausea experienced during cancer chemotherapy; recent evidence also indicates that cannabidiol (CBD), a compound from *Cannabis* related to THC, is of benefit in controlling symptoms of epilepsy. It has been debated whether or not *Cannabis sativa* is a toxic plant, harmful to human or animal health. Ingestion of fresh marijuana plants reportedly resulted in the death of horses in Greece (see page 225 in Kingsbury, selected references). However, by some accounts (see Coy W. Waller in Keeler and Tu, selected references) marijuana is not viewed as poisonous when fresh but only when damaged as by drying and/or smoking. Clearly, the opinions as to the harm (or potential benefit) of smoking marijuana are at variance as well.

Other significant phenolic (resinoid) molecules found in plants include urushiol (from poison ivy, poison oak, and poison sumac, *Rhus* spp.) and hypericin (from *Hypericum perforatum*, St. John's wort), both discussed in Chapter 11 under dermatitis. Urushiol, involved in contact dermatitis, is actually a mixture of very similar molecules, each consisting of a single hydroxylated phenyl ring with a rather long side chain (variously 15 or 17 carbon atoms long). The mixture of variants of urushiol differs slightly in poison ivy and poison sumac versus poison oak (with the C-15 chain form dominating in poison ivy and poison sumac, and the C-17 form being prevalent in the poison oaks). This could relate to slight differences in reactivity to the several allergenic species of *Rhus* in a given subject. Hypericin is a much larger, multiple-ringed phenolic molecule, lacking lengthy side chains. Its multiple double bonds

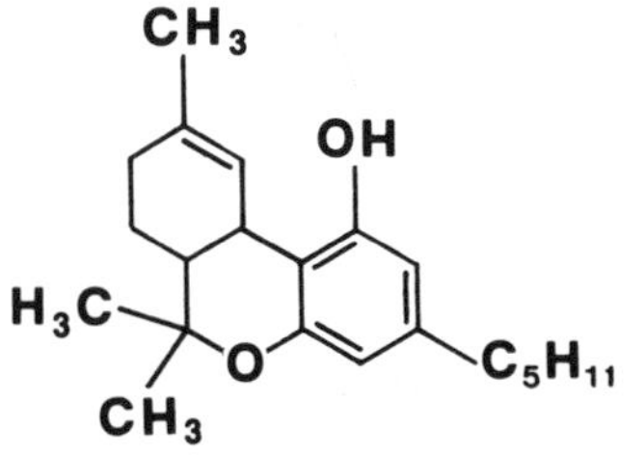

Figure 3–21 Tetrahydrocannabinol (from marijuana)

readily absorb ultraviolet radiation and increase skin sensitivity to sunlight, particularly in exposed facial areas of pale-skinned animals (for example, certain kinds of sheep), resulting in photodermatitis.

As a concluding tidbit to phenolic substances, it has recently been discovered that gossypol, a phenolic compound from cottonseed oil (expressed seed oil of *Gossypium*), may be quite valuable as a potential male contraceptive. This discovery was ultimately based on knowledge that a particular area of China, and one using (exclusively) crude cottonseed oil for cooking, had a remarkably low birthrate. Considered in total, clinical and laboratory studies in China and the United States have shown that gossypol effectively decreases sperm count by selectively blocking a major enzyme critical to the development of sperm, without lowering sex drive. Although more research, particularly into side effects, is necessary, gossypol appears very promising as a "male pill."

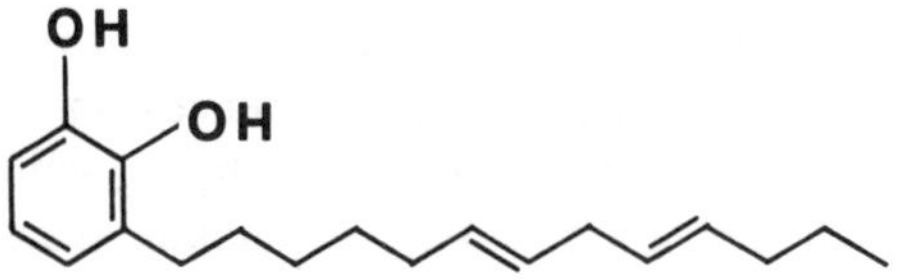

Figure 3–22   Urushiol (from poison ivy)

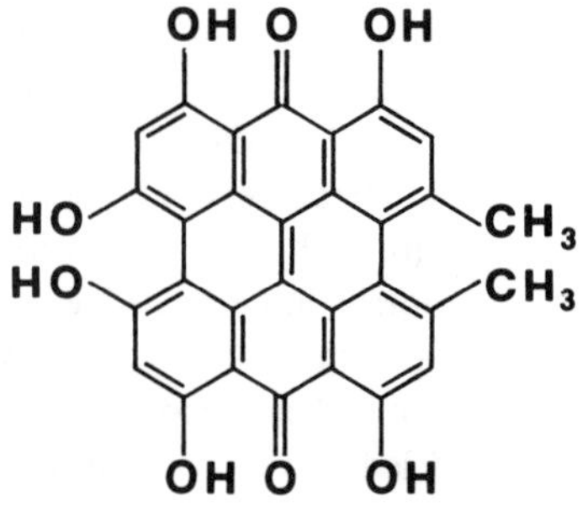

Figure 3–23   Hypericin (from St. John's wort)

Mention should be made of another group of resins, the terpenoids. In some cases superficially resembling phenolics, terpenoids derive from a different biochemical pathway and are classified by the size and configuration of the molecule (mono-, sesqui-, di-, tri- terpenes, and so on). Although most are harmless or even aromatically pleasant and beneficial (as in the essential oils or, more accurately, monoterpenes of mints and members of the citrus family), a few types are irritants of the skin. Diterpenoids isolated from acrid latex of members of the spurge family (such as species of *Euphorbia*) are not only irritant, but may have cocarcinogenic activity. Sesquiterpenes isolated from members of the sagebrush tribe (for example, species of *Artemisia*) of the sunflower family are known to be involved in dermatitis allergy. Plant steroid molecules such as diosgenin from Mexican yam (*Dioscorea*) are actually triterpenoid derivatives.

MINERAL TOXINS

In consideration of mineral toxicity of plants, nitrate poisoning of livestock is perhaps most significant. Certain weed species (for example, goosefoot or lamb's quarters,

Chenopodium album, and pigweed, *Amaranthus* spp.) have the capability of accumulating excess nitrate, often as potassium nitrate (KNO_3). Interestingly, this ability to uptake nitrate is increased by the application of certain herbicides, such as 2,4-D. Plants containing in excess of 1.5 percent nitrate by dry weight are considered potentially dangerous. In ruminant animals such as cattle, the nitrate is often converted to nitrite during digestion; nitrite is approximately ten times as toxic as nitrate. Nitrite in the bloodstream interferes directly with the ability of hemoglobin to carry oxygen, resulting in potential asphyxiation. Such oxygen-deficient blood turns a chocolate brown color; this color change is useful in diagnosis of nitrite poisoning. Although primarily a problem with livestock, nitrates can adversely, though indirectly, affect human beings. Forage such as corn leaves stored in silos often ferments to form silage. Side products of these fermentation reactions may result in the buildup of corrosive, yellowish-brown gases (oxides of nitrogen, for example, nitrogen dioxide and tetroxide), which are heavier than air (and hence remain in the silo). Irritation of the lungs caused by nitrogen oxides is known as silo-filler's disease. Additionally, nitrocellulose may form and, in combination with nitrogen gases, may cause the explosion of silos.

Finally, cattle on range in western states may be affected by selenium poisoning. Selenium is apparently recognized and utilized in the body in place of sulfur; sulfur bonds, essential to the integrity of many protein molecules, are disrupted. In particular, cells of the liver and kidney, lacking proper protein synthesis, may undergo relatively rapid degeneration. Certain plants (for example, some species of *Astragalus* known as poison vetches) selectively accumulate selenium from selenium-rich soils. Such selenium indicator plants are of interest to geologists because of the association between selenium and uranium. Cattle and other livestock feeding on ranges with selenium-rich soils, in addition to possible acute selenium poisoning, may develop a chronic syndrome known as blind staggers, indeed involving physiological blindness, followed by weakness, possible paralysis, and respiratory failure. Animals fed grain or forage grown on selenium-rich soils may develop the misnamed "alkali disease," which has nothing to do with alkali. The symptoms of alkali disease are somewhat different from those of blind staggers and involve, among other characteristics, hoof deformity and sloughing, starving, and emaciation. It is not clear why blind staggers and alkali disease, both resulting from selenium poisoning, should have rather distinct symptoms.

SELECTED REFERENCES

BROWER, LINCOLN P. 1969. Ecological Chemistry. *Scientific American* 220(2): 22–29. An interesting account of a particular type of glycoside molecule and its differential effect on animals.

HARBORNE, J. B. 1982. *Introduction to Ecological Biochemistry*, 2nd ed. Academic Press, New York. Chapter 3 deals with types of toxic plant chemicals and their effects on animals in ecological context, that is, animal predation of plants.

JACOBS, BARRY L. 1987. How Hallucinogenic Drugs Work. *American Scientist* 75(4): 386–392. A readable account of the possible mode of action of truly hallucinogenic drugs, such as LSD, psilocin, and mescaline, on nerve cells of the brain.

KEELER, R. F. AND A. T. TU (editors). 1983. *Handbook of Natural Toxins*: Volume 1—*Plant and Fungal Toxins*. Marcel Dekker, Inc., New York. For interesting but technical accounts, see Chapter 2, "Cardiac Glycosides 'Cardenolides' in Species of *Asclepias*, Asclepiadaceae" by James Seiber and others; and Chapter 15, "Chemistry, Toxicology, and Psychic Effects of *Cannabis*," by Coy W. Waller.

KINGHORN, D. A. (editor). 1979. *Toxic Plants*. Columbia University Press, New York. Chapter 7, "The Poisonous Anacardiaceae," by Harold Baer, contains a good account of the toxic substance in poison ivy and poison sumac; see also Chapter 6, "Cocarcinogenic Irritant Euphorbiaceae," by Kinghorn, and Chapter 8, "Contact Hypersensitivity and Photodermatitis Evoked by Compositae," by Neil Towers.

KINGSBURY, J. M. 1964. *Poisonous Plants of the United States and Canada*. Prentice Hall, Inc., Englewood Cliffs, N.J. Pages 17–59 contain an excellent overview of "poisonous principles" in plants.

MOLYNEUX, R. J., AND L. F. JAMES. 1982. Loco Intoxication: Indolizidine Alkaloids of Spotted Locoweed (*Astragalus lentiginosus*). *Science* 216: 190–191. Provides technical insight into the mechanism of locoweed intoxication or poisoning.

ROBINSON, TREVOR. 1959. Alkaloids. *Scientific American* 201(1): 113–121. An excellent popularized overview of this important group of secondary compounds, although evidence since has led to an increased appreciation of the role of certain alkaloids in chemical defense against herbivores.

———. 1983. *The Organic Constituents of Higher Plants*, 5th ed. Cordus Press, North Amherst, Mass. The standard reference on natural plant chemicals, emphasizing secondary compounds.

SCHULTES, RICHARD E., AND ALBERT HOFMANN. 1980. *The Botany and Chemistry of Hallucinogens*, revised and enlarged second edition. Charles C. Thomas, Springfield, Ill. Detailed information on the chemistry of psychoactive compounds of plants.

TYLER, VARRO E., LYNN R. BRADY, AND JAMES E. ROBBERS. 1988. *Pharmacognosy*, 9th ed. Lea & Febiger, Philadelphia. A textbook dealing with the various categories of natural, especially plant, chemicals employed as drugs.

WILEY, R. G., W. W. BLESSING, AND D. J. REIS. 1982. Suicide Transport: Destruction of Neurons by Retrograde Transport of Ricin, Abrin, and Modeccin. *Science* 216: 889–890. Technically written, but demonstrates potential clinical use of highly toxic plant proteins.

Poison Survey
of the Plant Kingdom

To wrestle with the seemingly endless diversity in nature, living organisms must be classified (the principles of classification will be dealt with in Chapter 7). The largest (most inclusive) groupings of organisms recognized are the kingdoms. In older, more traditional classifications, organisms were considered to belong either to the animal kingdom or the plant kingdom, even though some creatures (for example, *Euglena*) did not clearly fit one way or the other. Now the acceptance of five more or less distinct kingdoms is the dogma of the day. The five-kingdom system has merit and deserves mention at this point. The five kingdoms commonly recognized are Plantae (the plants), Animalia (the animals), Protista (unicellular organisms including a number of algae and protozoa), Fungi (molds, mushrooms, and the like), and Monera (the bacteria). A fundamental cellular distinction exists between the Monera (prokaryotic organisms, their cells lacking organized or at least compartmentalized nuclei) and the other four kingdoms (organisms placed in these all have eukaryotic cells, that is, with distinct nuclei). In the five-kingdom concept, the bacteria, the fungi, and a number of algae are not considered to be members of the plant kingdom. However, the aim of this book is to be inclusive, rather than exclusive. For the sake of appreciation of a wide variety of toxic plants, a simple and more classical (encompassing) outline of the plant kingdom is followed, in which bacteria, fungi, and algae are considered to "belong," alongside organisms that are unquestionably plants. The format used herein for coverage of the plant kingdom is consistent with that employed in other major coverages of medicinal or poisonous plants (for example, Walter H. Lewis and Memory P. F. Elvin-Lewis, 1977, *Medical Botany*, Wiley-Interscience, New York).

PLANT KINGDOM OUTLINE

A. Nonvascular plants
  1. Bacteria
  2. Fungi
  3. Algae
  4. Lichens
  5. Mosses and liverworts
B. Vascular plants (tracheophytes)
  1. Seedless
    a. Ferns
    b. Fern allies
  2. Seed plants
    a. Gymnosperms
    b. Angiosperms

NONVASCULAR PLANTS

Considering the nonvascular plants first, these as a group do not have special conducting tissues; that is, there is no tissue particularly specialized or designed to function primarily, as opposed to other tissues, in the conduction of food and water.

Bacteria

As indicated, bacteria are not truly plants in the modern sense of the term, having a different and simpler (prokaryotic) cell structure, but they are included here because of their significance and for the purpose of providing a broader overview of toxicity throughout the "plant kingdom." Bacteria are fundamentally unicellular, although small filaments or colonies may be formed; their tiny cells have various forms and shapes, with rods (bacilli) and spheres (cocci) being most common; a few, as in the syphilis bacterium, have a spiral shape. In addition to their morphology, bacteria are of necessity classified by various physiological or cytochemical traits, including the differential reaction of their cell walls to gram stain (that is, gram positive versus gram negative bacteria). As a generality, gram positive bacteria are sensitive to a broader spectrum of antibiotics than are gram negative bacteria.

Most bacteria are harmless and should not be called germs, and definitely not "bugs." Indeed, the majority of species are doubtless free-living saprophytes in the soil. Nonetheless a substantial number are infectious, such as the bacterium causing tuberculosis and the one resulting in bacterial pneumonia. The general condition produced by a bacterial infection is known as a bacteremia. On the other hand, only a few bacteria are actually toxic (to human beings). In these few types, a toxin (exo-

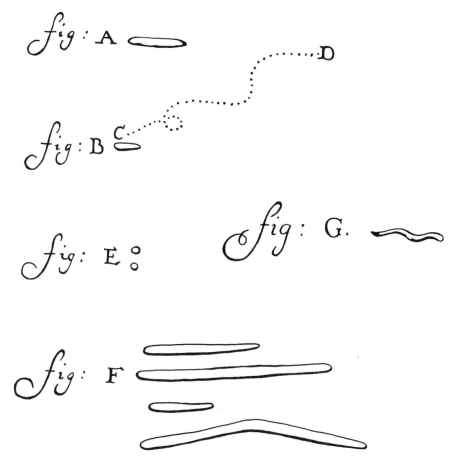

Figure 4–1   Leeuwenhoek's (1695) illustration of bacteria

toxin), usually a protein, originates in but diffuses out of the cell. The condition resulting from bacterial poisoning is called a toxemia, and not a bacteremia. Although the kinds of bacteria potentially causing toxemias may be few in number, they are significant, especially if viewed in historical perspective. Included in this list are organisms causing botulism, tetanus, diphtheria, and cholera; these are perhaps the major toxic bacteria and are discussed next.

Botulism was known in the past as "European sausage poisoning." This relates to the fact that botulism toxin can be present in spoiled meat; however, spoiled fish is a more likely source. The botulism bacillus (*Clostridium botulinum*) is associated with the rather broad category of diseases known as food poisoning. Fortunately, a low percentage (about 3 percent) of reported cases of food poisoning is actually botulism.

What one commonly encounters in the way of food poisoning (as, for example, at the local cafeteria) is the bacterial genus *Salmonella*, which is the cause of an infection (bacteremia) of the digestive system, not a toxemia. Although *Salmonella* can make you "sick as a dog," with symptoms of vomiting, diarrhea, and a high fever, recovery is usually complete and fairly rapid. Other commonplace food poisonings involve *Staphylococcus aureus*, which may develop in, for example, cream-filled pastries allowed to "sit out." A toxin is involved in staph poisoning; however, special therapy is typically not required for full recovery.

To return to our consideration of botulism, the greatest danger is home-canned produce, particularly home-canned beans (of various sorts) and corn (tomatoes are typically too acidic for effective growth of the botulism bacillus). If canning is merely done with normal stove heat, that is, the burners on top of the range, the resistant spores (endospores) formed inside the bacterial rods are not killed. The botulism bacillus thrives under anaerobic conditions (absence of oxygen). Hence, after the can (or canning jar) lid is closed, the resistant spores will germinate and the cells will begin to multiply. The bacterium will produce a toxin (exotoxin) that diffuses out of the eventual thousands or more likely millions of cells and accumulates in the canned vegetables. As in most other significant bacterial toxins, the poisonous substance is a protein. Botulism is particularly dangerous because it is difficult to detect. Its presence imparts no special color or odor to the contaminated produce. Indeed, botulism is dangerous, the death rate being about two of every three people afflicted with the disease. If death is the outcome, this will usually occur within a span of two or at most three days. The poisonous protein of botulism is a neurotoxin; more specifically, it will block nerve impulses to muscles. The eventual cause of death may well be failure of the muscles of respiration (diaphragm muscles) to function, thus resulting in asphyxiation.

A logical question is how to avoid the potential hazard of botulism. Pressure cooking will help. Pressure in addition to heat will tend to kill the spores, which are resistant to average stove heat. A simpler and perhaps more sure solution is to boil the home-canned produce, say for 10 to 15 minutes, when the can or jar is reopened. This "second" boiling is really the essential safeguard; it is effective because any quantity of toxin present, since the toxin is a protein, is rather quickly denatured (molecular structure disrupted) by the heat of boiling and loses its toxicity. If the toxin is destroyed and if the food is consumed soon thereafter, it is of little consequence whether or not living cells (or more likely spores) are still present. Although botulism antitoxins are available, simple prevention is clearly the best way to deal with botulism—boil the can goods before you eat them!

The tetanus bacillus (*Clostridium tetani*) is a close relative of botulism. "Botanically," botulism and tetanus bacilli are members of the same genus. What one must beware of in the case of tetanus is dirty puncture wounds, for example the wound of a rusty nail (or tooth of a rake) in the foot or hand. The rust has nothing to do with tetanus per se. It is simply that such objects are coincidentally associated with environments where tetanus is likely to occur. The tetanus bacillus lives anaerobically in soil (as in a pasture) and in manure as well. Hence, rusty nails or farm implements are likely to come into contact with the tetanus organism.

Although tetanus is rare as a human disease in the United States due to effective childhood tetanus toxoid immunization, the tetanus bacillus is probably just as prevalent as ever in the environment. Being anaerobic, the tetanus bacterium will not grow in a well-aerated, surface wound. However, down inside a puncture wound, in the absence of free oxygen, germination may occur, and a small infection will develop with an incubation period varying from several days to several weeks. The infection itself is harmless and does not spread beyond necrotic tissue at the base of the wound. However, as the bacteria multiply in the local infection site, an exotoxin is released, which enters the bloodstream and is distributed systemically.

It is the toxin and its spread that may indeed be hazardous. The toxic protein of tetanus is one of the most powerful toxins known. As little as 0.0002 gram can be fatal to a human being. Similar to the botulism protein, the toxic protein of tetanus is a neurotoxin. In the case of tetanus, nerve impulses to peripheral voluntary muscles may be altered. Symptoms can include severe spasms and contortions of facial muscles (hence the term lockjaw); facial muscles may become fixed so that the patient appears to be smiling sarcastically (the *risus sardonicus*). Complete muscle rigidity may eventually occur and concomitantly, respiratory paralysis. At a minimum, following a significant puncture wound received out-of-doors or otherwise potentially involving soil or feces, a physician should be consulted so that the patient's immunization record may be reviewed and evaluated for its adequacy.

The bacillus causing diphtheria (*Corynebacterium diphtheriae*) is frequently seen to be club shaped or dumbbell shaped in prepared microscope slides (smears); also, the appearance of characteristic granules aid in its microscopic identification. Diphtheria has been the cause of epidemics in the past; it is now a rare (due to childhood vaccination) but still present and dangerous disease. In the case of diphtheria, there is both a potentially serious infection and a toxin with which to contend. Infection typically occurs in the upper respiratory passages. As the infection progresses, a mishmash of blood, lymph, and tissue, and the bacterial cells themselves, may form a rather tough, membranelike structure (the pseudomembrane), potentially blocking respiratory passages. Additionally, the bacterial cells exude a toxin, which may be transported to various parts of the body, including the heart, kidneys, and liver. Although the action of diphtheria toxin is not entirely clear, it can cause damage in various body organs, leading to death. In fact, the exotoxin is typically the most dangerous aspect of diphtheria disease.

The cholera bacterium (*Vibrio cholerae*) is a curved, motile rod (bacillus). Cholera is one of the diseases that has periodically spread around the globe in epidemics (pandemics). Several strains of cholera are known, but they cause a similar disease etiology. Cholera spreads in contaminated food and water in association with poor public hygene (as in certain underdeveloped countries). The cholera toxin is a protein that irritates the lining of the digestive tract, resulting in severe abdominal pain, vomiting, and diarrhea. Cholera has a diuretic action on the digestive tract, causing potentially a great loss of fluids and electrolytes. The resultant watery, mucus-laiden stool is characteristic of the disease (rice water stool). If proper fluid (and ion) replacement is observed, cholera is typically not a dangerous disease, and death rates are quite low. However, when medical knowledge and attention are not available, death rates are much higher.

Fungi

As in the case of bacteria, the fungi as well are usually no longer classified within the plant kingdom. Many fungi resemble types of algae in their filamentous or even unicellular structure; however, unlike many algae (or plants in general), the fungi are not green (have no chlorophyll), they do not release oxygen into the environment, they do not store starch (rather, glycogen is their carbohydrate storage product), and the dominant constituent of their cell walls is typically chitin (in contrast to the cellulosic walls of most plants). Thus, on the basis of a number of significant distinctions, the fungi are presently placed in their own kingdom (kingdom Fungi).

Most fungi are neither poisonous nor of medicinal value, although exceptions to this statement seem numerous and in some cases significant. Many of the poisonous representatives of fungi occur among the group commonly known as the mushrooms, although, indeed, the majority of mushrooms are not toxic. Contrary to the opinion of some, there is no test by which one may distinguish mushrooms that are poisonous (that is, "toadstools") from those that are not. It is alleged that the "skin" of a poisonous mushroom is not readily peelable and also that a toxic mushroom will darken a silver spoon if contacted. These tests are unreliable, as neither test is applicable to the group of mushrooms (amanitas) most often involved in fatal human poisoning. Mushrooms must be carefully and often laboriously identified on an individual basis; there are no appreciable shortcuts to the time-consuming task of learning their taxonomy. If one is not skilled in mushroom identification and the knowledge of which are toxic and which are edible, then the practice of gathering wild mushrooms for food should be avoided.

Most dangerous among the mushrooms are several species belonging to the genus *Amanita* (the destroying angel and the death cap). Time should be taken to learn something of *Amanita*. Amanitas may be recognized by the persistence of a cuplike structure (volva) at or around the base of the stalk, in addition to a ringlike membrane

Figure 4–2 *Amanita*. Death cap, destroying angel

(annulus) encircling the stalk beneath the cap. The annulus may be worn away by weather, so it becomes critical to determine whether the volva is present or not. A little digging may be in order because the volva may be at or slightly below ground level. Even if one knows essentially nothing about identification of mushrooms, learning to look for the "death cup" (volva) of *Amanita* could have the benefit of avoiding serious difficulty. Indeed, it is species of *Amanita* that are most often involved in reported cases of fatal mushroom poisoning. However, it is true that a number of other types of mushrooms are toxic, some seriously, and some are hallucinogenic as well (for example, *Psilocybe*, the "magic mushroom"). This topic will be considered in much more detail in Chapter 5.

Toxic fungi also occur in a group of fungi that might be generally termed the sac fungi. In sac fungi, reproductive cells (spores) do not occur in umbrellalike bodies, as in the mushrooms, but often rather in an inverted-looking structure resembling an urn or saucer or in some cases resembling a tiny baseball bat (or even a tiny baseball). As in the case of mushrooms, most sac fungi are harmless. However, some are significantly toxic. An example of a toxic representative among sac fungi is ergot (the ergot fungus, *Claviceps purpurea*). Ergot is a parasite of cereal grains (grasses), especially cultivated rye. Dark, hard, somewhat elongated ergot bodies may replace the kernels of grain in infected plants. Ergot contains the ergot alkaloids and, in addition, closely related LSD-like substances. The ergot alkaloids and related compounds are toxic and are capable of inducing varied effects, including hallucinations, in a disease known as ergotism. Ergotism has been circumstantially related to the psychic aberrations alleged in the Salem, Massachusetts witchcraft trials in the late seventeenth century (see Linnda R. Caporael, "Ergotism: The Satan Loose in Salem?" *Science* 192: 21–26, 1976.)

Fungi are second only to the flowering plants in terms of their poisonous, medicinal, and historically intriguing representatives. Consequently, Chapter 5 is devoted solely to coverage of the fungi in relation to toxicity and medicine.

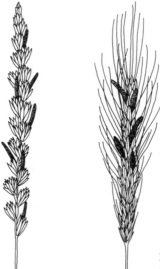

Figure 4–3 *Claviceps purpurea.* Ergot fungus (on rye)

Algae

Many algae are considered to be plants. Characteristically, they possess the special green substance, chlorophyll, and produce their own food (starch is the typical food storage product of green algae); they release oxygen as well. Their cell walls, if present, are usually composed of cellulose. Thus, the algae generally possess those features characteristic of the true (higher) plants. Algae are regarded as the most primitive among plants. They possess a simple body organization. Many algae are just single cells; some can swim, much in the manner of the motile protozoa. These one-celled, motile algae are often classified with protozoa, in the Kingdom Protista. However, the boundaries delimiting this kingdom (Protista) from the other kingdoms of eukaryotic organisms are not sharp. Other types of algae are small filaments or simple colonies or form large sheetlike growths; but even these often retain a one-celled stage in the life cycle. Algae can be quite abundant in the environment, although often as not they go unnoticed. Simple, one-celled or filamentous algae may become extremely abundant even in temporary pools of water; they will seemingly disappear when the pools dry, only to reappear, as by magic, when the shallow depressions fill with rainwater again. Major groups of algae are distinguished, among other features (including ultrastructural details), by their particular pigment complexes, for example, green algae, brown algae, red algae, and so on. Only a few species of algae are actually poisonous.

Figure 4–4   Filamentous blue-green alga

Toxic algae occurring in fresh (or in some cases "not so fresh") water include filamentous, unicellular, and gelatinous-colonial representatives of the so-called blue-green algae, whose pigmentation may indeed appear bluish-green under a microscope. Possible genera involved are *Anabaena, Aphanizomenon, Microcystis, Nostoc,* and *Gloeotrichia.* Although resembling true algae, and for many years classified as such, the blue-green algae actually comprise a category of bacteria, the Cyanobacteria. Regardless of their classification, some blue-green algae produce toxic substances, which are generally considered to be degenerative products of proteins: polypeptides, amines, and hydrogen sulfide (rotten-egg gas) may be produced. Although hydrogen sulfide will impart a foul odor to a pond, the truly toxic substance seems to be a type of polypeptide (cyclic polypeptide) that causes digestive upset and liver damage. Perhaps surprisingly, extensive loss of life of livestock, waterfowl, and even pets animals has been attributed to blue-green algal toxicity. Problems are typically encountered only in late summer or early fall when rainfall decreases, pond levels fall, nutrient levels increase, and the concentration of algae in ponds becomes great. For example, it is rather common to encounter an algal bloom in August and September, in which blue-green algae become so abundant as to discolor the water of cow ponds. Such concentrations of algae in farm ponds are prerequisite to the buildup of toxins in the water. Death may be rapid for animals drinking such water, and yet there is often no alternative water source.

In marine environments, toxic algae of concern belong to an unusual group of motile, unicellular algae known as the dinoflagellates. Microscopic examination reveals that, although single-celled, a transverse groove or furrow separates the cell wall into two halves. In some forms, the cell walls are composed of a tiny armor of

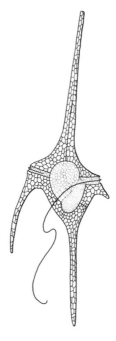

Figure 4–5 Representative dinoflagellate

plates. These characteristic forms usually swim as members of the plankton, often in nearshore environments, and may become abundant (causing a bloom or water discoloration). Species of the genus *Gonyaulax* occurring on both the east and west coast of North America have been implicated in numerous cases of human shellfish poisoning. Clams, scallops, and mussels may be involved. In this case, poisoning is not by spoiled but by healthy shellfish. The filter-feeding shellfish intake the dinoflagellate cells and accumulate a toxin produced by the alga (with no apparent harm to the shellfish). Poisonings are only encountered when the contaminated shellfish are consumed.

The toxin was originally considered to be an alkaloid and is still considered to be a complex, nitrogenous molecule. Rather rapid acting, the *Gonyaulax* toxin affects the peripheral and central nervous system. Within a few minutes a tingling (pins-and-needles) sensation of the face and fingertips may occur. Inside of 24 hours, the patient may be the victim, through action on the nervous system, of muscular paralysis and respiratory or cardiac failure. Patients surviving the first 24 hours of paralytic shellfish poisoning have a good chance of recovery. Intake of as few as five or six poisonous clams may prove fatal. Raw shellfish are more hazardous, but even cooked shellfish can retain dangerous levels of toxin. The white meat of a shellfish is the least dangerous part. A federal testing program for shellfish has helped reduce the dangers of shellfish poisoning.

Another genus of dinoflagellate, *Gymnodinium*, may accumulate off the west coast of Florida in sufficient numbers to impart a red or reddish-brown discoloration to the water. This particular bloom has been given the name red tide. The toxin produced by *Gymnodinium brevis* is not equivalent to that produced by *Gonyaulax* and seemingly has no direct or indirect connection to human internal poisonings. Although certainly not occurring every year, intermittent red tides have been associated with mass mortality of fish (fish kills) along the Florida coast. At a minimum, the rotting carcasses of dead fish washed ashore do not enhance the esthetic qualities of the coastal environment.

Lichens

A lichen is not a single organism. Rather, a lichen is a combination (symbiotic association) of two different kinds of organisms: a simple, often one-celled alga living with (inside the matrix framework of) a type of fungus (usually a member of the sac fungi). The close harmony between the two associates gives the superficial appearance that only one organism is present. Lichens appear as variably colored, often crustlike growths on the bark of trees or the surfaces of rocks. Some types are found to occur on open soil (especially in western rangelands). Ground lichen, *Parmelia molliuscula*, occurring from Nebraska west into the Rockies, grows on open soil and may accumulate in masses moved about by the wind. In this form, ground lichen may be consumed in some quantity by cattle, which suffer a usually mild toxic response of the nervous system, manifest in the form of ataxia. Large

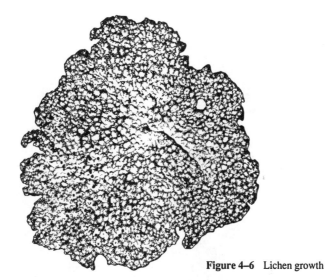

Figure 4–6   Lichen growth

quantities of ground lichen must be consumed before serious toxicity (in this case, paralysis) is encountered. The toxic substance in ground lichen, usnic acid, is well known and occurs in certain other lichens as well (these species usually not being consumed, or at least not in quantity).

Mosses (and Liverworts)

Mosses, possessing a "leaf and stem," may resemble small vascular plants. However, they do not contain any true vascular (conducting) tissue. In mosses, at a certain stage of their life cycle, an often stalklike, spore-producing plant is directly attached to the "leafy," formerly gamete-producing plant; interestingly, thus, these two generations in the life cycle may be seen together, appearing essentially as a single plant. No moss (or for that matter any of the related plants known as liverworts) is known to be toxic, but one type of moss has received a moderately substantial medicinal use (at least in folk medicine) over the centuries. Peat moss or bog moss, *Sphagnum* spp., is found in abundance in boggy or marshy areas of the Christmas tree forests of Canada and the moorlands of the British Isles. *Sphagnum* accumulates in these bogs, which eventually fill in, forming a highly organic, semicompacted soil known as peat, which may be burned for energy, much like coal. *Sphagnum* vegetation can hold tremendous amounts of water, due to special water-storage (hyaline) cells of the leaf. Because of its great ability to retain water, peat moss has been used as a moisturizer, particularly as a packing material applied to the surfaces of burns. A major problem with burns is their tendency to dry out or dessicate, and a peat moss wrapping is a significant aid in counteracting tissue dessication.

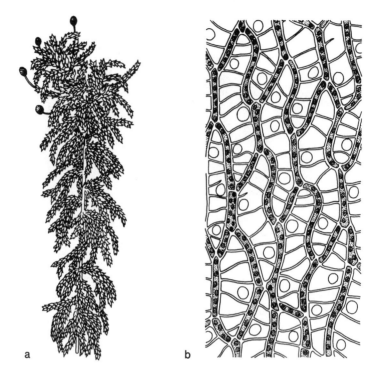

Figure 4–7 *Sphagnum*, peat moss: (a) whole plant; (b) microscopic view of leaf

VASCULAR PLANTS (TRACHEOPHYTES)

The vascular plants or tracheophytes possess specialized conducting (vascular or tra-cheary) tissues; of the two fundamental types of vascular tissues, the xylem functions in conduction of water and mineral nutrients, and the phloem functions in food conduc-tion. Both xylem and phloem are present in a given vascular strand (bundle) or vascular cylinder of a plant. Among the various kinds of vascular plants, first to consider are those forms that are seedless; in these, although reproduction does not result in the development of seeds, a usually visible display of spores on the leaf or the stem is a prelude to the establishment of the next generation.

Seedless Vascular Plants

Ferns and allies.   The most familiar group of seedless vascular plants is the ferns, with their characteristic pinnately compound leaves that typically arise at ground level, unfurling from their origin points along horizontal stems (rhizomes). When ferns are in a reproductive state, spores are most often seen to be borne in sporangial clusters (sori) on the backs of the leaves. Of the approximately 10,000 species of ferns in the world, only a very few kinds have been implicated in cases of poisoning. Best known is bracken fern, *Pteridium aquilinum*, which, unlike many reclusive ferns, can be common in open woods or even pastures and fields in various parts of the world, including portions of North America and the British Isles. Bracken is recognized by the fact that its spore-containing structures (sporangia), rather than occurring in distinct sori (small, dotlike clusters) on the backs of leaves, are spread along the back margin of the leaf, covered by the rolled edge of the leaf.

The consumption of bracken fern in quantity, especially in hay of poor quality, presents potential problems for livestock. Both monogastric animals (especially horses) and ruminants (animals with multiple stomach chambers, such as cattle) are affected, but apparently not in the same way. Bracken fern contains the protein (enzyme) thiaminase. Due to the activity of thiaminase, horses eating bracken in quantity (over a period of time) suffer a reduction in thiamin (vitamin B1) and develop a B1 deficiency. Approximately one month elapses before significant symptoms appear; from that point on, the animal may waste away over a number of days, exhibiting weakness and often also incoordination. Prior to death, convulsions may occur. The degeneration is often reversible if horses are fed B1 supplement. In cattle consuming bracken, to make a long story short, because of bacterial activity in the

Figure 4–8 *Pteridium aquilinum.*
Bracken fern

various stomach chambers, a significant reduction in thiamine level usually does not occur. Yet, even though thiaminase is seemingly not the culprit and B1 deficiency is apparently not involved, cattle may eventually die as a result of bracken consumption. In a still not understood process, the bone marrow is adversely affected, and a condition resembling aplastic anemia in human beings develops. White blood cell counts decrease (increasing susceptibility to disease), the blood does not clot properly, and internal bleeding occurs. In spite of much interest and research, the chemical "villian" present in bracken fern, affecting cattle, remains anonymous.

Of the very few ferns associated with toxicity, one other worthy of mention is jimmy fern, *Notholaena sinuata*, a smallish fern of drylands from West Texas to Arizona. The sinuous-margined leaflets of jimmy fern are covered beneath with brownish scales. The leaves fold or curl up when dry, opening up again under moister conditions. Commonly consumed by cattle, sheep, and goats in certain range areas, this plant may induce a violent trembling response (the "jimmies") in animals undergoing what would be considered a normal level of exercise. Symptoms may disappear when the animals rest, only to reappear when activity is resumed. Subsequent attacks may prove fatal, apparently due to respiratory paralysis. The poisonous principle in jimmy fern remains unknown.

The so-called fern ally *Equisetum arvense* (actually a member of a separate division or phylum from that to which ferns belong) is one of the most unique plants

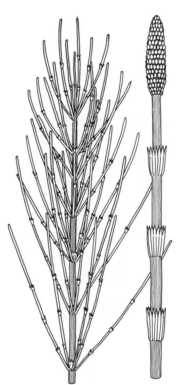

Figure 4–9 *Equisetum arvense.*
Horsetail

in appearance. Perhaps growing along a creek bank or some similar environment, an *Equisetum* population will look much like a bunch of erect, green sticks, a half-meter or so in height. Leaves are reduced to scarcely perceptible scales, and multiple branches may occur, whorled on the main axes. Some unbranched axes develop a terminal, conelike cluster of spore-laiden scales. Stems of *Equisetum* are ribbed and furrowed, and the outer cell walls contain silica (making the stems abrasive to the touch). In the past, *Equisetum* has been used, much like steel wool, for cleaning pots and pans; hence the common name scouring rush. Another perhaps more familiar common name is horsetail, an allusion to the whorled branches coming off at apparently all angles. It is interesting that *Equisetum* can induce a syndrome in horses similar to that caused by bracken fern (an unrelated plant). Although certain chemical details are lacking, the fact that a vitamin B_1 deficiency is developed after consumption of *Equisetum* (or hay containing a quantity of *Equisetum*) is indicative of the presence of thiaminase or thiaminaselike substances in the plant; additionally, tissue extracts of horsetail test positive for activity of this type of enzyme.

Seed Plants

Gymnosperms.   To complete our survey of toxicity throughout the plant kingdom, we now finally come to those vascular plants with seeds. Of the two main groups of seed plants (gymnosperms and angiosperms), the gymnosperms are clearly the lesser of the two groups in terms of overall numbers as well as toxic representatives. In distinction from angiosperms, the gymnosperms lack flowers (although a flower as a morphological entity is surprisingly difficult to define) and, perhaps more significantly, they lack fruit. As indicated by the name gymnosperm (gymnos = naked, sperm = seed), seeds of members of this botanical phylum are not surrounded at any time by a fruit (that is, by a fruit wall). However, in some cases the seed may itself resemble a fruit or else be surrounded by a structure that is fruitlike.

Indeed, seeds of the most definitively toxic representative of the gymnosperms, the yews (*Taxus* spp.), are surrounded (except at the apex) by a fleshy outgrowth of the seed coat, that is, by an aril. The red "fruits" (technically, arillate seeds) of yews and their dark, linear, evergreen foliage contribute to their popularity as ornamental shrub plantings around houses and buildings. Both the Japanese yew (*Taxus cuspidata*) and the English yew (*Taxus baccata*) are commonly planted; *Taxus canadensis* (ground hemlock) is native to the northeastern and northcentral United States. Yews contain alkaloid substances known as taxine (apparently, at least two alkaloids, taxine A and taxine B, may be present in a given plant). Yews (even hedge-clippings) are dangerous to animals, and unfortunately are readily consumed by livestock. The toxic alkaloid material in yew, functioning through the nervous system, acts as a depressant, causing the heartbeat to slow or stop. If a substantial quantity of yew foliage has been consumed, a rapid death (occurring in a few minutes time) with few perceivable, preceding symptoms may be expected. Human poisoning from yew is made more likely because children are attracted by the fleshy red covering of the seed and may consume these in quantity. The red aril itself is scarcely toxic; however, dangerous amounts of alkaloid

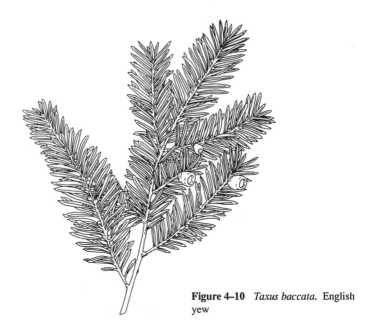

Figure 4–10 *Taxus baccata.* English yew

may occur in the dark gray seed inside the aril. Danger of poisoning is increased greatly if the seeds are bitten (breaking the seed coat) prior to swallowing.

Yews are apparently not the only poisonous gymnosperms. Information is accumulating (see P. T. Hooper, cited under Keeler and Tu, selected references) that certain of the gymnosperms known as cycads (tropical or subtropical gymnosperms recognized by their distinctly palmlike foliage) are toxic and capable of producing either neurotoxic or hepatic-gastrointestinal syndromes in cattle. Among cycads, species of *Macrozamia* and *Bowenia* have been implicated in neurotoxicity, and species of *Macrozamia* and *Cycas* in liver and intestinal disorders. Suspicious compounds have been isolated from these cycads, and the exact poisonous principle or principles involved in cycad toxicity are likely to be determined in the near future.

The toxicity of other gymnosperms is less clear, and indeed most are harmless. The fleshy, foul-smelling, orange-yellow seeds (resembling fruits) of the fan-leaved maidenhair tree (*Ginkgo biloba*) contain substances suspected of causing skin and gastric irritation; however, further investigation seems warranted. Finally, among the greatest group of gymnosperms, the cone-bearing trees or conifers (characterized, in addition to cones, by their needlelike or scalelike leaves), a handful seem tied together by a strange and questionably meaningful pattern. Abortion in cattle has been at least circumstantially related to consumption of foliage of ponderosa pine (*Pinus ponderosa*), Monterey cypress (*Cupressus macrocarpa*), and red cedar (*Juniperus virginiana*). The essential oils in the tissues of these plants have been suggested as playing a role in stillbirths and/or premature births in the cattle, but more research is needed to clarify any connection between compounds in the plants and abortion in animals.

Angiosperms.   The flowering plants, or angiosperms, constitute not only overwhelmingly the largest group of seed plants, but the largest division within the plant kingdom.   The majority of familiar and unfamiliar plants, both toxic and non-toxic, occur within this great group—the dominant botanical phylum on the face of the earth.   In all, more than 200,000 species swell the ranks of the angiosperms.   As distinguished from the gymnosperms, seeds of angiosperms develop within and usually remain surrounded for a time by a fruit. Of the many features that "make an angiosperm an angiosperm," the possession of true fruit (developing from the ovary of the flower) is among the most significant.

Angiosperms themselves are divided into two large groups, the monocots (including palms, grasses, lilies, and aroids) and the dicots (including such groups as mints, legumes, milkweeds, spurges, sunflowers, oaks, and maples); the dicots are decidedly the larger of the two main groups of angiosperms. Obviously differing by the number of cotyledons, features distinguishing the monocotyledonous and dicotyledonous plants will be stressed in Chapters 6 and 8.   Consideration of angiosperms, and especially their poisonous and medicinal representatives, is really the main course of this book and consequently will not be dealt with further in this chapter.   Chapters 12 and 13 provide, respectively, exclusive coverage to toxic and medicinal members of this great division of plants.   Chapter 8 is devoted to significant toxic families of angiosperms.

SELECTED REFERENCES

BARNES, R. S. K. (editor). 1984. *A Synoptic Classification of Living Organisms.* Blackwell Scientific Publications, Oxford, England.   As indicated in the editor's preface and introduction, this is a sort of "mini-encyclopaedia" in which the major groups and subgroups of organisms on earth are classified according to the relatively recent, five-kingdom concept. It is very useful in gaining an appreciation of a current consensus of classification of biological diversity encountered in nature.

BISACRE, MICHAEL, AND OTHERS (editors). 1984. *The Illustrated Encyclopedia of Plants.* Exeter Books, New York. The first section of the book is a beautifully illustrated account of the plant kingdom, including information on human uses of plants. The plant kingdom is enumerated in a traditional manner; that is, algae, bacteria, and fungi are included within the plant kingdom.

KEELER, R. F., AND A. T. TU (editors). 1983. *Handbook of Natural Toxins:* Volume One—*Plant and Fungal Toxins.* Marcel Dekker, Inc., New York. Contains technical but interesting review articles on toxins and the toxicity of several different plant groups; see, for example, Chapter 14, "Cycad Poisoning," by P. T. Hooper.

KLEIN, R. M. 1987. *The Green World*, 2nd ed.   Harper & Row, Publishers, New York.   An excellent consideration of the plant kingdom from an economic, ethnobotanical, and medicinal point of view.

MARGULIS, LYNN, AND KARLENE V. SCHWARTZ. 1988. *Five Kingdoms—An Illustrated Guide to the Phyla of Life on Earth*, 2nd ed. W. H. Freeman and Company, San Francisco. An outstanding, detailed, well-illustrated coverage of diversity of organisms, categorized under the five-kingdom concept.

SCAGEL, R. F., AND OTHERS. 1984. *Plants—An Evolutionary Survey*. Wadsworth Publishing Company, Belmont, Calif. A comprehensive, detailed morphological survey of the plant kingdom and the fungi.

SUGDEN, ANDREW. 1984. *Longman Illustrated Dictionary of Botany*. York Press and Longman Group Ltd., Essex. Pages 118–131 of this dictionary contain a simple and well-illustrated old-fashioned outline of the plant kingdom and associated terminology.

TIPPO, OSWALD, AND WILLIAM L. STERN. 1977. *Humanistic Botany*. W. W. Norton & Company, New York. A good review of general botany, including a survey of the plant kingdom, emphasizing the impact, harmful as well as beneficial, of plants on humans.

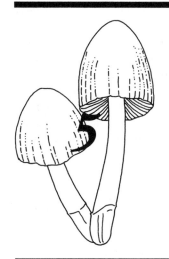

Poisonous and Medicinal Fungi

by MARTHA J. POWELL

Like plants, fungi can be either friend or foe. While one fungus produces the antibiotic penicillin, taming most bacterial infections, ingestion of the amiable-looking and reportedly delicious mushroom *Amanita phalloides* may end in an excruciatingly painful death. One can find fungi almost anywhere. You may already be familiar with mold growing on long-forgotten fruit harbored in your refrigerator; yeasts multiplying in the sugary exudates of plants; black spots covering leaves; shelves emerging from the trunks of ancient trees; cups, sponges, spines, and puffballs in forests, meadows and lawns; and mushrooms magically springing up following a rain only to disappear after a few days. In this chapter you will learn what all these organisms have in common and how diverse they are in form. Then you will discover fungi that produce toxins and poisons that can cause injury or death. Finally, the value of fungi in treating diseases will be explored.

CHARACTERISTICS OF FUNGI

You have already learned that, unlike plants, fungi do not produce chlorophyll; consequently, they cannot make their own food. They are considered heterotrophs because they must absorb their nutrients from outside sources, either nonliving organic material or a living cell. To do this, they release enzymes that break down complex compounds, such as the carbohydrates in wood, into simpler sugars that can be transported into the fungal cell. Although they have cell walls, the predominate carbohydrate is typically chitin and not cellulose as in plants. Like animals, fungi store carbohydrates as glycogen and not starch. Humans cannot produce the amino acid lysine, but they require it for proper nutrition. Plants and fungi, however, can make this essential amino acid. The pathways whereby fungi and plants produce lysine are not the same and include a whole battery of different enzymes and intermediate compounds. A key intermediate compound produced along the lysine production pathway in fungi is alpha aminoadipic acid (AAA); but in plants another compound, diaminopimelic acid (DAP), is the key intermediate. Thus, fungi have many unique characteristics that, when considered in their totality, support their classification in a separate kingdom from higher plants and animals.

The basic growth unit of most fungi is a microscopic filament, the hypha, which when clustered in vast numbers is called a mycelium. It is the mycelium of the fungus that you see with your unaided eye growing over moldy bread. Remarkably, hyphae may also become organized into fruiting bodies with definite forms and elaborate shapes. The well known mushroom, morel, puffball, and shelf are all fruiting bodies that arose from an amorphous mycelium and that will produce spores, aiding in the spread of the fungi into new territory.

GROUPS OF FUNGI

Most fungi that are toxic or produce medically important compounds are the molds (they do not produce conspicuous fruiting bodies) or fleshy fungi (they have easily observed fruiting bodies). Because there are so many kinds of fungi, we categorize them into subgroups based on the types of spores they produce in reproduction. For example the gills on the underside of the cap of the fruiting bodies of **Basidiomycetes,** such as mushrooms, are covered with sexually produced and microscopic basidiospores on club-shaped basidia. Rows of elongate sacs, asci, containing sexually produced ascospores cover the depressions or inner edge of a morel or cup fungus, common **Ascomycetes.** Although yeasts do not produce fleshy fruiting bodies, they are also Ascomycetes because ascospores can form from these single-celled fungi. Most Ascomycetes and molds produce short stalks (conidiophores) directly off the surface of the mycelium on which huge numbers of conidia form. Fungi that reproduce only with these asexually arising conidia are classified as **Deuteromycetes.**

TOXIC FUNGI

There are two types of fungal toxicity to animals, but both types usually occur in humans by accident. The first type we will consider is *mycetismus*, poisoning from toxic or fleshy-type fungi. Such poisonings may happen when mushroom hunters, in search of prized edible species, mistakenly identify a poisonous form as edible. According to the North America Mycological Association's (NAMA) registry of mushroom poisoning cases, most cases of reported mycetismus are young children who become victims as they indiscriminately explore the edibility of the world around them. Because Americans are becoming more aware of the delicacies among wild mushrooms and of their hallucinogenic properties, the incidences of accidental mushroom poisonings are increasing.

The second type of fungal toxicity is *mycotoxicosis*. Some molds growing on grains and nuts, either in the field or in storage, produce a variety of toxic secondary products called mycotoxins. Thus, mycotoxicoses may occur unknowingly when contaminated food is eaten, because the unseen toxin persists in food after the fungus has disappeared. Mycotoxins are not now believed to represent a major human health hazard in developed countries, such as the United States, because poorer quality grains, which are most susceptible to invasions by toxigenic fungi, are typically used for livestock rather than human foods. But because mycotoxins can be present in trace amounts and their effects are most dramatically noticeable only when ingested in large dosages, their long-term effects on human health may not be evident. Among livestock animals, it is known that low dosages of mycotoxins can reduce growth rates and increase susceptibility to other diseases. Without question, mycotoxins are a widespread and persistent hazard to the quality of grains stored for long time periods. Thus, we will also examine several types of mycotoxins and their biological effects on animals.

MYCETISMUS

There is no simple sign to warn if a fungus is poisonous. Thus, one cannot depend on a silver spoon tarnishing when stirred in a pot of mushrooms, or garlic turning blue-black when fried with fungi, or mushrooms bruising blue when crushed to alert one of danger. The only way to know for certain is to learn with the help of an expert the macroscopic and microscopic features used for identification of fungi. Varro Tyler in 1963 grouped poisonous mushrooms and other fleshy fungi into four categories based on the effects of their toxic compounds. We will follow this scheme, adding to it a fifth category.

1. Protoplasmic poisons

Amatoxins. The most lethal mushroom toxins are found among species of *Amanita*, *Conocybe*, and *Galerina*. The common names of some of these species bode of their destructive powers, such as "death cap" (*Amanita phalloides*) and "death angel" (*A. verna* and *A. virosa*). The genus *Amanita* can be distinguished from other genera because it produces white spores and has a cup or sack-shaped structure at the base of its stalk and a skirtlike ring encircling the stalk just below the cap (Fig. 5–1). One problem with identifications, however, is that the cup and ring may weather away. *Amanita phalloides* (Fig. 5–1) stands 8 to 20 cm tall, and its cap is smooth and has a green tint.

The two toxic agents, amatoxins and phallotoxins, are cyclopeptides, ring-shaped molecules composed of amino acids.At the center of the molecule (Fig. 5–1), the amino acid tryptophan connects to the outside amino acid with a sulfur link. There are six forms of amatoxins and five of phallotoxins, and different species may have different complements of the toxins. For example, *A. phalloides* has alpha, beta, and gamma

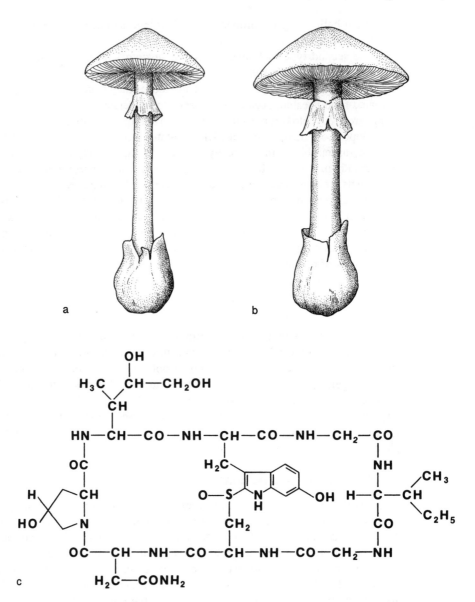

Figure 5–1   (a) *Amanita virosa*, death angel; (b) *Amanita phalloides*, death cap; (c) alpha amanitin

amanitin.   Although phallotoxins injected into experimental animals are deadly and cause cellular membranes to break, they do not appear to be active if ingested. Thus the amatoxins are believed to be the killer compounds.

The primary diagnostic symptom of amanitin poisoning is the long time delay between eating the mushroom and the onset of symptoms. The latency period is 6 to 24 hours after mushroom consumption. Initial symptoms are principally gastrointestinal (GI) disturbances. There are severe stomach pains, violent vomiting, diarrhea, and tenderness and enlargement of the liver. These are serious and prolonged enough that medical aid is typically sought. For a few hours the GI symptoms subside, and the victim feels relatively healthy again. But just when the worst seems over, new, more serious symptoms occur. In this phase the toxin has already attacked and damaged the liver, kidney, and intestine; hence related symptoms occur, including jaundice, hypoglycemia, and kidney failure. There are painful headaches, mental confusion, coma, and convulsions. Fluid may collect in the lungs. Death occurs in over half the cases and within the fourth to eighth day.

As for many toxins, liver cells are the target of amanitin attack. In the cell's nucleus, the nucleolus (the site of ribosome sub-unit production) is destroyed. Amanitin interferes with the enzyme RNA polymerase II as it binds to DNA. This in turn obstructs messenger RNA transcription from chromosomal DNA. With no messenger RNA, ribosomes produce no proteins. Thus, in 48 hours liver cells begin to die. As the toxin continues to circulate in the blood from the liver to the kidney, the glomeruli of the kidney filter out amanitin. Rather than being excreted from the kidney, the toxin remains and destroys cells of the convoluted tubules. Because amanitin can then reenter the blood and circulate back to the liver, the liver receives repeated dosages of the toxin. When death comes, therefore, it is from hepatic coma or kidney failure. Survivors may have long-term organ damage.

Gyrotoxins.   Although less commonly leading to death than amanitin poisoning, false morels also contain cytoplasmic poisons. False morels include species of *Gyromitra* (Fig. 5–2), *Helvella*, and *Verpa* and can be easily mistaken for true morels. All these fleshy fungi are hollow-stalked Ascomycetes with complex-shaped caps. Whereas the caps of morels are covered with craters, looking somewhat like a sponge on a stalk (Fig. 5–8), the cap of *Gyromitra* is convoluted like a brain (Fig. 5–2), that of *Helvella* is saddle-shaped, and on *Verpa* it attaches only at the apex of the stalk. *Gyromitra esculenta* from some regions, such as the western United States, is one of the choice edible fungi, while in other regions it is toxic and fatal in about 15 to 35 percent of the cases of ingestion. In Europe, this type of poisoning leads to 2 to 4 percent of all fungal poisonings. Because the toxin is volatile, some believe that drying the fungus or boiling it in repeated changes of water will extract the toxin. Detoxification, however, is not always certain.

False morels contain gyromitrin, a hydrazine-type compound. When a false morel is eaten, the body hydrolyzes gyromitrin into monomethylhydrazine (MMH). This later toxin is similar to hydrazines used as rocket and jet engine fuels from which exposed workers have reported symptoms similar to those after *Gyromitra* poisoning. MMH inhibits enzyme systems requiring the coenzyme pyridoxal phosphate (one of the B vitamins).

Symptoms from gyromitrin poisoning appear faster than those from amanitin poisoning, but there is still typically a 2- to 8-hour delay after consumption. The earliest symptoms include abdominal pains and a feeling of "being full." Then watery or bloody

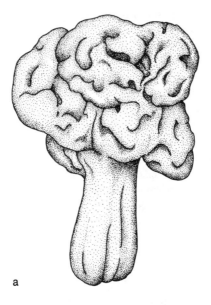

a

CH₃—CH==N—N(CH₃)—C(=O)H

b

H₂N—N(CH₃)H

c

Figure 5–2 (a) *Gyromitra esculenta*,
false morel; (b) gyromitrin;
(c) monomethylhydrazine

diarrhea, nausea, and vomiting start. There may also be headaches, dizziness, and loss of coordination. In cases with fatalities, there are severe fevers, convulsions, and irregular pulse, and most importantly the liver is damaged. When death occurs, it is in 2 to 10 days from liver or heart failure.

2. Neurotoxins

Muscarine. Muscarine is a toxin working on the autonomic nervous system. Although muscarine was first isolated from *Amanita muscaria*, the fly agaric, from which the compound received its name, it is present in concentrations too low for physiological activity. Species of *Clitocybe* and *Inocybe* contain much larger amounts of this compound. One species, *Clitocybe dealbata* (Fig. 5–3), has a white

Figure 5–3 *Clitocybe dealbata*, sweating mushroom

stalk that is mealy in texture when crumbled. The cap is grayish white with a depression in the center and has a wavy margin. This mushroom is called the sweating mushroom because of the symptoms it produces. Because it often grows in fairy rings, it can be confused with the edible *Marasmius oreades*. At the center of the cap of *Inocybe fastigiata* (Fig. 5–4), there is a prominent protrusion. The cap is yellowish, shiny, and sometimes cracked from the edges, with the edges curved upward.

a

b

Figure 5–4 (a) *Inocybe fastigiata*; (b) muscarine

The alkaloid muscarine (Fig. 5–4) is a potent cholinergic activator, stimulating the parasympathetic nervous system. Symptoms appear soon after eating the mushrooms, generally within 15 to 30 minutes, but may take up to 2 hours. Typical symptoms are profuse sweating, nausea, and vomiting. Characteristically, there is excessive salivation and nasal and eye discharge. Diarrhea can occur, and blurred vision has been reported. In severe cases, asthmalike symptoms arise, the pulse slows, blood pressure lowers, and the victim goes into shock. Death can occur within 9 hours and happens in about 5 percent of cases. When death occurs, it is from difficulties in breathing and heart functions.

Psilocybin and Psilocin.   These neurotoxins (Fig. 5–5) effect the central nervous system and are found in species of *Psilocybe, Panaeolus, Conocybe, Stropharia*, and *Gymnopilus*. Spores of these genera are dark, ranging from rusty brown in *Conocybe* and purple in *Psilocybe* to black in *Panaeolus* and *Stropharia*. When some of these mushrooms are bruised, they turn blue because enzymes released from injured cells oxidize psilocin to a blue metabolite, but such a color change is not restricted to these mushrooms. Those who collect and intentionally ingest psilocybin-containing mushrooms should take note that some of these species closely resemble "little brown mushrooms" containing amatoxins (such as *Galerina* and *Conocybe filaris*).

The body apparently hydrolyzes psilocybin, the indole alkaloids contained in these mushrooms, into psilocin, the bioactive compound. The psychic activity is based on interference with the neurotransmitter, serotonin, which is structurally similar to psilocin.

Hallucinations and psychic symptoms appear within 30 to 60 minutes of mushroom ingestion and continue for several hours. Hallucinations are of kaleidoscopic-colored visions in different patterns and shapes, often of art and architectural motifs. Perceptions of time, space, and sensory stimuli are altered. There may be a feeling of separation between body and spirit, where the spirit is suspended in air looking down. Euphoria, depression, or a state of introspection may develop. Clinical trials show that 4 to 8 mg of psilocybin produce hallucination, and toxicity in rats is at 28 mg/kg. Deaths are reported more commonly in children than in adults.

Gordon Wasson, a banker by trade but ethnomycologist by passion, popularized knowledge of the important role of these psilocybin-containing mushrooms in past and isolated cultures. Wasson's investigations revealed that many cultures had used hallucinogenic mushrooms in rituals, but had carefully developed taboos that prevented abuse of the mushrooms. In the early 1950s, he traveled to remote Indian villages in the southern mountains of Mexico and participated in religious ceremonies where natives consumed "magic mushrooms" to divine God's truths and messages. The Indian's link between the mushroom and God is clear from their word for the mushroom, Teonanacatl, meaning God flesh. The natives believed that the mushrooms were gifts from God, and through the mushroom, God communicated with them. In Guatemala, archeologists have also discovered mushroom-shaped stones with carved effigies. These religious relics have survived since 1000 B.C. and attest to the importance of mushrooms in some of humanity's early awareness of a God. Tribes engaged in the ceremonial use of hallucinogenic mushrooms today are living remnants of a religion

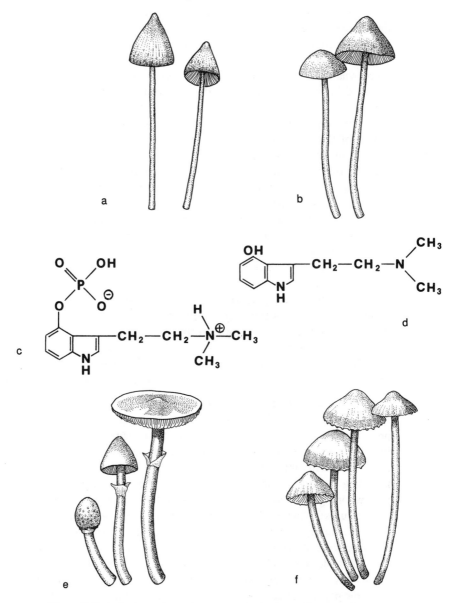

Figure 5–5 Hallucinogenic mushrooms: (a) *Psilocybe semilanceata*, liberty cap;
(b) *Panaeolus (Psathyrella) foenisecii*, haymaker's mushroom; (c) psilocybin;
(d) psilocin; (e) *Psilocybe (Stropharia) cubensis*, magic mushroom;
(f) *Panaeolus subbalteatus*, belted mushroom

dating back to the Aztec and Mayan empires. Through time, beliefs of the ancient
religion became infused with the Catholic teachings, forcibly introduced by the
Conquistadors and Spanish missionaries.

Gordon Wasson described in a *Life* magazine article his experience in one of these ceremonies, including hallucinations and visions where geometric patterns, imbued in rich pastel colors, transformed into architectural structures. Ceremonies began at night in huts illuminated only with candle light. On one side of the room there was a Christian alter. Knowledge of which mushrooms were sacred was invested in the *curandero*, the priestess who presided over the ritual. The Indians named these sacred mushrooms according to their psychic effects, religious symbol, or where they could be found: landslide mushroom, mushroom of superior reason, crown of thorns, and children of the waters. Kneeling on a mat, the *curandero* cleaned the mushrooms and passed each through copal incense as she prayed. She then distributed them to the participants and to herself. Each participant had to be ceremonially clean or it was believed that they would "go crazy" after eating the mushroom. This meant that they had to abstain from certain foods and sexual intercourse before the ceremony. Each person drank chocolate, and then slowly chewed the mushrooms. The Spanish had reported that natives drank chocolate before consuming mushrooms during the coronation ceremony of Montezuma in 1506. Presumably, the chocolate makes the rancid-smelling and acrid-tasting mushrooms easier to eat. Next the *curandero* extinguished the candle and prayed to God for insight and asked questions. Will the young boy live or die? Will the crops be good? Is the visitor's son in good health?. The *curandero* hummed, sang, clapped her hands or spoke, imploring God for answers.

By dawn, answers to the *curandero's* questions came as the mushroom spoke to her. The young boy would die, and later he did. Wasson's son was not at home. Later the father learned the son had driven to another state for a party.

Ibotenic Acid and Muscimol.   *Amanita muscaria* is called the fly agaric because flies, reportedly attracted to the mushroom, are putatively killed by the insecticidal property of ibotenic acid contained within the mushroom. When humans eat fly agaric, ibotenic acid is readily broken down into muscimol (Fig. 5–6), the compound more active in causing intoxication. The distinctive fruiting body of *A. muscaria* (Fig. 5–6) is among the most commonly illustrated mushrooms for popular items. It has a broad yellow, orange, to red cap covered with a layer of white warts that look like cottage cheese curds. Whereas the cup at the base of *A. phalloides* fits loosely around the stalk, that of *A. muscaria* makes a close fit around the bulbous base. The gills, stalk, ring, cup and spores are all white. Above the cup, several ridges ornament the stalk.

Ibotenic acid is an amino acid (Fig. 5–6) that can be decarboxylated to muscimol in the body or simply by heating. Clinical studies show that purified muscimol produces the same psychic effects as the mushroom, particularly the sleep symptoms.

Symptoms come on relatively quickly, about 20 to 60 minutes after eating the mushrooms, and last for several hours. Many symptoms resemble those of alcohol inebriation, but additional symptoms can be very serious, including epileptic-type seizures. At first there is dizziness, a loss of coordination, and drowsiness. Then there is a period of deep sleep with vivid dreams. Sometimes there are GI problems, such as nausea and vomiting. On awakening there is a delirious or manic phase with a feeling of elation and hyperactivity, including some extraordinary physical feats.

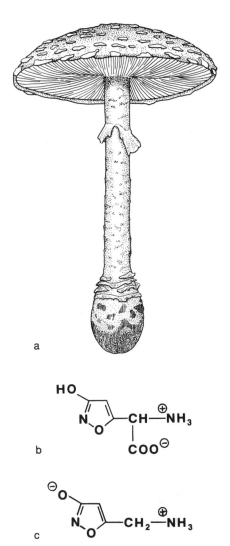

Figure 5–6   (a) *Amanita muscaria*, fly agaric; (b) ibotenic acid; (c) muscimol

People have also reported hearing voices or echos, seeing colored visions, and becoming confused or disoriented. Perception of size is changed; a large object may seem small, and a small object large. Accompanying these symptoms, particularly after large dosages of mushrooms, there may be skeletal muscle spasms and convulsions. Richard Haard and Karen Haard refer to muscimol as the toggle-switch intoxicant because the reaction can go two ways. In some cases the activity affects the cerebellum portion of the brain, causing sleep and mood changes. In others the effect is on the medulla, scrambling the motor control center of the brain and causing epileptic-like fits. Estimates of the rate of death from eating *A. muscaria* are controversial and range from 0 to 5 percent.

Because this mushroom is capable of producing visions (although quite different from the hallucinations psilocybin-containing mushrooms induce), it has had a cultural role in religious ceremonies, although today some tribes use it recreationally because of its inebriating potency. Gordon Wasson proposed that the intoxicating beverage, Soma, revered 4000 years ago in the *Rig Veda*, a Hindu collection of spiritual psalms, is *A. muscaria*. As a part of social gatherings among some tribes in Siberia, the mushroom is dried, rolled into a ball, and eaten whole as an intoxicant. The body concentrates the toxins and excretes them in the urine. Among these tribes, urine is collected after eating the mushroom and drunk for a second dosage, presumably without the GI discomfort accompanying consumption of the mushroom itself. The Ojibway tribe in the Great Lakes areas of North America and Canada also knew of the inebriating potency of this mushroom. In the 1600s, a Jesuit priest recorded that natives of an Algonkian group believed that after death you go to heaven and eat mushrooms.

3. Coprine

The genus *Coprinus*, the inky cap mushroom, contains some good edible species, but drinking alcohol after eating one species, *C. atramentarius* (Fig. 5–7), causes illness. The mushroom has a bell-shaped cap on a sturdy stalk and black spores. As the mushroom ages, the cap degenerates into a watery black mass from

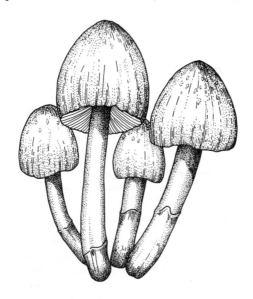

Figure 5–7 (a) *Coprinus atramentarius*; (b) coprine

the bottom up. This species typically grows in clusters, unlike the edible shaggy mane, *C. comatus*.

Coprinus atramentarius contains the compound coprine (Fig. 5–7). Under normal conditions, the liver oxidizes ethanol to acetic acid, which can be additionally respired. Coprine interferes with the enzyme aldehyde dehydrogenase in the liver so that ethanol oxididation is incomplete and toxic acetaldehydes accumulate. Coprine's activity is similar to Antabuse, a disulfiram compound used to treat alcoholism. Because coprine is heat stable, even cooking the mushrooms does not make them safe to mix with alcohol consumption.

Symptoms occur within 10 to 15 minutes of alcohol consumption after mushroom ingestion. The face and neck flush red, the heart beats rapidly, breathing is deep, legs and arms feel numb, and hands swell. A metallic taste develops in the mouth. Recovery is usually within 4 hours. The latency period after eating mushrooms before ethanol can be consumed without coprine activity varies according to the person, but can last for 2 to 5 days. Recovery requires excretion or catabolism of coprine and new synthesis of aldehyde dehydrogenase.

4. Gastrointestinal (GI) irritants

Without knowing the chemical basis of their bioactivity, this is a catchall grouping of poisonous mushrooms, including mushrooms that are very dangerous, causing liver or kidney damage, and others that cause only mild discomfort. The adage "one man's poison may be another man's delight" is most appropriately applied with the latter group. Some fungi that may be eaten with impunity and pleasure by some people may produce nausea, vomiting, and diarrhea if eaten by another person. Even a "safe" mushroom collected from another region or at another time of year may cause illness when eaten. Some mushrooms can be eaten after cooking but not raw. Others are a problem only if consumed with alcohol. The general rule when eating wild mushrooms, particularly for the first time, is to consume a small portion to see how it affects you. It is always a good rule to eat mushrooms in moderation. An absolute rule is never to eat a mushroom if you are unsure of its identification. Gastrointestinal symptoms start 30 minutes to 2 hours after eating the mushrooms. There is nausea, vomiting, stomach cramps, diarrhea, and weakness.

True morels, *Morchella* (Fig. 5–8), are among the most prized edible fungi, but some people report nausea when morels are eaten in association with alcohol consumption. One couple reported in the journal *Mycologia* that they and their two daughters had eaten morels at a party. The two adults became nauseated and sick enough to seek medical attention, but the children had no adverse effects. The only difference was that the children had not drunk alcohol. Thus, the sensitivity to the morels was associated with alcohol, but the chemical basis of the sensitivity is not known. An often collected mushroom is *Laetiporus sulphureus* (Fig. 5–9), known as the sulphur shelf or chicken mushroom because of its yellow to orange coloration on all surfaces. It is a common fall fungus found growing as clustered shelves on living or rotting trees. Gastrointestinal discomforts with this fungus are also associated with alcohol consumption, but not in all cases of poisonings. Individuals may also develop allergies to specific mushrooms or several related species. Nausea, vomiting, and intestinal cramps are the most common symptoms.

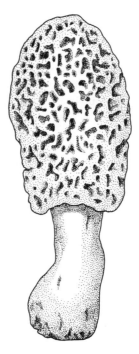

Figure 5–8   *Morchella* sp., morel

The North American Mycological Association Case Registry of Poison Incidences shows that *Chlorophyllum molybdites* (Fig. 5–10) is the most commonly reported

Figure 5–9   *Laetiporus sulphureus*, sulfur-shelf fungus

Figure 5–10   *Chlorophyllum molybdites*, green-spored parasol

cause of poisoning. This is a showy mushroom, often found in fairy rings in lawns. The sturdy stalk has a ring but no cup. The cap is covered with brownish scales and is large, up to a foot in diameter. The gills start out white, but turn green as spores are released. Typical symptoms are vomiting, nausea, diarrhea, intestinal cramps, weakness, and sweating.

In search of the gourmet's delight, chanterelles, an orange, funnel-shaped fungus, one may mistakenly collect the jack-o'-lantern mushroom, *Omphalotus olearius*. Whereas the underside of the cap has cross-linked ridges on the chanterelles, they are predominantly lamellate in the latter mushroom. Ingestion of *O. olearius* produces vomiting, nausea, salivation, and diarrhea.

5. Carcinogenicity

Because the time between contact with a cancer-causing compound and the induced cancer may be decades, knowledge of carcinogenic compounds in fungi is limited. Basically, most discoveries have come from broad-spectrum screening programs and clinical studies using animals. It is significant that some carcinogens in mushrooms have been identified. For example, fresh raw samples of the common edible mushroom *Agaricus bisporus* (Fig. 5–11) contain a phenylhydrazine compound called agaritine that induces cancer in test animals. You will recall that this is the same type of compound as gyromitrin (Fig. 5–2). Mice fed uncooked *Agaricus bisporus* developed cancer from agaritine. Although human sensitivity or dose levels cannot be extrapolated from the experiments, they do indicate areas where new toxins may be discovered.

6. Lichens as poisons

Lichens are generally considered nonpoisonous, but there are a few exceptions. Two lichens that grow in alpine regions, *Letharia vulpina* and *Cetraria pinastri*, are used to poison wolves. In the winter the carcass of an animal is filled with the lichen and powdered glass. When the wolf dines on the dead animal, wounds from the ingested glass make the organs sensitive to the acids of the lichens, and the wolf dies.

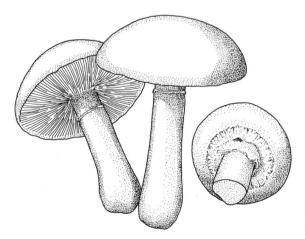

Figure 5–11 *Agaricus bisporus*, common cultivated mushroom

Treatment

With serious cases of mushroom poisoning, emergency medical attention is required. The first action is to induce vomiting with ipecac emesis to expel the ingested mushrooms. Activated charcoal in sorbitol is given to remove any unabsorbed poison. These procedures are useless with protoplasmic poisons, because symptoms appear too long after the mushroom is digested.

For most intoxications, only supportive measures can be taken. If there has been vomiting and diarrhea, fluid and electrolyte balances must be carefully controlled. The delirium phase of muscimol intoxication can have convulsive activity or depression; hence, restraint and reassurance may be required. A muscle relaxant such as diazepam controls seizures accompanying muscimol ingestion. A sedative, such as chlorpromazine, can be used with psilocybin intoxication if panic develops from hallucinations. Complete recovery from amanitin poisoning has been achieved in some cases with repeated dialysis of the blood and maintenance of high carbohydrate levels. Antibiotics should be used to avoid secondary bacterial infections of injured tissues. Lives have also been saved after amatoxin poisonings by liver transplants.

For some types of poisonings, there are specific antidotes. Thioctic acid has been used to control amanitin poisoning, but this drug is controversial. Atropine sulfate (an alkaloid derived from nightshade) is used to counter cholinergic symptoms of muscarine poisoning. It is important to note that atropine exacerbates the effects of ibotenic acid and muscimol and should never be used to treat *A. muscaria* intoxication. Because of the mode of action of gyromitrin, pyridoxine injections can counter symptoms of gyromitrin.

MYCOTOXICOSIS

Mycotoxicosis is a poisoning from eating food contaminated with toxic fungi or their toxic metabolites. Because mold growing in and on foods is a common occurrence, the question can be raised at the onset, does eating moldy food hurt? The simple answer is sometimes yes and sometimes no, but one cannot tell for sure just by looking at the fungus. Because it is not possible to test the effects of mycotoxins on humans under controlled experimental conditions, the adverse effects of these agents on humans have been questioned. Despite skepticism by some, experimental results in animals have led governments throughout the world to place "safe limits" of contamination for at least one mycotoxin, aflatoxin B (Fig. 5–12). Cows and goats fed grains with aflatoxins can carry over the toxins to their milk; hence, there are additional limits for diary animal feed. For other mycotoxins, because of technical difficulties in measurements and lack of data as to human hazard, there are no regulated limits. Symptoms of mycotoxicoses are variable and are influenced by dosage levels. Low dosages can be easily overlooked and attributed to other factors, such as nutrition and disease. It is the high dosage that results in the most striking and readily diagnosed symptoms. Thus, we distinguish *chronic* poisonings of low dosages over a long period of time and *acute* poisoning of large dosages from a single or limited number of feedings.

Although not restricted to these Deuteromycete genera, many toxigenic fungi belong to *Aspergillus*, *Fusarium*, and *Penicillium*. One strain of a given species may produce toxins and another strain produce none. Complicating the story even more, a strain may produce toxins under one set of environmental conditions and not others. Finally, several different species may produce the same mycotoxin, and conversely a single species may produce multiple types of mycotoxins. Among the free-floating spores in the air, there may be conidia of toxigenic molds. So be cautious; the mold growing on the bowl of rice left out on the kitchen counter may be releasing mycotoxins.

Because molds are also important in food-ripening processes, such as the ones involved in the production of Roquefort and Camembert cheese or fermentation of soy sauce, there has been concern whether commercially used strains are toxigenic. Because of reports in Wisconsin, for example, of toxigenic strains of *Penicillium roqueforti* on silage associated with abortion of calves or placenta retention, the obvious question is if this strain is also found on cheeses. Under conditions of usage, no toxigenic strains have been reported for commercially used fungi. Some strains used commercially, however, can produce toxins on substrates other than those used for the industrial process.

What types of foods are most likely to be contaminated with mycotoxins? Grains, oil seeds, cotton seed meal, and ground nut meal are important livestock feed and possible substrates for toxigenic molds. Wheat and rye, the basic grains for breads and pastas, can also become contaminated with toxigenic molds. These molds also grow along surfaces of cheeses and cured meats. When does food and feed become contaminated? Although contamination can occur on living plants, most problems arise when food is stored for long time periods. The two most important environmental factors affecting mycotoxin production are temperature and excessive moisture (ranges greater than 20 to 28 percent for living tissue and 12 to 18 percent for stored). This means that mycotoxins are particularly a problem in tropical and subtropical agriculture, but are also a persistent difficulty in temperate zones. Now lets look at a few specific examples of mycotoxins. Most documented effects are on livestock or laboratory animals, but coincidences between human diseases and mycotoxin consumption warn of potential dangers to human health.

1. Aflatoxins

Aflatoxins are the most comprehensively studied mycotoxins. The name is derived from the species first shown to produce the toxin, *Aspergillus flavus* (*A. fla.* toxin = aflatoxin). The discovery of aflatoxins brought about a burgeoning awareness of mycotoxins as hazards to animal health and product safety. For a time, the cause of "turkey X disease" that killed 100,000 turkey poults in England in 1960 was a mystery. Turkey poults lost appetite, became lethargic, and, in a few weeks of these symptoms, died. Thousands of partridges, pheasants, and ducklings also suffered fatalities.

Autopsies revealed hemorrhaging and necrosis of the liver, as well as kidney lesions. Through experimentation and some detective work, scientists correlated supplementation of feed with ground peanut meal imported from Brazil with the deaths of the young birds. When fungal growth was found on feed implicated in the death of the animals, the possibility of mycotoxin poisoning was considered. Analysis of the feed revealed toxic metabolites identical to those produced by the mold *A. flavus*.

Aflatoxins are a group of compounds that can be separated on thin layers of absorbents covering glass plates when partially immersed in a mixture of organic solvents. The names of the aflatoxins reflect their fluorescence (either blue or green) under ultraviolet light and the order of separation on the thin layer plates: aflatoxin B_1, B_2, G_1, and G_2. Aflatoxin B_1 is the most toxic type and can be converted into another form when ingested by cows. The converted aflatoxin is secreted into milk and is named aflatoxin M_1 (milk toxin). All these compounds are coumarin derivatives and have in common difurofuran ring structures, pentagons with one double bond and an oxygen in the ring structure (Fig. 5–12).

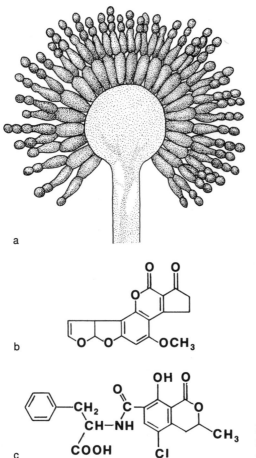

Figure 5–12 (a) *Aspergillus flavus*, microscopic view; (b) aflatoxin B_1; (c) ochratoxin A

Sometimes fungal contamination may be evident as radiating threads terminating in yellow-green globules covering grains such as corn. The fungus is particularly able to grow in grains damaged mechanically or by insects. With the light microscope, one can see that the greenish masses consist of upright shafts terminating in swollen vesicles from which emerge bowling-pen-shaped cells and rows of conidia (Fig. 5–12). The vast numbers of conidia are carried by air, insects, or mites into new uncontaminated areas. After the fungus dries up, however, the toxin remains.

Aflatoxins are the most carcinogenic and among the most potent toxic compounds occurring naturally. In addition, aflatoxins are mutagens, causing chromosomal aberrations, and teratogens, causing malformations in embryos. As expected from this introduction, aflatoxins in animal feed are a major problem in livestock production. Acute poisonings result in subcutaneous hemorrhages and cause death by damage to the liver and kidney, as well as lung congestions. Affected livers are fatty and pale in color with large, mottled lesions. Chronic toxicity results in reduction of appetite and growth. With extended feeding, liver carcinomas develop, leading to death. Animals have different levels of susceptibility to aflatoxins, and all tested mammals are sensitive. Ducklings, turkey poults, and trout are highly susceptible, but poisonings also occur in cows, pigs, rats, mice, and monkeys. In addition, the nutritional status of animals influences susceptibility. Animals with protein-deficient diets are increasingly more sensitive to the toxicity.

Aflatoxins have multiple sites of activity in the cell. They bind to DNA and block the transcription of RNA, impairing protein synthesis. Thus protein deficiencies in diets augment toxicity from aflatoxins. Aflatoxins also compete with hormones for cellular binding sites and consequently have antireproductive effects. Aflatoxins interfere with the immune systems of animals, making them more susceptible to disease. Even vaccinations of animals are not effective with aflatoxin consumption. The carcinogenic effects of aflatoxins are related to their interactions directly with DNA.

Aflatoxins are monitored on a global scale, and in the United States there are regulations for "safe" levels for different uses of contaminated grains. For example, each batch of raw, shelled peanuts in the United States must be analyzed and certified as to their aflatoxin content by the U.S. Department of Agriculture (USDA) and the Food and Drug Administration (FDA). According to the Peanut Marketing Agreement for raw, unprocessed peanuts, batches with over 50 parts per billion (ppb) aflatoxins are not allowable for human consumption. When dairy cows are fed feed rich in aflatoxins, their milk becomes toxic because ingested aflatoxin B_1 is hydroxylated into aflatoxin M_1, which is secreted into the milk. Consequently, feed for dairy cows and goats has more stringent standards (0.5 ppb aflatoxins). Highly contaminated grains are not allowed for feed and are rerouted for other functions, such as fertilizers.

Although association of human cancer with aflatoxins has not been proved experimentally, there is enough circumstantial evidence to warrant caution. Typically, there is a higher incidence of human liver cancer in regions where rates of aflatoxin contamination of food are high. This is particularly true in economically or agriculturally stressed areas where food of lower quality (damaged and hence more likely to have mold growth) is used for human food. Human sensitivity was shown in India in 1974, when about 400 people became ill after eating corn containing aflatoxins at concentrations of 6 to 15 ppb. One hundred and six of those affected died.

2. Citrinin

This nephrotoxin is a product of *Penicillium citrinum* and other molds growing on cereals such as barley and oats, as well as on corn. At first there was interest in this compound as an antibiotic, but soon it was found that it was too toxic to animals to be pharmacologically useful. Pigs are highly sensitive to this compound, which damages the kidney, causing lesions and enlargement of collecting tubules. Liver lesions can also accompany other tissue damage.

3. Fumigaclavines and other tremorgenic compounds

The alkaloidal fumigaclavines cause tremorgenic effects and is a neurotoxin. *Aspergillus fumigatus*, one mold producing the compound, is commonly found in corn silage. Cattle that ingest contaminated silage become uncoordinated and walk with a stiff-legged gait as skeletal muscle tremor and paralysis set in. Because the paralysis also affects muscles of the digestive system, constipation of the animal leads to additional toxic responses.

Paspalam staggers is induced in sheep and horses when the animals eat grass containing sclerotia of the ergot fungus *Claviceps paspalum*. Animals have muscle tremors and are excitable when made to move. Because of the lack of coordination, animals often die of dehydration, drowning, or injury.

4. Ochratoxin

Ochratoxins are a group of isocoumarin derivatives linked to phenyalanine and are produced by molds such as *Aspergillus ochraceus*. Ochratoxin A (Fig. 5–12) is the most destructive form and is both a teratogen and kidney toxin, particularly in chickens, sheep, and pigs. A kidney disease (Balkan nephropathy) of people in Slavic countries in Europe was so similar to the mycotoxin-induced disease in animals that human toxicity is possible. Ochratoxins and ochratoxigenic molds are found on a variety of foods, including rice, oats, wheat, chili peppers, legumes, sorgum, dried fish, fermented sausage, and cured ham. An array of additional symptoms are associated in ochratoxin poisoning in diverse animals, including paralysis, respiratory failure, induced abortions, and delay and reduction in egg production.

5. Patulin

This diphenol derivation is one of the smallest of the mycotoxins (Fig. 5–13) and has antibiotic properties. Because it is an inhibitor of mitosis, its side effects on animals are too dangerous for application in animals as an antibiotic. The toxin was first isolated from *Penicillium patulum*, but is known from several molds, including *P. expansum*, a fungus that grows on damaged and rotten apples.

With acute poisonings, there are lung hemorrhages and congestion. In the blood the toxin can be distributed through liver tissue within 23 seconds, causing degeneration. Patulin is carcinogenic, but only in tissue surrounding the area where the compound was injected.

Patulin has been detected in commercial apple juice and apple butter when rotten apples were used in their production. Patulin is a relatively stable compound and is protected by the acid condition and sulfhydryl groups occurring naturally in apple juice.

6. Sporidesmins

When there are hot and dry periods ending with warm rains and overgrazing of pastures, the fungus *Pithomyces chartarum* grows in grass. This fungus produces a compound that attacks the liver of sheep and cows. In these herbivores, the liver

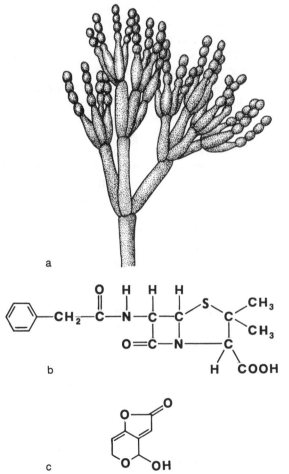

Figure 5–13   (a) *Penicillium* sp., microscopic view; (b) the antibiotic, penicillin G; (c) the mycotoxin patulin

normally breaks down phylloerythrin, a metabolite derived from chlorophyll consumed with the grass. Injured livers are unable to catabolize the compound. In livestock that has eaten contaminated grass, phylloerthrin alters the permeability of capillaries under the skin when exposed to the sun. As a result, sheep and cattle develop photosensitivity and may exhibit facial eczema. Eyes become inflamed, there is nasal discharge, and ears, eyelids, and face swell. The animals weaken, shun the sun, and die.

7. Trichothecenes

This is a large group of toxins that have in common their sesquiterpenoid structure. They inhibit protein and DNA synthesis and may have phytotoxic, cytotoxic, and dermal activities. Livestock, particularly pigs and cattle, are frequently poisoned from grains contaminated with these compounds.

Early in the 1980s, controversy surrounded reports that the Soviet Union had used one type of trichothecene produced by *Fusarium tricinctum*, T-2 toxin, as a chemical weapon in wars in Southeast Asia and Afghanistan. Victims described airplanes spreading "yellow rain" over villages. People became ill with the same symptoms associated with T-2 toxin poisoning. Hemorrhagic skin rashes, bleeding from the nose, mouth, and throat, depletion of the bone marrow, and death were all reported. The United States supported these claims of mycopoisonings with a Soviet gas mask found contaminated with T-2 toxin and with measurements of T-2 toxins in blood and urine samples of victims. Unequivocal evidence was never presented. The charges are interesting because earlier in the century, during a food shortage in the Soviet Union, there was an epidemic of alimentary toxic aleukia after people ate moldy millet and cereal rather than face starvation. This disease was associated with trichothecene-producing fungi. The toxin caused hemorrhagic and necrotic lesions in the digestive system and damaged bone marrow. Thus, it was known that the country had studied this toxin for a number of years and was involved in its production.

Another trichothecene compound is vomitoxin, an emetic material. The plant pathogenic fungus *Gibberella zeae* causes two important diseases of plants, wheat scab and stalk-ear rot of corn. While the grain is still in the field, the fungus releases vomitoxin into the plant tissue. When the infected wheat or corn is feed to pigs, they will refuse to eat it, or if they do, they vomit. After eating a few bad kernels, pigs will sort through the grain, selecting the better kernels. Although little is known as to human sensitivity to vomitoxin, the FDA has set the "level of concern" at 1 ppm vomitoxin for wheat products to be used as human food.

8. Zearalenone

The fungus *G. zeae* also produces another compound, called zearalenone, an estrogenic factor formed when grain is stored. Among pigs, which are particularly sensitive to this compound, zearalenone poisoning is an important cause of infertility and reduction of litter size. After female pigs eat contaminated grain, ovaries shrink, mammary glands enlarge, the vulva swells, and the vagina and/or rectum falls down. Males may exhibit female traits, such as enlarged mammary glands after eating contaminated feed. Zearalenone is also detected in human food in the United States, where 14 to 20 ppb has been measured in corn flakes and white corn meal.

9. Endophytic toxins

Commonly during periods of droughts or heavy grazing in pastures, certain fungi grow inside the blades of grass (endophytic fungi) and produce toxins. Thus there is no visible sign of fungus or damage to the grass, but the grass is toxic to livestock. One of these fungi is the Ascomycete *Acremonium coenophialum*, which grows in tall fescue grass. The toxins produce a number of animal health disorders, such as sore feet, reproductive problems, lower milk production, and reduced efficiency of feed in meat gain. This is an insidious disease that damages animal growth without killing the animal.

10. Ergot

The last mycotoxin poisoning that we will discuss is probably the oldest known example. On open-pollinated grains such as rye, *Claviceps purpurea* infects the flower and replaces the grain with a hard, brittle, banana-shaped, black sclerotium (Fig. 4–3). The sclerotium is rich in many types of alkaloids, some of which are toxic; others, as we will see later, are medically valuable. When contaminated rye is harvested and ground into flour, the sclerotia are ground up also. This means that any bread or other baked goods made from the flour will also contain these dangerous alkaloids. Many types of pasture grasses can also become infected with species of *Claviceps*. Thus animals grazing on ergotized grass may become ill. When animals eat contaminated grain, two types of illnesses can strike due to presence of the ergot alkaloids.

Acute poisonings result in nervous system disorders. Tingling sensations occur as if insects were crawling under the skin. The skin itches and limbs become numb. Then muscles begin to twitch, cramp, and go into spasms. Hallucinations and convulsions occur. Between convulsions, victims have a voracious appetite and insomnia. Death may follow in a few days or few weeks. Survivors may experience mental impairment.

With chronic poisoning, alkaloids cause constriction of the vascular system, restricting the flow of blood and setting up the gangrenous form of the disease. Victims feel tired and have severe muscle pains and prickling sensations. Limbs swell and burning pains alternate with a feeling of being ice cold. Extremities of the limbs then become numb and turn black with gangrene. Necrosis and withering continues up the limbs. The degree of gangrene varies depending on dosage. One may merely loose a nail or a few fingers and toes. In more severe cases, the whole foot, hand, or limb may fall off. Months may pass before death occurs.

Ergot holds an important role in human history. In the Middle Ages, thousands of people died of ergotism. Because in the gangrenous form the extremities burn as if on fire, St. Anthony became the patron saint of the disease, which became known as St. Anthony's Fire. In 1720, Czar Peter the Great of Russia led troops down the Volga valley to take from the Turkish empire an ice-free port for his land- and ice-locked nation. But the army never made it to the coast. Horses and soldiers ate ergotized grain growing in the valley and became ill. Thus, the ice-free port in the south was never obtained.

Ergot poisoning may have lead to the hysteria that culminated in the witch trials in late seventeenth-century Salem, Massachusetts. Recently, a psychologist probed the historical records to find some rational explanation for the bizarre range of behavior limited to such a short time span. The growing season preceding the witch trials was ideal for ergot parasitism of rye; consequently, stored grain may well have been contaminated. Symptoms thought to be due to bewitchment are quite similar to those for ergotism. Common complaints made by those who thought they had been bewitched were a feeling of being pinched, muscle pain, muscle spasms, a feeling of chills in the limbs, convulsions, and death. It is known that death from ergotism is more likely in children than adults. In Massachusetts, deaths said to be from bewitchment were most common among children. Thus the symptoms the citizens of Salem reported may have been due to consumption of ergotized grain and not from mere hysteria and superstition.

MEDICINAL FUNGI

The importance of fungi as sources of compounds to prevent and cure disease is becoming increasingly recognized. Antibiotics of fungal origins, purified or chemically modified from natural fungal compounds, are now commonplace as cures for bacterial infections. Each year scientists are discovering new fungal complex carbohydrates that protect animals from cancer. Even with these laboratory advances in the medical use of fungi, important revelations of herbal uses of fungi as medicines among diverse cultures are still giving us a storehouse of new compounds with medicinal potentials.

Herbal Uses

In traditional systems of medicines, certain fungi have particularly important roles. Current oriental medicine has preserved many aspects of traditional medicine and serves as a basis for some of our present understanding of the role of fungi in the prevention and control of disease. Fungi are often not used as a sole cure in oriental herbal medicine but are mixed with other fungi or plants to amplify activities or counteract side effects. It is believed that some compounds interact synergistically to produce their bioactivity. Thus discovery of the chemical bases of many of these remedies is difficult because of the vast numbers of compounds potentially involved. For other cures, great strides have been made in isolating bioactive compounds and in clinically documenting their effectiveness to cure disease. First you will read about fungal remedies widely used in folk medicine and applied against a wide range of symptoms. Then we will explore examples of fungi targeted against specific symptoms.

1. Tuckahoe

This polypore fungus, *Wolfiporia extensa* (*Poria cocus*), is known by many common names such as hoelen, China root, Indian bread, Virginia truffle, and tuckahoe. The fruiting body forms a white crust on trees and is covered with numerous, clustered, shallow pores (Fig. 5–14). Most medical interest is in the large, hard, resistant underground sclerotium (Fig. 5–14), which looks something like a huge, rough potato or irregularly shaped coconut. The sclerotium is reddish brown on the outside and white to tan on the inside and may be associated with tree roots.

The importance of this fungus is reflected in its inclusion as a component in over one-third of the blended oriental medical recipes and enumeration among the ancient remedies of the *Divine Husband's Classic of the Materia Medica* (A.D. 25 to 220, later Hun Dynasty). Tuckahoe is used as a general tranquilizer and is said to quiet the heart and calm the spirit. Compounds contained in the central portion of the sclerotium are thought to target the central nervous system. Thus, it is used to control heart palpitations, overcome insomnia, and decrease forgetfulness. In clinical studies, extracts from

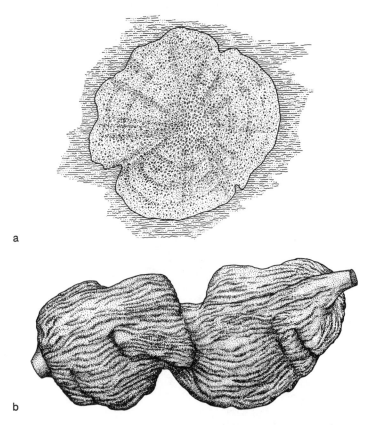

a

b

Figure 5–14 *Wolfiporia extensa*, tuckahoe: (a) fruiting body; (b) sclerotium

tuckahoe protected against stress-induced ulcers in mice. Because it relaxes the smooth muscles of the intestines, it is used as a stomachic and antispasmodic. It is believed to reduce the acidity of the gastric system and stop vomiting.

Another use of tuckahoe is as a diuretic to promote urination. The outer layer of the sclerotium is considered a stronger diuretic than the inner tissue. This layer is a rich source of potassium, which stimulates sodium secretion and urination. A final application of tuckahoe is in the control of chemically induced contact dermatitis.

Extracts of tuckahoe are used to treat breast and uterine cancer, particularly in Chinese medicine. We will see later that the clinical basis of activity is now known.

2. *Ganoderma lucidum*

A second cure-all fungus is also a polypore and in crude drug form is known as reishi. The distinctive fruiting body of *Ganoderma lucidum* consists of a cap, ranging from maroon to black, and laterally attached to a stalk (Fig. 5–15). The fruiting body is hard, and the surface is glossy, looking as if it were painted with lacquer. The bottom of the cap is tan to buff and is covered with tiny pores. This fungus is applied against general malaise and problems such as anorexia and insomnia. One traditional therapeutic effect of *G. lucidum* is control of heart disease. Recently, this fungus has attracted clinical interest because it has been experimentally shown to contain a hypolipidemic agent, lowering serum cholesterol but having no effect of triglycerides. Moreover, compounds in this fungus improve liver function. Glycopeptide compounds (composed of sugar and protein) called ganoderans lower blood sugar and are the basis of its use as an antidiabetic medicine.

There are a wide range of maladies that *G. lucidum* has been reported to allay but for which the pharmacological basis is unknown. It may protect against radiation injury and protect against high-altitude reactions. This is one of the many fleshy fungi containing carbohydrates that in clinical tests result in inhibition of tumor growth.

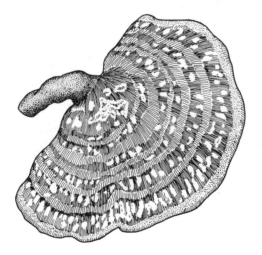

Figure 5–15 *Ganoderma lucidum*

3. **Wood ear fungus**

The ear fungus (*Auricularia auricula*) and black tree fungus (*A. polytricha*) are jelly fungi with dark violet to black gelatinous fruiting bodies. The fruiting body is shaped like a very wrinkled ear with a funnel-shaped protuberance on the back of the ear attaching to wood. When moist, the fruiting body is flexible and rubbery; but when it dries down, it is a thin, brittle sheet (Fig. 5–16). When rehydrated, the "ear" returns to its gelatinous state.

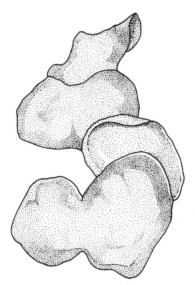

Figure 5–16 *Auricularia auricula* in dried-down form

This fungus inhibits platelet aggregation and is used as a blood anticoagulant to control blood clots in the circulatory system, which can lead to strokes or general bleeding. It also contains compounds that are anticholesterol agents. Because this is an edible fungus, inclusion in the diet may have health benefits. As stated in a Chinese proverb, "Nature cures the disease, the doctor collects the fee."

4. *Cordyceps* **species**

The interesting species of the Ascomycete *Cordyceps* (*C. hawkesii*, *C. militaris*, *C. sinensis*) infect bodies of insect larvae (for example, grubs and caterpillars) and render them mummified. A short stalk grows up from the insect body and terminates with a conical cap (Fig. 5–17) in which sexually produced ascospores in asci are contained in flask-shaped structures. In oriental medicine, this fungus is used for "eternal youth."

The entire assemblage of the fungus and mummified body of the larvae is used for medicine. A tonic, often mixed with other tonic herbs, is concocted from the assembly to rehabilitate patients after an illness or improve the constitution of the

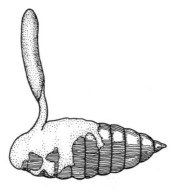

Figure 5–17 *Cordyceps militaris*

elderly. *Cordyceps* species are also used to treat serious coughs, and it has a tranquillizing effect. Research has focused on the chemical nature of anticancer agents in this fungus, particularly those effective against lung cancer.

5. Iceland moss

One lichen widely used as a general tonic has the misleading common name Iceland moss (*Cetraria islandica*). The gray to light olive-brown thallus of this lichen is a dichotomously branched strap with coarse, hairlike projections coming off the margins (Fig. 5–18). The margins roll inwardly, making the upper surface of the thallus a trough. Because this lichen was regularly used as a food in traditional cultures, particularly in countries in the north such as Iceland, some of its medicinal benefits were additional to its role in nutrition. In most modern cultures, this lichen is not considered a food staple. One of the many compounds found in the lichen is the carbohydrate lichenin. When the lichen is boiled in broth and then cooled, carbohydrates in its thallus form a jelly. Milk can be added to this jelly for a soup.

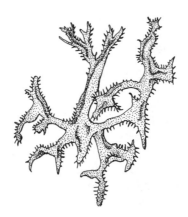

Figure 5–18 *Cetraria islandica*, Iceland moss

Lichenin and bitter substances from the lichen make a general tonic, stimulating appetite. Cetrarin, also contained in the lichen, is a nerve exciter and induces peristaltic movement of the intestine. The jelly or mucilagelike substance produced when the lichen is boiled soothes irritated and inflamed respiratory membranes. Recently, anticancer compounds have been found in this lichen.

Many other lichens used in traditional medicine have not withstood the test of time. Their selection was strongly influenced by the doctrine of signatures. For example, because *Parmelia saxatilis* was found on skulls left exposed to nature, this lichen was thought to cure epilepsy. The long, pendulous strands of *Usnea barbata* look like hair, and it was used to strengthen hair. The thallus of *Lobaria pulmonaria* resembles lungs in its pitted, reticulate surface, and hence was used to treat lung diseases. The yellow thallus of the lichen *Xanthora parietina* was used to cure jaundice.

6. Fungi used to control hemorrhages and inflammations

A number of fungi are important because of their hemostatic properties. Many of these are Basidiomycetes. Medicinal members of the puffball group are common in the genera *Calvatia* (Fig. 5–19) and *Lycoperdon*. Puffballs range from the size of ping-pong balls to bean-bag chairs. At maturity they contain olive-brown or black spores enclosed in their fruiting bodies. For medicinal purposes, the flesh of the fruiting body prior to spore formation or the spores themselves are used to control bleeding. In the traditional medicine of the Cherokee Indians, puffballs were inserted into the naval of newborn infants to control bleeding (and infection) after the umbilical cord was severed. Fruiting bodies of the desert puffball, *Battarrea*

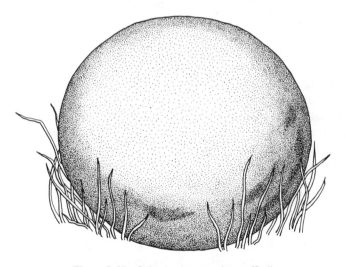

Figure 5–19 *Calvatia gigantea*, giant puffball

Figure 5–20   *Battarrea phalloides*, desert
puffball

phalloides, have a stalk at maturity (Fig. 5–20). Slices of young fruiting bodies and
spores of the mature puffball were used by Indian tribes in Nevada as a dressing for
sores, burns, and swellings. In Appalachian folk medicine, as well in other cultures,
spores of puffballs were applied topically as a powder to relieve the discomfort of
hemorrhoids or packed into the nostrils to stop nosebleeds.

The large white galls of corn smut (*Ustilago maydis*) filled with jet black
spores can be found on any part of the corn plant, including kernels on the ear (Fig.
5–21). Corn smut is used to control bleeding after childbirth or bleeding in the
lungs and bowels.

Polypores are also used as hemostatics. *Fomes fomentarius* is known as
amadou, tinderwood, or surgeon's agaric (Fig. 5–22). These shelves are perennial
and hard and corky in texture. The fruiting body is grayish and concentrically
ridged on the upper surface, with a tan and velvety margin representing the most
recent growth (Fig. 5–22). Slices of the shelf are beaten into a thin layer, soaked
in nitric acid, and dried. Ingrown toenails are treated with fragments inserted
between the flesh and nail. Whole pieces can be applied to areas of hemorrhages.
Smoldering slices were applied in early surgical practices to cauterize incisions.
The Ojibway Indians had another method to cauterize wounds. They ground this
fungus into a powder, mixed it with gunpowder, applied it to infected areas, and
then ignited it.

The important Ascomycete ergot, *Claviceps purpurea*, produces sclerotia
(Fig. 4–3) containing alkaloids that stop bleeding. These agents were widely used
to control hemorrhages after childbirth.

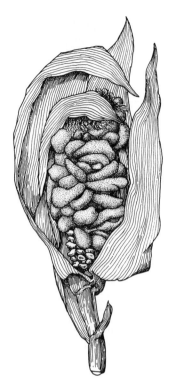

Figure 5–21 *Ustilago maydis*, corn smut

Figure 5–22 *Fomes fomentarius*,
surgeon's agaric

7. Other medicinal applications of fungi

One fungus is found to kill worms. The underground sclerotium from the polypore
Polyporus mylittae is rich in a protein-destroying enzyme, protease, which has been

given the name mylittine. This compound is effective in curing animals of worms (taenifuge), such as tapeworms and pinworms. Because mylittine is a heat-labile enzyme, heat must be avoided in preparations. Consequently, only ground powders of sclerotia are used.

In India, the polypore *Fomitopsis officinalis* is reported to be applied to the breast to control milk secretions when weaning. Small dosages are used to control heavy sweating during sleep. Large dosages are given as a purgative. The Ojibway Indians found that this fungus was effective against pneumonia, but an overdosage could cause paralysis and death. This fungus is also used to treat cancer, particularly malignant ulcers.

In addition to their use in the control of bleeding, puffballs can be used externally or internally against a number of other ailments. Some appear to have antiseptic properties. When spores are mixed with water and honey and drunk, the mixture soothes sore throat, laryngitis, tonsillitis, and throat infection. The mixture also functions as an expectorant. Spores of puffballs and the related fungi called earth stars are used for healing ear infections, eye infections, and boils. Preparations of puffballs as well as corn smut can also be used orally and are reported to promote menstrual cycles in females.

The toothed fungi are Basidiomycetes with spines on the spore-bearing surfaces of their fruiting bodies. One of these toothed fungi, *Echinodontium tinctorium*, is found in the western North America and produces reddish, shelf-fruiting bodies. It is best known as the "Indian paint fungus" because it served as a source of red dye for war paint among Native American tribes; but, in addition, the shelves were ground into powders, mixed with animal fats or tree saps, and used as a barrier cream to protect the skin from insect bites.

Since the Middle Ages, alkaloids contained in ergot (*Claviceps* sp.) have been used to induce uterine contractions, stimulating the process of childbirth. This practice was common in Europe, but also occurred in the United States. A herbal doctor in 1846, J. D. Cobb, wrote of the dangers of overdosages with ergot and advised that ergot should not be given to women bearing their first child who were "nervous and very irritable." He described the violent contractions induced with an overdosage of ergot and the fetus ripping through the uterus into the stomach, killing the mother. Indian tribes in North America used corn smut, a common parasite on one of their staple crops, in a manner similar to ergot to aid in stimulating childbirth.

8. Modern significance of herbal fungal remedies

The empirical selection of herbal remedies by our ancestors has left a rich legacy of herbal medicinal uses of fungi. But clinical research is needed to differentiate myth from fact and placebo effects from bioactivity. Progress is now started in defining the chemical and physiological bases as well as side effects of many of these remedies.

The prime example of modern science's exploitation of ancient remedies is the current widespread therapeutic uses of natural alkaloids from the ergot fungus and their synthetic derivatives. Ergotamine is the vasoconstriction agent in ergot that contributes to its gangrene effect when eaten; but in controlled dosages, this alkaloid is an effective medicine to control bleeding after childbirth. Because ergotamine tartrate constricts intracranial arteries, it is a treatment for migraine headaches. D-Lysergic acid diethylamide (LSD) affects midbrain activity and has been used beneficially in psychotherapy to treat mental illness. Unfortunately, the drug has unpredictable side effects, induces hallucinations, and has long-term mind-altering activity. Ergocornine is a birth-control agent that prevents proper attachment of fertilized eggs to the wall of the uterus. Ergonovine (Fig. 3–8; also known as ergometrine) stimulates smooth muscles. In the third trimester of pregnancy, the smooth muscles of the uterus selectively increase in their sensitivity to this compound, and hence it is an effective medication to induce and stimulate a weak labor. Ergotoxine has just the opposite effect of ergotamine; it causes vasodilation. Consequently, it is a medicine to treat high blood pressure and cerebral circulation problems.

Exciting new applications for fungal compounds are now being discovered, and one of these is based largely on knowledge of traditional medical applications of fungi to treat cancer. A whole group of complex carbohydrates has been discovered from several fleshy fungi that may help control cancerous tumor growth. The causes of cancer are complex and are not limited to just a few agents. Biological (including viruses) as well as chemical and environmental factors interplay with animal molecular machinery to induce cancer. Insight into fungi as sources of compounds against viral-induced cancer comes from a history of their antiviral applications. The milky latex of the mushroom *Lactarius piperatus* and decoctions from species of the lichen *Usnea* have been used against viral warts. Now we know that compounds from fungi can also stimulate the immune system to aid in the body's defense against cancer. Many of these same anticancer fungi also have compounds that reduce cholesterol and may help control cardiovascular diseases. We will now examine the role of fungi in cancer control.

Metabolites of Fungi Used against Cancer

Several different polysaccharides from fungi have strong activity against transplanted tumors in animals and against cancer cells carried along in artificial growth media. These complex carbohydrates are not cytotoxic and do not kill the cancer cells directly, but they stimulate the natural immune system of the animal, enabling it to ward off cancer cells. Different carbohydrates activate different parts of the immune system; however, all responses are classified as nonspecific immunostimulants. The paramunity takes place rapidly but does not affect the "immunological memory" of organisms. Consequently,the compounds must be administered repeatedly to continue host-mediated action.

Progress has been slow in the actual application of these compounds because of the stringent testing required for human safety. Calvacin, a potent antitumor glycoprotein, extracted from the giant puffball *Calvatia gigantea* (Fig. 5–19) held much excitement as a possible antitumor agent, only to be found later to be too toxic to animals. But the number of compounds with possible applications is increasing.

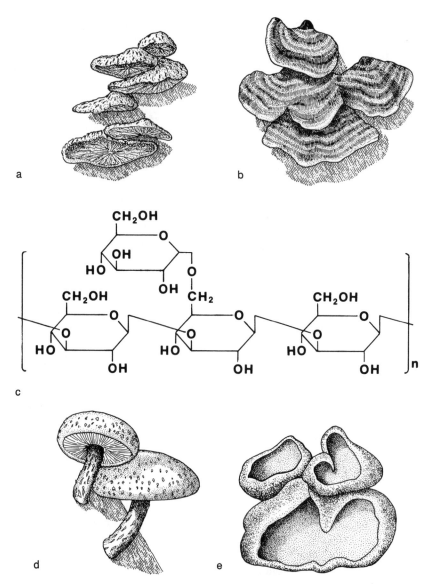

Figure 5–23 Anti-cancer fungi: (a) *Schizophyllum commune*, split gill fungus;
(b) *Coriolus versicolor*, turkey tail; (c) schizophyllan; (d) *Lentinus edodes*,
shiitake mushroom; (e) *Peziza vesiculosa*, cup fungus

1. Schizophyllan

The split gill fungus *Schizophyllum commune* (Fig. 5–23) is the source of this
glucan (a polysacharide composed of linked glucose sugars). Schizophyllan (Fig. 5–23)
is composed of a backbone of beta 1, 3 linked glucose sugars with branches coming off
with beta 1, 6 bonds every third sugar. Schizophyllan stimulates the complement system

in blood plasma, increasing protective proteins. Because of its high viscosity, the compound is difficult to administer, but ultrasonic treatment breaks it into a less dense solution without altering anticancer properties.

2. PSK

This is a structurally complex glycoprotein (proteins bound to polysaccharide) extracted from the shelf fungus *Coriolus versicolor*, sometimes known as turkey tail because of the alternating dark and light concentric banding on the upper surfaces of fruiting bodies (Fig. 5–23). Into the media in which it grows, the fungus releases the glucan, which is a highly branched molecule with both alpha and beta 1-3, 1-4, and 1-6 linkages. The compound has few side effects and stimulates the host macrophages and other cells in the immune system, which increases phagocytosis of foreign material. Hence it also impedes the growth of invading organisms and viruses.

3. Lentinan

Similar to schizophyllan, lentinan is a glucan, composed predominantly of beta 1, 3 glucose molecules. A popular edible mushroom, the forest mushroom or shiitake (*Lentinus edodes*, Fig. 5–23), is the source of this compound, which it releases into the culture medium in which it grows. In experiments where the compound was injected into mice with transplanted tumors, there was 50 percent total regression of solid tumors. The fungal carbohydrate activates T-lymphocyte cell activity.

4. Pachymaran

Wolfiporia extensa (tuckahoe, Fig. 5–14) contains a glucan called pachyman. Although this compound is not active against cancer, it can be chemically modified to another form, pachymaran. Pachymaran is active against tumor cells, particularly lung tumor cells and the cells derived from them that spread the cancer to other areas.

5. Vesiculogen

An Ascomycete and cup fungus, *Peziza vesiculosa* (Fig. 5–23), is the final example of fungi used to control cancer. Vesiculogen from this fungus acts as an immunoadjuvant; that is, it enhances the production of antibodies without acting as an antigen itself.

These few compounds, representative of a much longer list of anticancer compounds from fungi, illustrate the diverse activities of fungal carbohydrates and the potential to manipulate animal immune systems for prevention and control of cancer development.

Antibiotics

Many fungi produce compounds that are toxic to other microorganisms. In nature, these metabolites are the fungi's way of competing with other organisms for space to grow and reproduce. Technically, one could consider these fungi as poisonous; but because their toxins are used to kill microbes, without hurting animals, they constitute one type of medical fungus. These toxins targeted to control infections are called antibiotics. Among the many promising fungal metabolites with antibiotic properties, only a limited number have proved safe for animal use.

1. Penicillin

The discovery of the antibiotic penicillin is a story of how serendipity in science can lead to revolutionary new discoveries. Sir Alexander Fleming was a microbiologist from Scotland studying the bacterium *Staphylococus aureus*, a common agent of boils and postsurgicial fatal infections. In the late 1920s, he noticed that a Petri dish of this bacterium growing on nutrient media was contaminated with an airborne Deuteromycete, *Penicillium notatum*. Rather than merely throwing the culture away, he observed it more closely and found that, as the fungus grew, growth of the bacterium was arrested. Fleming astutely recognized that the accidental contamination had medical importance. He isolated the fungus and found that the liquid media in which the fungus grew contained the antibiotic. The avenue for production of the antibiotic called penicillin was beyond the expertise of Fleming's laboratory.

It was the work of the pathologist Howard Florey and the chemist Ernst Chain of the University of Oxford that produced the method to purify this unstable compound. Using purified penicillin, clinical tests demonstrated that penicillin was effective in treating bacterial infections of humans with limited side effects, except for individuals who were allergic to the antibiotic. The need for an effective antibiotic agent was exacerbated with the outbreak of World War II and the need to treat the wounds of war.

Final work in the United States resulted in the commercial-level production of penicillin. Workers at the U. S. Department of Agriculture laboratory in Peoria, Illinois, scouted for *Penicillium* species on moldy fruits at local groceries. They then isolated the molds and tested them for levels of antibiotic production. The big breakthrough came with an isolate of *Penicillium chrysogenum* picked off a moldy cantaloupe that produced 200 times the amount of penicillin as Fleming's first isolate. Researchers exposed this isolate to X-rays and created thousands of genetic mutants, which were then screened for antibiotic production. One isolate was found that produced many times the amount of penicillin of the original strain and was consequently used in the beginning of the industrial production of penicillin.

It was soon discovered that the mixture of molecular forms of penicillin produced could be altered by adjusting the contents of growth media. The original form with the highest antibiotic activity was penicillin G. It consists of two interlocked ring structures with several groups coming off the sides of the ring (Fig. 5–13). A four-membered ring contains nitrogen (beta-lactam ring), and a five-membered ring contains sulfur (thiazolidine ring). The presence of the beta-lactam ring is required for antibiotic activity. When phenoxyacetic acid is added to culture media, the mold produces a form of penicillin that can be administered orally, rather than by shots, because it is not broken down by the acids of the digestive system.

Penicillin G is effective against one category of bacterium, the gram positive bacteria. These bacteria stain blue-violet with the gram staining procedure because of the structure of their walls. It is wall production in gram positive bacteria that penicillin G blocks, resulting in the death of the organism. The beta-lactone ring of the antibiotic binds to the active site of the bacteria's enzyme, transpeptidase, inhibiting its activity. Bacteria need this enzyme for wall assembly and cross-linking its parts. The walls are thus weakened, and the bacterial cells burst and die.

Problems arose when it was discovered that the bacterial agent of postoperative infections and boils, *Staphylococcus aureus*, could become resistant to the activity of penicillin G. By chance mutation, they derived the ability to produce enzymes, beta-lactamases, that would break down the beta-lactam ring of the antibiotic. Another breakthrough came about when chemists took the basic structure of penicillin and chemically modified side-chain structures to semisynthetically produce new forms of penicillin. In these new forms, chemical groups were added to the molecule to protect the beta-lactam ring from beta-lactamase activity of bacteria. Other semisynthetic forms, such as ampicillin, impart antibiotic activity against gram negative bacteria.

2. Cephalosporins

Cephalosporium acremonium (*Acremonium chrysogenum*) also produces antibiotics with a beta-lactam ring. The lactam ring is joined to a six-membered sulfur-containing ring. One of these compounds, cephalosporin C, has become an important antibiotic because it is not affected by the beta-lactamases of bacteria, and people allergic to penicillin do not necessarily show sensitivity to this antibiotic. As with penicillin, chemical modifications of the natural compound result in a spectrum of new antibiotics.

3. Griseofulvin

Griseolfulvin is important because it is one of the few antibiotics safe to use against filamentous fungal infections in animals. Griseofulvin is produced by several species of *Penicillium*, including *P. griseofulvum* from which the name of the antibiotic is derived. Commercial production now uses a high-yield strain of *P. patulum*. The drug can be administered orally, where it is effective in inhibiting nuclear division and growth of dermatophytic fungi (those infecting skin, hair, and nails). Because the antibiotic only arrests fungal growth and is not lethal to the fungus, treatments must be continued until the fungus is scaled off from animal tissue. Caution must be used with this antibiotic when administered orally because it has teratogenic activity, causing malformed offsprings in animals.

4. Fusidic acid

This is a steroidlike antibiotic first isolated from the Deuteromycete *Fusidium coccidium*. Fusidic acid is most effectively used to control penicillin-resistant strains of *S. aureus*. Although the antibiotic is unable to penetrate the walls of gram negative bacteria, its inhibits protein synthesis in gram positive bacteria.

5. Other antibiotics

As might be expected, given their success in the invasion of habitats, mushrooms are a source of many antibiotic compounds. Thus the honey mushroom *(Armillariella mellea)* and jack-o-lantern mushroom *(Omphalotus olearius)* both grow on wood and produce antibiotics effective against gram positive bacteria and other fungi. The activity of many of these compounds is based on their sesquiterpene structure and orsellinate group. None of these compounds has become commercially important.

This survey points out only a few examples of the many fungi with medical importance. The need for medicine and antibiotics propels the continued search for sources of new and useful compounds.

ACKNOWLEDGMENTS

Appreciation is expressed to Dr. Kenneth W. Cochran for supplying the author with information from the NAMA registry of poison cases and references on medical uses of fungi. The staff at the Lloyd Library diligently located reference material that would have been otherwise difficult to acquire. Mike Vincent aided in locating fungal specimens for illustration from the Turrell Herbarium, Miami University. Loans from the National Fungus Herbarium and University of Arizona Herbarium were used for the illustration of *Wolfiporia extensa*.

REFERENCES

GENERAL MYCOLOGY

ALEXOPOULOS, C. J., AND C. W. MIMS. 1979. *Introductory Mycology,* 3rd ed. John Wiley & Sons, Inc., New York, 632 pp.

ARORA, D. 1986. *Mushrooms Demystified,* 2nd ed. Ten Speed Press, Berkeley, Calif., 959 pp.

LINCOFF, G. H. 1981. *The Audubon Society Field Guide to North American Mushrooms.* Alfred A. Knopf, Inc., New York, 926 pp.

MILLER, O. K., Jr. 1979. *Mushrooms of North America.* E. P. Dutton, New York, 368 pp.

POISONOUS FUNGI

ANONOMYOUS. 1982. *Mycotoxin Surveillance: A Guideline.* Food and Agriculture Organization of the United Nations, Rome, pp. 1–68.

CHRISTENSEN, C. M. 1975. *Molds, Mushrooms, and Mycotoxins.* University of Minnesota Press, Minneapolis, 264 pp.

CIEGLER, A. 1975. Mycotoxins: occurrence, chemistry, biological activity. *Lloydia* 38: 21–35.

DIENER, U. L., R. L. ASQUITH, AND J. W. DICKENS. 1983. Aflatoxin and *Aspergillus flavus* in corn. Southern Cooperative Series Bulletin 279. Auburn University, Alabama, 112 pp.

FULLER, T. C., AND E. MCCLINTOCK. 1986. *Poisonous Plants of California.* University of California Press, Berkeley, pp. 15–55.

HAARD, R., AND K. HAARD. 1977. *Poisonous and Hallucinogenic Mushrooms.* 2nd ed. Cloudburst Press of America, Seattle, Wash. 126 pp.

HATFIELD, G. M. 1979. Toxic mushrooms. In *Toxic Plants.* A. D. Kinghorn, ed. Columbia University Press, New York, pp. 7–58.

KEELER, R. F., AND A.T. TU. 1983. *Handbook of Natural Toxins,* Vol. 1. Marcel Dekker, Inc., New York, 934 pp.

LINCOFF, G., AND D. H. MITCHEL. 1977. *Toxic and Hallucinogenic Mushroom Poisoning. A Handbook for Physicians and Mushroom Hunters.* Van Nostrand Reinhold Co., New York, 267 pp.

LITTEN, W. 1975. The most poisonous mushrooms. *Scientific American* 232: 91–101.

MATOSSIAN, M. D. 1982. Ergot and the Salem witchcraft affair. *American Scientist* 70: 355–357.

MOREAU, C. 1979. Moulds, Toxins and Food. John Wiley & Sons, Inc., New York, 477 pp.

PURCHASE, I. F. H. 1974. Mycotoxins. Elsevier North-Holland, Inc., New York, 443 pp.

SMITH, J. E., AND A. HACKING. 1983. Fungal toxicity. In *The Filamentous Fungi,* Vol. 4. J. E. Smith, D. R. Berry, and B. Kristiansen, eds. Edward Arnold Ltd., London, pp. 238–265.

TYLER, V. 1963. Poisonous mushrooms. *Progress in Chemical Toxicology.* 1: 339–384.

WASSON, R. G. 1957. Seeking the magic mushroom. *Life* 42: 100–120.

———. 1979. Traditional use in North America of *Amanita muscaria* for divinatory purposes. *Journal of Psychedelic Drugs* 11: 25–31.

MEDICINAL FUNGI

CHANG, H.-M., AND P. P. BUT. 1987. *Pharmacology and Applications of Chinese Materia Medica,* Vol. 2. World Scientific Publishing Co., Pte Ltd., Singapore, 1320 pp.

———, H. W. YEUNG, W.-W. TSO, AND A. KOO. 1985. *Advances in Chinese Medicinal Materials Research.* World Scientific Publishing Co., Pte Ltd., Singapore, 742 pp.

COBB, D. J. 1846. The Medical Botanist and Expositor of Diseases and Remedies, Vol. 2. The Mother's Guide. Castile, N.Y., 112 pp.

COCHRAN, K. W. 1978. Medical effects. In *The Biology and Cultivation of Edible Mushrooms.* S. T. Chang and W. A. Hayes, eds. Academic Press, Inc., New York, pp. 169–187.

HARTWELL, J. L. 1982. *Plants Used against Cancer.* Quarterman Publications, Inc., Lawrence, Mass. 710 pp.

KAVASCH, E. B. 1985. Puhpohwee: The mushrooms of the Amerindians. *Garden* (Sept./Oct.), pp. 14–23.

KEYS, J. D. 1976. *Chinese Herbs. Their Botany, Chemistry and Pharmacodynamics.* Charles E. Tuttle Co., Tokyo, 388 pp.

LOWE, D. A., AND R. P. ELANDER. 1983. Contribution of mycology to the antibiotic industry. *Mycologia* 75: 361–373.

WAGNER, H., AND A. PROKSCH. 1985. Immunostimulatory drugs of fungi and higher plants. In *Economic and Medicinal Plant Research*, Vol. 1. H. Wagner, H. Hikino, and N. R. Farnsworth, eds. Academic Press, New York, pp. 113–153.

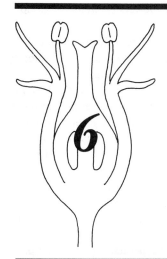

Form and Structure
of Poisonous and Medicinal
Flowering Plants

Since the overwhelming majority of poisonous and medicinal plants are flowering plants (angiosperms), it is important to learn the basics of flowering plant form, structure, and life-cycle phenomena. Such knowledge is not only key to the understanding of various parts of this book, but also to using identification guides or manuals dealing with the flora of a particular region, that is, books essential to the determination of the identity of plant species, poisonous or otherwise.

FLOWER STRUCTURE

We can begin with the flower itself, doubtless by most considered to be the characteristic "organ" of a flowering plant. A flower may be interpreted as a modified and compressed branch (stem axis), with nodes and much shortened or telescoped internodes, bearing more or less leaflike appendages. The upper, perhaps slightly expanded tip of this branch axis is the *receptacle*, a small, convex (thimblelike) structure. It is to the receptacle that the various appendages of the flower are attached. The receptacle per se may or may not be easy to perceive; even if not obvious, the position of the receptacle may be inferred by the point of attachment of the floral appendages. The appendages of the flower are interpreted as being modified leaves, although some are clearly more leaflike than others. These appendages usually exhibit a cyclic or whorled arrangement on the receptacle, each cycle having a definite number of parts; however, flowers possessing larger, indefinite numbers of parts, sometimes spirally arranged, are occasionally encountered. The following will describe the appendages of a typical flower.

The outermost or lowermost of the sets of appendages inserted upon the receptacle are the *sepals*, known collectively as the *calyx*. The sepals are typically the most leaflike of the floral appendages and usually have the appearance of little green leaves. The sepals may serve a protective function in the unopened flower bud. The *petals*, collectively the *corolla*, constitute the next (inward and/or upward) set of appendages on the receptacle. The petals are typically not green, but rather often exhibit an attractive coloration, perhaps useful in luring insects or other animals to the flower. The petal texture is usually delicate in comparison to the sepals, and the petals are typically relatively more ephemeral. Neither the sepals nor the petals participate directly in the reproductive processes of a flower, and hence are termed *accessory* floral structures. The term floral envelope is applied to the sepals and petals collectively; however, a better collective term is *perianth* (meaning "around the flower").

The *stamens*, located internal to (or upward of) the petals, are the male parts of the flower. (Some object to use of the term male for the stamens and female for the pistil, since both sexual structures, technically, most directly produce spores rather than gametes; however, for simplicity, the terms male and female will be used in this text for the stamens and pistil, respectively.) Each stamen is usually comprised of two substructures, the *filament* (or stalk of the stamen) and the *anther* (the abruptly expanded terminal portion); pollen is produced (as a result of spore formation) in the chambers (sacs) of each anther. Within each pollen grain are two minute sperm (sperm nuclei).

The female part of a flower, the *pistil*, is located at the center (or uppermost portion) of the receptacle. The pistil has three externally visible regions: The *stigma* (uppermost) is an expanded tip, serving as a pollen-receptive surface. The *style* is the stalklike portion of the pistil, leading from the stigma to the ovary. The *ovary* is the expanded basal portion of the pistil. Immature seeds, or *ovules*, develop in the ovary; the tissue within the ovary that provides, specifically, a place for attachment of the ovules is known as the *placenta*. Each ovule contains an egg cell (the egg cell actually develops in an enclosed, microscopic female plant, which in turn originated from the female spore). Ovules are stalked structures; to the distil end of the stalk, the often recurved ovule body (sporangium) is attached; eggs cells are positioned more or less toward the apex of the ovule body.

Although the pistil has three externally recognizable regions, a close look may reveal that it is composed of longitudinal subunits running throughout its length (recognized perhaps as branches of the stigma or style or partitions in the ovary). These modified leaves of which pistils are composed are termed *carpels*. If a pistil is composed of but a single carpel, the pistil is simple. If, however, the pistil is formed by two or more carpels fused together, then the pistil is compound. The number of carpels per pistil and the nature of their fusion has a direct bearing on fruit structure (considered later in this chapter). Also, perception of carpel number in a compound pistil is often essential to the effective use of more technical keys or guides to the identification of flowering plants.

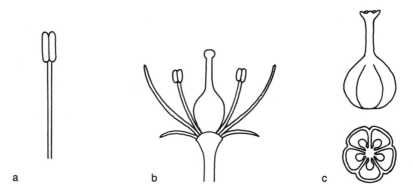

Figure 6–1   Flower parts: (a) stamen; (b) flower; (c) pistil, above; ovary cross-section, below

POLLINATION AND LIFE CYCLE

In pollination, pollen is transferred from the anther of a stamen to the stigma of a pistil. Most often, pollen is transferred from the anther of one flower to the stigma of another (often located on another plant, in the process of cross-pollination). In North America, pollination is most commonly accomplished either by insects (entomophily) or by the wind (anemophily). In comparison to wind-pollinated flowers, flowers pollinated by insects (or generally by animals) may be expected to possess a more showy perianth, to be more fragrant, and to have a greater supply of nectar. Pollen of entomophilous flowers is often more highly ornamented and more sticky (less easily blown up into the wind), as compared to anemophilous flowers. Pollen grains, landing on the appropriate stigma (that is, stigmas of flowers belonging to the same species), will germinate as a consequence of chemical recognition (these recognition chemicals from pollen grains play a role in respiratory allergy, as will be discussed in Chapter 11).

Pollen tubes (the everted protoplasts of pollen grains) will grow out through weak areas in the pollen grain wall and grow down through the style. In the ovary, a pollen tube will enter the apex of the ovule (usually, only one pollen tube is successful per ovule), releasing sperm in the vicinity of the egg cell. Typically, one sperm (remember, there were two per pollen grain) will fertilize the egg; the other sperm may fuse with an additional cell produced by the little female plant, sometimes triggering the formation of endosperm, or nutritive tissue, within the developing seed. This double fertilization is a phenomenon apparently unique to the angiosperms (flowering plants). It should be obvious that pollination and fertilization, as phenomena, are not one and the same, and that pollination is a prerequisite to the subsequent process of fertilization. The fertilized egg (*zygote*) develops into the embryo of the seed, the seed as a whole coming from the ovule. When the seeds mature, they often detach from their stalks, leaving a scar (the *hilum*), usually visible on the mature seed surface (seed coat or covering). The ovules are contained within the ovary; the ovary itself develops into the fruit.

Seeds are released from fruit by various mechanisms (an involved "ecological" topic somewhat beyond the scope of this book). After a certain interval of time (sometimes involving an obligate period of cold weather), seeds will germinate if they happen to have landed in a suitable habitat. In germination, the embryo grows (usually root first) out of the seed coat (leaving it behind), establishing the seedling stage.

VARIATION IN FLOWER STRUCTURE

Although the preceding paragraphs sum up the typical flower (and flowering plant life cycle), great variation exists in flower structure and morphology. If a flower possesses all four categories of floral appendages (sepals, petals, stamens, and pistil), the flower is said to be complete. If any set is missing, it is referred to as incomplete. Typical angiosperm flowers are bisexual (that is, one flower possesses both stamens and pistil); however, there are many examples of plant species with unisexual flowers, in which the pistil is lacking (or greatly reduced) in male flowers and the stamens are lacking (or greatly reduced) in female flowers. If unisexual flowers of both sexes are present on the same plant (for example, hickories), the plant is termed monoecious (meaning "one household"); if, on the other hand, male flowers occur on one plant and female flowers on another (for example, willow), the plant is said to be dioecious ("two households").

Flowers vary significantly in their fusion of parts, especially the petals. The petals are commonly entirely free (from each other), as in bloodroot (*Sanguinaria*) or poison hemlock (*Conium*). However, in many other cases the petals are united (at least toward the base) to form a corolla tube. Examples of striking tubular (united) corollas are seen in tobacco (*Nicotiana*) and morning-glory (*Ipomoea*).

The symmetry of flowers also varies. Flowers such as buttercup (*Ranunculus*) and marsh marigold (*Caltha*) have equal and evenly spaced floral parts and are termed radially symmetrical or, more appropriately, actinomorphic. On the other hand, flowers of sweet pea (*Lathyrus*) and many other legumes, for example, are decidedly bilaterally symmetrical and are referred to as zygomorphic.

Additionally, the position of the ovary within a flower exhibits variation. In flowers of St. John's wort (*Hypericum*) and many other species, the sepals, petals, and stamens (which are numerous in St. John's wort) attach to the receptacle below the point of attachment of the ovary; such a flower is termed hypogynous (meaning "below the gynoecium" or female part), and the ovary is referred to as superior. If, however, as in an apple flower (*Malus*) or a flower of water hemlock (*Cicuta*), the floral appendages arise (or appear to arise) from the top of the ovary, the flower is then termed epigynous ("above the gynoecium"), and the ovary is considered to be inferior. In yet other types of flowers, for example, wild cherry (*Prunus*), the sepals, petals, and stamens may be attached not directly to the receptacle (or to the top of the ovary) but to an extra cuplike

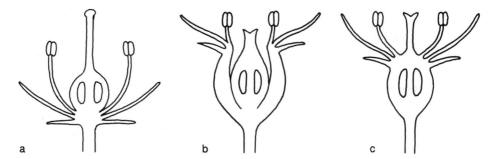

Figure 6–2   Flower types: (a) hypogynous; (b) perigynous; (c) epigynous

structure (the floral cup or hypanthium), which surrounds but is not fused with the ovary, and which in turn attaches to the receptacle below the ovary. Although the ovary is technically superior in such a flower, the flower is not termed hypogynous, but rather is referred to as perigynous ("around the ovary or gynoecium").

Finally, a meaningful pattern of variation in the numbers of floral appendages per flower is to be seen if the two great groups of flowering plants (monocotyledonous plants and dicotyledonous plants) are compared: In monocots, the floral appendages usually occur in threes or multiples thereof; in dicots, the number is much more likely to be fours, fives, or perhaps twos (or multiples of fours or fives, or even a large indefinite number). Basic knowledge of variation in flower structure is critical to the proper use of most identification guides to flowering plants.

INFLORESCENCES: GROUPING PATTERNS OF FLOWERS

Flowers often do not stand alone on a plant but rather are clustered in various grouping patterns, or *inflorescences*. Familiarization with the basic floral grouping patterns of plants is helpful in deciphering the identity of many plants, whether poisonous or not. Terminology pertaining to inflorescences is often lacking in precision; however, in general, the *pedicel* of a flower is its immediate stalk (if lacking a pedicel, the flower is termed sessile). A common parent stalk (that is, bearing several or many flowers) is the *peduncle*. Modified leaves associated with inflorescences are termed *bracts*. A leafless flowering stalk arising at ground level (for example, bloodroot and autumn crocus) is termed a *scape*.

The basic patterns of inflorescences, although not uncommonly showing intergradation and intermediacy when many examples are examined, are indeed easy enough to perceive and, as indicated, often provide useful clues to the identity of a given plant. In some cases (carrot family and sunflower family), entire families of plants are recognizable (characterized) by the particular nature of their inflorescence. In addition to simply looking at pictures and matching the plant in hand with the most likely illustration, it is well to understand that (at least theoretically) there are two fundamental categories of inflorescences. In determinate (or centrifugal) inflorescences, the central or terminal flower opens first, essentially arresting further elongation of the inflorescence. Hence, the order of bloom or flower opening (anthesis) in a determinate inflorescence is from the inside out (or from the top down if the inflorescence achieved some elongation prior to opening of the terminal flower). Also, determinate inflorescences, when branched, often exhibit opposite branching. The dichasium (or cyme) is a fundamental type of determinate inflorescence.

In the case of indeterminate (or centripetal) inflorescences, which are often alternately branched, the central or terminal flower is the last flower to open, and the direction of anthesis is thus from the outside in (or from the bottom up); some indeterminate inflorescences are capable of continued elongation (until the terminal flower has developed). The panicle is a basic type of indeterminate inflorescence. Some major types of inflorescence are diagrammed in Figure 6–3 (an open circle, that is, half-circle, indicating an open flower, and a closed circle signifying a closed flower).

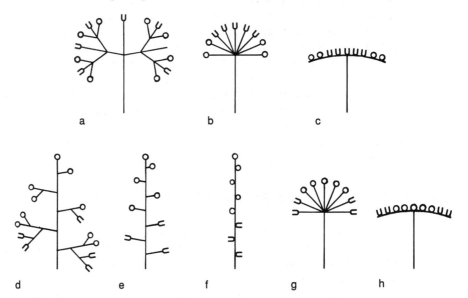

Figure 6–3 Inflorescences: (a) cyme or dichasium; (b) determinate umbel; (c) determinate head; (d) panicle; (e) raceme; (f) spike; (g) indeterminate umbel; (h) indeterminate head

FRUITS

As with inflorescences, one should be aware of the types or categories of fruits that might be encountered when the study of flowering plants is undertaken. When the word fruit is used, most people doubtless think of certain favorite sweet and tasty plant parts that may be eaten without cooking and even served as dessert. It is perhaps not widely recognized that some of the common vegetables of the dinner table are actually fruits in the botanical sense. The gardener or farmer who grows snapbeans, tomatoes, eggplants, cucumbers, squash, or sweet corn is actually harvesting the fruits of the plants. Strictly speaking, vegetables (for example, lettuce, radishes, turnips, brussel sprouts, spinach, and carrots) are edible plant parts (such as edible leaves, roots, or stems) that are not encompassed by the following definition of a fruit.

Botanically a fruit is a ripened ovary (or ovaries). In some instances, flower (or other) parts in addition to the ovary may contribute to the structure of the mature fruit (when parts additional to the ovary are modified and become part of a fruit, the fruit is termed an accessory fruit, for example, an apple). The ripened ovary (fruit) wall is termed the *pericarp*. The pericarp may or may not be divisible into distinct subunits, that is, exocarp, mesocarp, and endocarp (for example, a wild cherry fruit possesses a skin or exocarp, the flesh or mesocarp, and a stone or endocarp; however, the endocarp is lacking in a grape and no subdivisions are recognizable in the fruit wall of a walnut). The pericarp can be fleshy or dry at maturity; if dry, the pericarp may possess a mechanism to split open (dehisce), or it may be indehiscent and perhaps dependent on external agents, such as animals, for opening.

The majority of fruits come from a single pistil (ovary); such fruits are termed simple (regardless of whether or not the pistil itself was a simple or compound pistil). If a given fruit derives from more than a single pistil, it is a compound fruit. A compound fruit arising from a number of initially separate ovaries in a single flower is called an aggregate fruit; one involving the concrescent ovaries of a number of flowers is termed a multiple fruit. In a very few cases, for example, *Caulophyllum* (blue cohosh), the ovary wall does not develop normally, and a fleshy seed coat replaces the fruit in appearance and in function.

The following list is an introductory guide to some common fruit types. An observant trip to the grocery store can clarify most of these types. In no way, however, can it be assumed that if a plant structure is a fruit, especially if found in the wild, that it is necessarily edible. One should never consume any plant or plant product unless its edibility is known with certainty. This point should be brought home by the inclusion of some toxic as well as nontoxic examples of fruits in the following key. For practice, determine which of the examples given are those of potentially toxic representatives and which are not.

Key to Common Fruit Types

1. Fruit developed from the ovary of a single pistil (*simple fruit*)
    2. Pericarp fleshy (moist, sometimes juicy)
        3. Fleshy throughout: *Berry* (grape, tomato, nightshade)
        3. Inner pericarp (endocarp) stony or cartilaginous
            4. Endocarp stony: *Drupe* (olive, peach, poison sumac)
            4. Endocarp cartilaginous, fruit accessory: *Pome* (apple)
    2. Pericarp dry (papery, leathery, or woody)
        5. Fruit dehiscent (opening) at maturity
            6. Derived from a simple pistil

       7. Splitting on one side: *Follicle* (milkweed, larkspur, Indian hemp)

       7. Splitting on two (opposite) sides: *Legume* (green bean, wisteria, Kentucky coffee tree)

    6. Derived from a compound pistil, opening by valves, teeth, or pores: *Capsule* (buckeye, jimson weed, soapwort, poppy)

  5. Fruit indehiscent

       8. With winglike outgrowths: *Samara* (maple, ash, tree-of-heaven)

       8. Lacking wings

          9. Pericarp united with seedcoat: *Grain* (*Caryopsis*; grasses such as corn)

          9. Seed coat free from pericarp

             10. Pericarp papery or cartilaginous, fruit small: *Achene* (sunflower, sycamore, buttercup)

             10. Pericarp very hard, fruit larger, husk present: *Nut* (walnut, oak, hickory)

1. Fruit developed from the ovaries of several to many pistils (*compound fruit*)

  11. Derived from the separate simple pistils of a single flower: *Aggregate fruit* (raspberry, blackberry)

  11. Derived from the pistils of a number of flowers: *Multiple fruit* (mulberry, osage orange, pineapple)

LEAVES

When building knowledge of plant structure to bolster one's ability to identify and classify, attention must be given to vegetative parts of the plant (leaf, stem, root) as well as to reproductive features (flower, fruit, seed). Learning something about the nature of leaves is particularly helpful in identifying plants. Basic parts of a leaf are the *blade* or *lamina* (the expanded sheetlike portion) and the *leaf stalk* or *petiole*. Leaves lacking petioles are termed sessile. If the leaf blade (or the petiole) extends around the stem, the leaf may be termed sheathing (or, in some cases, clasping). Little flaps of leaflike tissue of dubious function, the *stipules*, may or may not be present at the leaf base (the base of the petiole). The upper angle between the leaf base and the stem is the *leaf axil*. Branch buds (axillary buds) occur in the axil of the leaf.

    A leaf with an undivided blade is a simple leaf, as in pokeweed (*Phytolacca*), wild cherry (*Prunus*), and bloodroot (*Sanguinaria*). However, anyone familiar with the preceding three examples will know that, although they all have simple leaves, they look little alike in detail. In pokeweed, the leaf margin lacks teeth or lobes (that is, the margin is entire), in wild cherry the margin is toothed, and in bloodroot it is substantially lobed (palmately lobed in this case). In addition to the leaf's margin, the vein pattern (externally visible vascular bundle pattern) may vary as well. In the redbud tree (*Cercis canadensis*), the rather large, entire, heart-shaped leaves are palmately veined (that is, the leaf's main veins arise and spread equally from a common point at the leaf base); by contrast, the pinnately lobed leaves of the white oak (*Quercus alba*) are pinnately veined as well (that is, possess a midvein or midrib, with the main lateral veins arising at various points from the midvein, like the branches of a feather). Leaves of monocots are often parallel veined and lack the detailed small-vein network often seen in dicot leaves.

The occurrence of compound (versus simple) leaves adds additional complication to the consideration of leaves. Put simply, if a leaf blade is completely divided into separate parts (leaflets), the leaf is compound. That each leaflet of a compound leaf is not itself a leaf is attested by the fact that no axillary bud is to be found in the axils of leaflets. Compound leaves may be palmately (or digitately compound), with leaflets arising from a point, much like the fingers of a hand, for example, buckeye (*Aesculus*); or they may be pinnately (feather) compound with leaflets arising (more or less at right angles) at points down the *rachis* (extension of the petiole into the blade area), for example, black locust (*Robinia*). Less frequently, leaves may be uniformly divided into

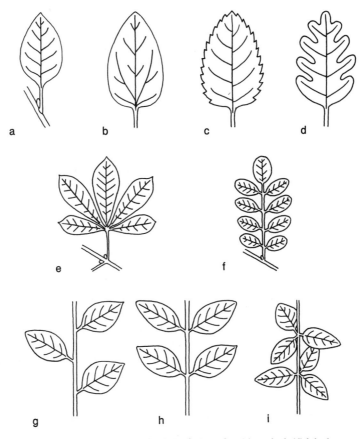

Figure 6–4   Leaf form: (a) simple leaf; (b) entire; (c) toothed; (d) lobed; (e) palmately compound; (f) pinnately compound; (g) alternate; (h) opposite; (i) whorled

threes (ternately compound), as in poison ivy (*Rhus*). Furthermore, leaves may be more than once compound (decompound), for example, pinnately decompound, as in poison hemlock (*Conium*), and ternately decompound as in baneberry (*Actaea*).

Leaves arise from the stem at points called *nodes*; typically, longer internodal areas of the stem occur between the nodes. In terms of positioning or arrangement of leaves, one of three general patterns usually pertains: there may be one leaf per node (alternate leaves, as in black locust), two leaves oppositely placed per node (opposite leaves, as in buckeye), or, less commonly, three or more equally spaced leaves per node (whorled leaves, as in oleander, which often has both opposite and whorled leaves on a branch). When leaves are alternate, they may describe a spiral around the stem; less commonly, alternately placed leaves occur in two linear rows (two-ranked condition). Opposite leaves may be two-ranked or else the leaf pairs are rotated 90 degrees node to node (four-ranked, or decussate, condition). Not uncommonly in monocotyledonous plants, for example, garden hyacinth (*Hyacinthus*), the leaves are entirely basal (not present at all on the flowering stalk or scape; that is, stem or cauline leaves are lacking). Additionally, leaves may be evergreen, that is, persisting more than a single season, as in species of *Rhododendron*, or deciduous, as in wild cherry (*Prunus*) and most of the native broadleaf trees of the eastern United States. A tree or shrub that is truly deciduous loses all its leaves each fall and must produce all new leaves the next season.

STEMS

Stems of plants, especially underground stems, deserve some consideration in our context. A plant that is both perennial and herbaceous (nonwoody) will possess some sort of specially modified, and usually underground, stem. Erect underground stems may take the form of a bulb (for example, hyacinth and onion), which is mostly leaf tissue, or a corm (for example, jack-in-the-pulpit), a corm being composed primarily of stem tissue. Various types of horizontal underground or ground-level stems encountered include rhizomes (cylindrical underground stems) as in bloodroot, tubers (fat rhizomes) as in the Irish potato, or slender runners (stolons) as in strawberry plants. Regardless of the form, an underground stem functions as a perennating organ, allowing the regeneration of aerial or aboveground stems (and leaves) in subsequent seasons. A general distinction is made between woody and herbaceous (softer, nonwoody) aboveground stems. Aboveground (aerial) stems may or may not have armature in the form of thorns (for example, hawthorn), which are modified branches, or spines (for example, black locust, with paired spines at each node), which are modified leaves (or modified stipules), or prickles (simple stem-surface outgrowths, as in roses). Tendrils are modified stems (or branches or even leaves) especially adapted for climbing (for example, grape vines).

LIFE-FORM OF PLANTS: THE HABIT

Consideration of stems leads us to the final topic of this chapter, the habit or growth form (life form) of plants. It is easy enough to confuse the term habit with habitat; put simply, the distinction is that habitat is where the plant grows, and habit is how (the form in which) it grows. Plant growth form is a matter of some complexity. For example, although we can designate a plant's growth form or life form simply as "tree," in reality there are several types of tree growth-forms (for example, a vaselike broadleaf tree versus a pyramidal, coniferous evergreen). Nonetheless, the following relatively simple classification of habit is useful.

A. Herbaceous plants; aerial stems nonwoody, relatively slender and soft; never obtaining the height (or width) of most woody plants.

   1. *Annuals*: Live but one year (more accurately one season). Perennial (or overwintering) stems or buds of any type are lacking. Reproduction usually depends on the successful production of seed (to carry on to the next season). For example, flax (*Linum*), corn cockle (*Agrostemma*).

   2. *Biennials*: Live two years (that is, through two successive growing seasons). Often a rosette of leaves (with an overwintering bud at their center) is produced close to the ground in the first season. In the second season, the stem bolts (from the bud) to produce a flowering shoot. For example, poison hemlock (*Conium*), mullein (*Verbascum*).

   3. *Perennials*: Live an indefinite (not infinite!) number of seasons, usually more than two. Some sort of perennial, usually underground stem is present, sustaining the plant from season to season. For example, bloodroot (*Sanguinaria*), jack-in-the-pulpit (*Arisaema*). The majority of members of the spring flora of the deciduous forest of the eastern United States are herbaceous perennials.

   4. *Vines*: Climbing or twining plants, which may be annual (as in cucumber and various other members of the gourd family) or perennial, as in bindweeds (*Convolvulus*).

B. Woody plants (possessing perennial, woody, often larger aboveground stems).

   1. *Trees*: Rather than absolute height, trees are more properly distinguished from shrubs by growth form. In trees, a dominant trunk or main stem occurs, to which the side branches are subordinate in size and position. For example, red oak, shagbark hickory, wild cherry, sugar maple, tulip tree.

   2. *Shrubs* (bushes): Shrubs, expectedly, would not reach the ultimate height of most trees. However, shrubs are better distinguished (from trees) by the fact that a number of more or less coequal stems arise at ground level (often in a more or less fastigiate manner). For example, mountain laurel (*Kalmia*), hazelnut (*Corylus*), coralberry (*Symphoricarpos*).

   3. *Vines*: Climbing or twining plants. Grape vines constitute good examples of vines that are not only perennial, but whose aerial stems become woody, increasing in diameter with age through the action of a cambium.

SELECTED REFERENCES

HOLM, EIGIL. 1979. *The Biology of Flowers*. Penguin Books Ltd., Harmondsworth, Middlesex, England. A good account of flower structure in relation to floral biology, especially pollination mechanisms.

PORTER, C. L. 1967. *Taxonomy of Flowering Plants*, 2nd ed. W. H. Freeman and Company, San Francisco. Chapter 8 constitutes an excellent survey of plant form and structure pertinent to classification.

RADFORD, ALBERT E. 1986. *Fundamentals of Plant Systematics*. Harper & Row, Publishers, Inc., New York. Chapter 5 constitutes a detailed survey of descriptive terminology utilized in plant identification and classification; quite valuable as a reference for plant description.

RAVEN, PETER H., AND GEORGE B. JOHNSON. 1986. *Biology*. Times Mirror/Mosby College Publishing, St. Louis, Mo. Chapter 30, "Flowering Plants," presents an excellent overview of flower structure and the flowering plant life cycle.

SUGDEN, ANDREW. 1984. *Longman Illustrated Dictionary of Botany*. York Press and Longman Group Ltd., Essex, England. Pages 70–100 give an outlined account of the reproductive features of a plant (flowers, inflorescences, fruits) as well as vegetative components, such as leaves and stems.

Classification of Poisonous and Medicinal Plants: Taxonomy

The topic of plant taxonomy (the science of plant classification) constitutes a course unto itself, and several excellent college-level texts deal with the topic. Hence, the present chapter is intended only as a brief introduction to the principles of taxonomy, designed specifically to show the relevance of the topic to the study of poisonous and medicinal plants. This chapter can do no more than "light the path" toward the goal of achieving competence in proper identification of families, genera, and species, a capability crucial to the scientific approach to the study of poisonous and medicinal plants. First-hand experience in plant identification and other aspects of taxonomy is of course the best teacher.

Taxonomy is surely the oldest botanical discipline, dating from prehistoric time, when human beings encountered the need to identify plants for food, shelter, clothing, weapons, tools, and even medicinal uses (as may be surmised from plant remains in ancient burial sites). Coming forward in time, taxonomy is evident, in one form or another, in all major civilizations of antiquity, and from there on throughout the historical record (the reader is referred to Chapter 2 for historical context).

THE TAXONOMIC PROCESS

Taxonomy is both a science (or an art as some would have it) and a process. The process of taxonomy consists of the following separable but interrelated phenomena, occurring mentally in the order given: (1) identification, (2) systematics, and (3) nomenclature. Identification is more or less synonymous with recognition, the so-called "ah-hah!" response when the identity of a plant is realized. Mental abstraction or generalization is central to plant recognition; that is, we form a general mental picture of a plant species from having seen a number of individuals of that species, much as we unconsciously derive an abstraction (mental image or pattern perception) of a chair from having seen many examples of chairs in our lifetime. It may well be that in no case is the mental abstraction of two people regarding a particular plant species (or a chair for that matter) precisely the same.

Systematics, or grouping, is the phase of the taxonomic process in which objects (plant species, or whatever) are ordered, or placed in mental categories. Our brains will automatically systematize or categorize objects, or even people, although we may scarcely think about it. When we walk down the street, aware of other people, we doubtless group them in our minds as male/female, tall/short, blond/brunette/gray/bald, loud/quiet, friendly/unfriendly, or what have you. In systematizing plant species, as our knowledge becomes more sophisticated, we may quickly sense to which genera and/or to which families particular species belong.

The final stage of the taxonomic process is nomenclature or naming plants. Simply put, when we have recognized a plant (and perhaps categorized it mentally), it is logical (and virtually unstoppable if one know's the name) to apply a name to that plant. This part of the process is in no way fundamentally distinct from greeting people by name on the street. If we do not know the name (of a plant or person) already, we may seek to find it out. Thus, it should now be apparent that the taxonomic process, composed of three often rapidly sequential and connected stages, is commonplace, being essentially an automatic process that we could doubtfully prevent our minds from going through even if we wanted to do so. Whether we realize it or not, we are all taxonomists, at one level or another, even without special training. Becoming an expert in plant taxonomy, thus, is simply an addition of knowledge and a refinement of skills and techniques already present in the human mind (virtually from birth). In summary, the taxonomic process, basically, is inherent in human thought and communication.

SCIENTIFIC NAMES: THE TWO-NAME SYSTEM

In the practice of formal taxonomy, we use a two-name system for the scientific names of plants and animals. This is substantially similar to our practice in everyday communication in which we might well introduce a brother and sister as John Doe and Jane Doe, respectively. Hence, using the two-name method, we communicate the name of poison ivy as *Rhus radicans* and of poison sumac as *Rhus vernix*. The family name Doe, indicating relationship of siblings, has much the same import as the generic name *Rhus* (likewise indicating relationship, in this case of somewhat similar species). This very logical two-name or binomial method, the initiation of which (for plants) is credited to Linnaeus (1753) in his *Species Plantarum*, has now been the standard and official practice for scientific names of plants for well over 200 years. The binomial method was actually employed prior to the time of Linnaeus, and scholars argue over whether or not Linnaeus intended the formal adoption of this method; however, the point is relatively moot since Linnaeus is given essentially full credit for its official origin.

In the binomial method, the scientific species name of a plant has two parts, the genus (generic) name followed by the species (specific) epithet. For bibliographic purposes, the name of the original publishing author (authority) of the name is provided following the specific epithet. Scientific names of plants are in Latin or, if derived from other languages, they are latinized (have proper Latin terminations). Also, the first letter of the generic name (always a singular noun, treated as a subject) is capitalized, and both the generic name and the specific epithet are underlined (or italicized in print). Hence, the correctly cited scientific name for the species known as poison hemlock is *Conium maculatum* L. (the L. is for Linnaeus). Although certainly not always, scientific names often have some appropriate meaning, perhaps describing a feature or features of the plant. *Conium*, the latinized genus name, is actually derived from the Greek common name, *koneion*, for poison hemlock. The epithet *maculatum* is an adjective meaning spotted or dappled, doubtless in reference to the purple blotching characteristic of the lower portion of the stem of poison hemlock.

The ending *-um* of *maculatum* is a neuter termination (as opposed to *-a*, which is feminine, and *-us*, masculine). Thus we can surmise that *Conium* is a noun of neuter gender in Latin. If (and only if) specific epithets are adjectives (as in the case of *maculatum*), they must conform in gender to the generic name. A case of gender disagreement, such as the name of the onion, *Allium cepa*, is explained by the fact that the epithet *cepa* is not an adjective at all, but rather, is itself a noun in the same Latin case as *Allium*, a "noun in apposition." Such nouns in apposition, used in forming a particular species name, do not necessarily agree in gender. On the other hand, the

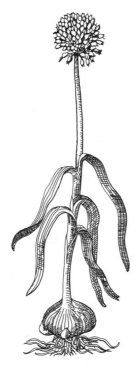

Figure 7–1 *Allium cepa.* Onion

seeming gender disagreement in the name of yarrow, *Achillea millefolium*, has a different explanation than that of the onion, since *millefolium* is truly an adjective (meaning thousand-leaved).   In this case, *Achillea*, although apparently feminine, is actually a neuter noun (and thus there is no disagreement with *millefolium*, which bears a neuter ending); hence, it is not always possible to ascertain the gender of a Latin noun (that is, generic name) simply by looking at the word on a page.   Still other apparent discrepancies of agreement, for example, the name of the peyote cactus, *Lophophora williamsii*, may be explained by the fact that the specific epithet is a possessive noun (ending in *i* or *ii*), named after a person (thus, Williams's *Lohophora*).

It is not feasible, given the objective of the present book and chapter, to explain all types of situations of gender, case, and word type involved in scientific names. Suffice it to say that the complexities of botanical Latin grammar (actually, simpler than classical Latin grammar) do come into play in the total picture of the names of plants. However, a great knowledge of this Latin grammar and of etymology (study of word origins, as from other languages) is not essential to the appreciation of scientific names. Much information of pertinence is readily available and understandable in a good (and definitely unabridged) dictionary.

WHY SCIENTIFIC NAMES?

Instead of going further into the details of Latin or Greek words and grammar, our time would likely be better spent in this chapter by gaining an appreciation of why we bother to have latinized scientific names for plants in the first place! If we know that a given plant is poison ivy (poison ivy being the common name), why should we impose a scientific name on it? Why should we call it *Rhus radicans*? Does this not add to the confusion? Believe it or not, scientific names may actually help avoid confusion! To take the case of poison ivy, in addition to the common name poison ivy, additional common names are employed in colloquial usage, for example, poison oak (which is actually another species), poison vine, and markweed, among others. So which common name is correct, one might ask? To this question, there is no ready answer and no authoritative source to which to turn. As an added complication, poison ivy is not a true ivy in the sense of Boston ivy or English ivy (which are unrelated to poison ivy); poison ivy is much more closely akin to sumacs than to ivys. Thus, is it not misleading to call this sumac relative "ivy"?

The way out of this dilemma is the use of the scientific name.   Through the employment of carefully wrought rules set forth in the *International Code of Botanical Nomenclature*, we can eventually establish, with reasonable certainty, the correct scientific name for each species of plant we encounter; and there should be only one such name per species. The experienced reader of botanical literature may now argue that he or she knows the plant called poison ivy by another scientific name, *Toxicodendron radicans*, and so has not this writer contradicted himself in asserting that only one correct scientific name may exist for a species? No, because the group of sumacs to which poison ivy belongs is sometimes recognized as a genus (*Toxicodendron*) distinct from *Rhus* as a whole, and if this is the case, we would be dealing with two genera, *Rhus* and *Toxicodendron*. It is a matter of informed opinion (taxonomic judgment) as to whether or not *Toxicodendron* is recognized as distinct from the genus *Rhus* and is thus worthy of its own status as a genus.

The beauty of the official rules of nomenclature is that they permit us to establish the correct scientific name for poison ivy, regardless of the genus to which it is considered to belong. Thus, everyone can be satisfied as to the scientific name, depending on their particular interpretation of the *Rhus/Toxicodendron* generic complex; one has only to pick a genus! If *Rhus* is chosen as the genus to which poison ivy belongs, then *Toxicodendron radicans* becomes merely a synonym of the correct name, *Rhus radicans*, and vice versa if *Toxicodendron* is selected. Hence, proper generic selection is often the key to the solution of cases where more than one scientific name is seemingly being used for a given species; that is, upon choosing the genus, only one correct scientific name for poison ivy will exist.

An additional point of value in the use of scientific names, as opposed (or at least in addition) to common names, is that scientific names have the power of indicating relationships. We know, simply from the names, that *Rhus radicans*, *Rhus vernix*, and *Rhus toxicodendron* are related species; that is, they belong to the same genus (*Rhus*). Use of common names for these three plants, respectively, poison ivy, poison sumac, and poison oak, in no way confers to the uninitiated reader or listener any hint of relationship. That is, ivys, sumacs, and oaks would probably be assumed to be unrelated plants if one did not already know better. Latin or latinized scientific names are also of value in world-wide communication. A decision to proclaim that all scientific names would henceforth be in English, or Russian, or German, or French, or Spanish would probably initiate heated debate, in level of intensity not far beneath that of discussion of nuclear arms control. On the other hand, adoption of a dead (unspoken) language (Latin) as the official language of nomenclature of plants (and animals) causes scant political turmoil. As a final point, Latin has been traditionally the language of scholars. The bulk of the rich history of botanical writing (and naming) through the centuries has been in Latin. Preservation of this wealth of tradition and convention is probably alone enough to warrant retention of the usage of Latin scientific names. So, whether a person wants to learn the scientific names of plants or not, he or she should at least learn how and why they are constructed and appreciate their use, value, and the fact that they are most likely here to stay.

WHAT ARE SPECIES?

So, we have learned something of the names of species, but what *are* species, biologically? This is a very different question indeed. We must in fact determine what constitutes a species and which species are which (that is, what entities in nature should be recognized as species) before we can effectively apply scientific names to them. Probably as much has been written about species concepts and definitions, that is, simply, what is a species, as on any topic in biology. Out of this substantial body of writing has filtered a more or less accepted working definition of a species, biologically, as being: An interbreeding or potentially interbreeding population (population implying similar individuals) or group of such populations, reproductively isolated from other such groups. A species is thus viewed as a natural breeding group or unit (that is, members of a species can "recognize" each other reproductively, as opposed to members of other species). This definition is clearly stated in *Methods and Principles of Systematic Zoology* (Mayr, Linsley, and Usinger, 1953). It is the zoologists who developed the "biological definition" of a species, in special reference to animal species. However, botanists have generally adopted the definition as well, although its application in plants can be fraught with difficulties. This definition (of Mayr) is biological, not morphological, since it does not attempt to tell us what a species must look like, but rather what species behavior is expected to be. As such, it constitutes a widely applicable (although not universal) and testable definition of a species.

There are really two related parts to the biological definition of species: (1) we are to expect reproduction or fertility within species, but (2) infertility (reproductive isolation) between species. Although as a working hypothesis the biological concept (definition) of a species is probably here to stay, problems arise if it is applied too rigidly in all situations in nature, especially when dealing with plant species. Quite a number of plant species are prone to hybridization. For two examples of many, several species of dogbane (*Apocynum*) will hybridize with each other, as will various species of sunflower (*Helianthus*); intermediate species forms (even hybrid species) are recognized in these and a large number of other plant genera. Species in problematical genera such as these can be difficult to delimit, as the species boundary becomes very fuzzy. As botanists, considering (accepting?) the biological definition of a species (which calls for reproductive isolation), may we allow any hybridization between two (or more) species and still call them species? And if so, how much? There is no pat answer or solution to this particular problematical question. We must examine every problem species situation individually, in each case attempting to answer questions such as what is the extent of the intergradation between the potentially hybridizing species, do the hybrids persist and reproduce under natural conditions, and do the hybrids reproduce (backcross) with the parent forms (parent species)? Answering such demanding questions is a time-consuming task, often requiring substantial research effort. In this regard, it is probably not an overassertion that taxonomists will never run out of plants to study and data to gather.

In general, animal species more frequently conform to the biological definition of a species than do plant species. In initially understanding what is meant (by most taxonomists) by a species, it is probably profitable to think in terms of animals or even human beings. Characteristics of biological species are in fact well illustrated with *Homo sapiens*, a virtually perfect biological species. At a minimum, we can make these comments about the human species:

1. Interbreeding potential exists within the human population group (this is not saying that all people will reproduce, and hence emphasis should go to the word potential).

2. Reproductive isolation (in terms of production of viable offspring) is in force, as far as we know, between the human population group and all populations of other species. Hence, the human population (in total) maintains its reproductive (and morphological) integrity.

3. It would be seen that a virtual continuum of minor morphological variability exists within the world-wide human population if the entire spectrum of human phenotypes could be placed side by side in a lineup, although some prevailing, general phenotypes (that is, races) would be more common than others.

4. Morphological discontinuity (major morphological differences, or morphological "gaps") exist between the human population group and populations of any other species (for example, gorillas and orangutans).

It is really the morphological discontinuity between most species, in spite of the minor variations within species, that permits our mental (abstractive) discrimination of one species from another, as alluded to earlier in this chapter. The morphological discontinuities typically associated with species boundaries allow the writing of descriptions of and identification guides to various kinds of organisms, for example, the writing of floras describing the plant species of a given region. Once understanding the alleged properties of biological species (in humans or animals), these concepts may be applied to plants. However, again, one should heed the admonition that in situations involving plant species difficulties will be encountered with an inflexible application of the biological species definition.

Time has been spent on the naming and defining of species because, in taxonomy and in considerations of poisonous and medicinal plants, what we are very often dealing with are plant species. Additionally, although its definition is admittedly problematical, the species is nonetheless the taxonomic category (taxon) that is most definable, among all other categories. In fact, all other taxonomic categories or ranks are in essence defined relative to the species; that is, a genus may be viewed as a group of related species, a family as a group of related genera, an order as a group of related families, and so forth; all these relative definitions depend on our ability to define species adequately. Whether or not we can adequately define a species is, as has been indicated, debatable; regardless, this point will not be further discussed, as gains in so doing, relative to the topic of poisonous and medicinal plants, would likely be minimal. However, prior to the chapter's conclusion, a few comments about the nature of taxonomic categories other than species would seem in order.

NAMES OF FAMILIES AND GENERA

Of the taxonomic categories (taxa) other than species, families and also genera deserve some special attention. Families of flowering plants, representing assemblages of related genera and species, often stand out in the taxonomic hierarchy (rank listing; see below) as entities somewhat more distinct than certain other categories (for example, order or class). Whether or not we can adequately define "what a plant family is," families are often clearly perceivable, major morphological/taxonomic units (especially in terms of floral and inflorescence structure), representing distinct nodes in the entire system of plant classification. The ability to sight recognize major families of flowering plants provides a substantial boost to one's facility for identifying plants (poisonous or not), especially with reasonable rapidity. Also, a person's awareness of the botanical landscape is greatly enhanced by knowledge of flowering-plant family identification. These are reasons, thus, that a separate chapter (Chapter 8) has been devoted specifically to this topic.

Names of angiosperm families are readily recognized, because, of the more than 300 families, the vast majority of their names end in the Latin termination -*aceae*, for example, Rosaceae (rose family), Solanaceae (nightshade family), Ranunculaceae (buttercup family), Papaveraceae (poppy family), Euphorbiaceae (spurge family), Caryophyllaceae (pink family), and Anacardiaceae (poison ivy family). Family names ending in -*aceae* are based on the names of genera included in the family; the name Solanaceae, for example, is based on the stem of the genus name *Solanum* (nightshades, Irish potato); thus Solan -aceae. A few (eight in total) family names do not end in -*aceae*, but rather end in -*ae*, for example, Labiatae (mint family), Umbelliferae (carrot family),

Figure 7–2 *Rhus radicans.* Poison ivy

Compositae (sunflower family), Cruciferae (mustard family), and Leguminosae (legume family), and are not based on generic names. These are large families, long-recognized, bearing historically older names. The use of these older, "non-aceae" names, is permitted for these few families because of long-entrenched use in the literature, and common usage among professional botanists. The rules of nomenclature, however, also permit the use of alternative -*aceae* names (which are based on generic names) for each of these historically old and revered families, indicated as follows in parentheses: Labiatae (Lamiaceae), Umbelliferae (Apiaceae), Compositae (Asteraceae), Cruciferae (Brassicaceae), Leguminosae (Fabaceae). We are free to choose either the -*ae* or the -*aceae* name (for example, either Compositae or Asteraceae) for each of these special families, and it is well to be aware of the existence of both names, since either may be encountered in current literature.

Names of genera may be derived from virtually any language source, although a large number were initially Greek common names for plants (for example, *Anemone* for the windflower, and *Daucon*, latinized to *Daucus*, for the carrot). Generic names are pertinent to the present discussion not only because some constitute the basis (stems) of family names, as discussed above (and hence explain the origin of those family names), but also because the common names of natural plant product chemicals (including toxins) are frequently named in accordance with the genus name. Such compounds often end in -*in* or -*ine*, as in abrin, the toxic protein from *Abrus* (precatory bean); digitoxin, a toxic and medicinal glycoside from *Digitalis* (foxglove); solanine, a poisonous alkaloid from *Solanum* (nightshades and Irish potato); and coniine, the toxic alkaloid from *Conium* (poison hemlock).

IDENTIFICATION AND TAXONOMIC KEYS

Although rarely necessary, complete identification of plants would involve a progression of identification stages through the entire taxonomic hierarchy, from kingdom through species, or even variety. A good analogy to the process of pinning down a classification is that of tracing an at first totally unknown address (through successively smaller geographic units). A total classification of poison ivy, progressing through sequentially smaller systematic units, is as follows:

Taxonomic Hierarchy

Kingdom: Plantae

Division (equivalent to phylum in zoology): Tracheophyta

Class: Angiospermae

Subclass: Dicotyledoneae (subcategories are permitted for essentially all the taxonomic ranks)

Order: Sapindales (orders often end in -*ales*)

Family: Anacardiaceae

Genus: *Rhus*

Subgenus: *Toxicodendron*

Species: *Rhus radicans*

As indicated, such total classification is typically unnecessary, and it is usually enough to identify the family, genus, and species of a given plant. Family-through-species identification is accomplished with various types of taxonomic keys (found, for example, in regional floras). Keys are written devices serving the specific purpose of identification; they are usually constructed as a series of paired statements, requiring the user of the key to make a choice in each instance; that is, does the feature(s) of the plant conform to the statement of the first choice, #1, or does it fit better the statement in the second choice, #1? As a hypothetical example, a key might well look something like the following:

Sample Taxonomic Key

1. Leaves simple
   2. Leaves entire
      3. Flowers hypogynous: Species A
      3. Flowers perigynous or epigynous: Species B
   2. Leaves toothed: Species C
1. Leaves compound
   4. Leaves alternate
      5. Leaves pinnately compound (and with many leaflets per leaf): Species D
      5. Leaves palmately or ternately compound
         6. Leaves palmately compound (five or more leaflets per leaf), tree: Species E
         6. Leaves ternately compound (three leaflets per leaf), herb, shrub, or vine: Species F
   4. Leaves opposite or whorled
      7. Leaves opposite, petals fused: Species G
      7. Leaves whorled, petals free: Species H

Which species would *Rhus radicans* (poison ivy) key out as in this key? The reader is referred to Chapter 6 for assistance with terminology used in this key.

Whether one wishes to identify poisonous plants, edible plants, or simply plants in general, familiarity with the use of taxonomic keys in various manuals (floras and the like) becomes essential, as well as an understanding of terminology of plant structure involved in their usage. In addition to the informational content of this chapter, material presented on plant structure (Chapter 6, as indicated) and on plant families (Chapter 8) should take the person interested in plant identification well down the road toward the initial facility necessary to put taxonomic keys to good use.

SELECTED REFERENCES

GLEDHILL, D. 1985. *The Names of Plants*. Cambridge University Press, Cambridge, England. A handy little book; the first part is devoted to the need for and development of the rules for naming plants, including some insights into Latin grammar; the second is a listing of the meanings of a large number of scientific names.

JONES, SAMUEL B., JR., AND ARLENE E. LUCHSINGER, 1986. *Plant Systematics*, 2nd ed. McGraw-Hill Book Co., New York. Chapter 1 introduces the topic of taxonomy, including a discussion of taxonomic objectives. Chapter 4, dealing with principles of taxonomy, provides a good discussion of various taxonomic categories: species, genera, families, and so on. Nomenclature or naming is covered in Chapter 3.

MABBERLEY, D. J. 1987. *The Plant-Book - A Portable Dictionary of the Higher Plants*. Cambridge University Press, Cambridge, England. A comprehensive dictionary of plant names, containing a list of name authorities at the end.

MAYR, ERNST, E. GORTON LINSLEY, AND ROBERT L. USINGER. 1953. *Methods and Principles of Systematic Zoology*. McGraw-Hill Book Co., New York. Although a number of years old now, Chapter 2 still provides the foundation for our current concept and definition of species.

STACE, CLIVE A. 1980. *Plant Taxonomy and Biosystematics*. Edward Arnold, London. Chapter 1, The Scope of Taxonomy, clearly addresses the need for classification, as well as outlining some taxonomic basics.

Flowering Plant Families
of Toxic Significance

As an initial and sometimes quick aid to identification of common poisonous (and medicinal) plants, it is well to learn something about the recognition characteristics of the major families of flowering plants containing toxic representatives. This is no substitute for the careful keying out of a plant in question, but can nonetheless be very helpful in the process. Only those characteristics aiding in spot recognition of families will be stressed in the family descriptions in this treatment of the subject.

The assumption should never be made that, because one member of a particular plant family is nontoxic, all other members are nontoxic as well. Conversely, even if a family is noted for its toxicity, it is essentially never true that all members (species) of that family will prove to be poisonous. One must also not assume that, if a given poisonous representative of a family causes a particular toxic reaction, this same effect exactly will be necessarily produced by other toxic members of that family. Finally, it should be borne in mind that toxic plant species are to be found in families in addition to those described here.

In the present listing, the objective is to focus on the flowering plant families that are considered most significant in poisonous and/or medicinal membership. The discussion of families is divided into dicotyledonous and monocotyledonous families, dicots and monocots being the two major divisions of flowering plants; dicots constitute decidedly the larger of the two groups, in general and in terms of toxic representatives. Beyond that, the order of listing follows the system of classification of Charles Bessey (1915), as modified by Lyman Benson (1957); the Bessey system, in one form or another, has probably constituted the major system of classification employed for the teaching of plant families in the United States in the twentieth century.

DICOT CHARACTERISTICS

Dicotyledonous plants generally possess the following features: The stem vascular bundles usually form a ring or concentric configuration when the stem is viewed in cross section (best observed in young and/or herbaceous stems). The leaves are pinnately or palmately veined, the ultimate (small) vein pattern usually being reticulate (a network). The flower parts (sepals, petals, and so on) occur in whorls of fours or fives (less commonly in twos or some other number), or else in a large, indefinite number (sometimes spirally arranged). The embryo in the seed possesses two cotyledons. Dicots run the gamut of growth form, ranging from herbs or vines to shrubs or large trees (increasing in girth due to the activity of a vascular cambium), and of leaf position and form (alternate, opposite, whorled; simple or compound; and so on).

DICOT FAMILIES

Major dicot families with poisonous/medicinal representatives are presented next. For convenience, these dicot families are divided into four informal groups, A to D, based on ovary position in the flower and fusion or nonfusion of the petals. For explanations of the terms hypogynous, perigynous, and epigynous and also of petal fusion, see Chapter 6; Chapter 7 deals with the derivation of family names; toxic compounds and effects are discussed in Chapters 3 and 11, respectively.

A. Flowers Hypognous; Petals Free (Not Attached to Each Other) or Lacking

Crowfoot (buttercup) family: Ranunculaceae.   Herbs with leaves that are usually deeply palmately (or ternately) lobed or compound, said to resemble a "birdsfoot." Stamens are numerous in a flower and often spirally arranged (on a sometimes thimblelike receptacle); several or a number of separate simple pistils may be present. Flowers often possess only a single cycle of perianth parts (two cycles are present in *Ranunculus*), these usually being petallike in appearance (although technically probably constituting sepals). Fruits are achenes (sometimes numerous in a convex, headlike arrangement) or else small follicles or berries. Poisonous substances may be either of two distinct types of alkaloids or a potentially toxic glycoside; in a few cases the toxic substance is unknown. Toxic effects are highly variable, but may include severe irritation of the digestive tract and alterations in the rate of the heartbeat. The buttercup family is commonly represented in the spring flora of the eastern United States. Included in the numerous toxic members of this family are monkshood *(Aconitum)*, baneberry *(Actaea)*, windflower *(Anemone)*, marsh marigold *(Caltha)*, virgin's bower *(Clematis)*, larkspur *(Delphinium)*, Christmas rose *(Helleborus)*, golden seal *(Hydrastis)*, and buttercup *(Ranunculus)*.

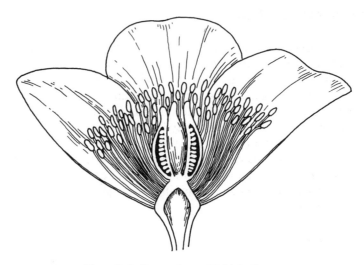

Figure 8–1   Ranunculaceae (*Caltha*): flower

Poppy family: Papaveraceae.   Herbs with colored or milky sap (latex). Flowers are usually large, solitary, and showy. Although both perianth cycles are initially present, only the petals are seen on a mature flower, since the sepals typically fall off as the flower opens. Stamens are numerous but cyclic in arrangement. One compound pistil is present per flower, giving rise to a capsular fruit opening by valves or sometimes by a ring of pores underneath the persistent stigma head. The toxic substance is the opium or morphine type of alkaloid (see Chapter

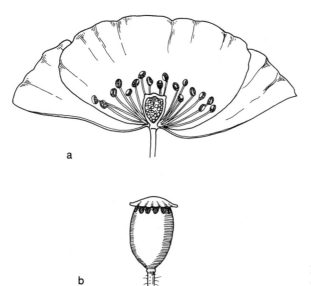

Figure 8–2   Papaveraceae (*Papaver*): (a) flower; (b) capsule

3), which typically acts as a depressant on the central nervous system. Toxic representatives include introduced plants such as opium poppy and certain other poppy species (*Papaver*) and bloodroot (*Sanguinaria*), a native plant; the European celandine poppy (*Chelidonium*) is rarely planted in American gardens and is probably toxic as well.

Mustard family (the crucifers): Cruciferae or Brassicaceae.
Herbs, usually with a pungent taste. Flowers possess four cruciform petals (that is, the petals exhibit a crosslike configuration if viewed face on). Stamens have a characteristic arrangement in the family; there are four longer and two shorter stamens per

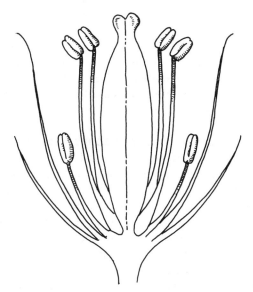

Figure 8–3 Cruciferae: diagrammatic flower

flower. The fruit is a modified capsule known as a silicle or silique. Toxic substances are mustard oils, which are components of glycoside molecules. Mustard oils may cause gastrointestinal irritation. Representatives include various species of wild mustard (*Brassica*).

Spurge family: Euphorbiaceae.
A large and diverse family. Flowers of spurges are unisexual, with male and female flowers often occurring on the same plant (monoecious). In the genus *Euphorbia*, the tiny male flowers (each consisting of but a single stamen) and the single, three-carpeled female flower are contained together in often diminutive, cuplike inflorescences (the cyathia) superficially resembling individual flowers. The fruit is capsular (the three parts of the capsule often separating). Leaves sometimes bear either red or white blotches or markings. A number of species contain an acrid milky latex that is caustic to the skin and eyes (causing burns). Poisonous substances in the family vary from diterpenoids (especially in representatives

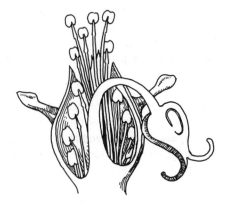

Figure 8–4   Euphorbiaceae (*Euphorbia*): cyathium

with milky latex) to toxic proteins and even saponins. Poisonous or at least potentially harmful representatives include tung nut (*Aleurites*); tread-softly (*Cnidoscolus*); snow-on-the-mountain, cypress spurge, and wartweed (*Euphorbia*); manchineel (*Hippomane*); and castor bean (*Ricinus*). Poinsettias, which belong to this family, contrary to popular opinion, are either nontoxic or else only very mildly so.

Poison ivy (sumac) family: Anacardiaceae.   Mostly smallish woody plants with alternate, pinnately or ternately compound leaves and small, 5-merous, numerous flowers in sometimes large panicles; in a flower, a ring of swollen tissue (the nectar disc or hypogynous disc) often occurs between the base of the stamens and the ovary base. The fruit is most typically a drupe. Resin ducts are present in all tissues (especially the leaves), the resin being readily brought to the plant surface by bruising or brushing against the plant. The resin is lacquerlike (similar to shellac or varnish) and is difficult to remove from the skin. Probably the majority of people are allergic to some degree to the resin produced by various members of this family and will develop a dermatitis (skin rash) as a consequence of contact with the substance. Toxic representatives include poison ivy, poison oak, and poison sumac (all belonging to the genus *Rhus*). "Good" sumacs (harmless species of *Rhus*) have reddish, erect, pubescent (hair-covered) fruit clusters. "Bad" sumacs (those causing dermatitis, including poison ivy) have drooping, whitish (perhaps green- or yellow-white) fruit clusters, which are frequently glabrous (lacking pubescence). Astringent substances in good sumacs have been used to treat hem-

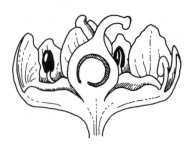

Figure 8–5   Anacardiaceae (*Rhus*): flower

orrhoids (but by all means, don't get your good and bad sumac species confused in this regard!).

Nettle family: Urticaceae.   Herbs with opposite or alternate, simple, toothed leaves and watery sap. Clusters of small, often greenish, unisexual flowers are numerous in the leaf axils, imparting a congested appearance to the axils. Stinging trichomes (hairs), constructed like little hypodermic needles, may be present and especially prevalent toward the base of the stem. These stinging hairs are thought to contain a variety of substances, including histamine and acetylcholine. Tips of the hairs may break off under the skin, resulting in a burning or stinging dermatitis response that may persist a matter of minutes or even hours. Representatives are stinging nettle (*Urtica*) and wood nettle (*Laportea*).

a

b

Figure 8–6   Urticaceae (*Urtica*): (a) male flower; (b) female flower

Pink (carnation) family: Caryophyllaceae.   The pink family gets its common name because each of the petals often has an apical notch or split (as though it had been cut or pinked, as with pinking shears or scissors). Additional useful characters in recognition of this herbaceous family are the simple, entire, opposite leaves, which are lightly sheathing around the stem, and the slightly swollen nodes. A technical feature of the family is that the numerous ovules (immature seeds) are attached to a placenta in the form of a central rod passing up through the ovary ("hitching post" placenta); if a cross section is made through the ovary, the central placental rod is seen to be surrounded by one unified ovary chamber. The fruit is a capsule opening by valves or by apical teeth. The majority of members of the pink family are nontoxic. However, two toxic representatives, corn cockle (*Agrostemma*) and bouncing bet or soapwort (*Saponaria*), may be common and merit inclusion of this family. Both corn cockle and soapwort contain saponins (soaplike substances) that may cause severe gastroenteritis, and possible damage to red blood cells as well, if absorbed into the bloodstream.

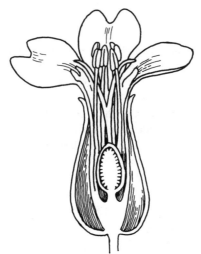

Figure 8–7 Caryophyllaceae: diagrammatic flower

B. Flowers Hypogynous; Petals Fused (at Least at the Base) to Form a Corolla Tube

Heath family: Ericaceae.   Mostly shrubs, found naturally on acid soils; often with somewhat leathery, evergreen foliage. The usually whitish or pinkish petals are often fused into a funnel-shaped or urnlike corolla (which may be broadest at the

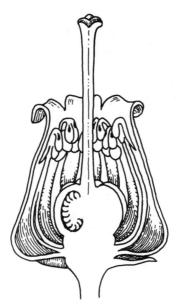

Figure 8–8 Ericaceae (*Andromeda*): flower

middle); anthers commonly open by terminal pores. Fruit is a capsule or berry. The toxic principle is a poorly known resinoid (possibly terpenoid) substance, andromedotoxin, affecting the nervous system and the heart. Andromedotoxin (also called grayanotoxin) is found in most toxic members of the family. Representatives that are poisonous or probably so include bog rosemary (*Andromeda*), mountain laurel (*Kalmia*), dog laurel (*Leucothoe*), Japanese andromeda (*Pieris*), and rhododendrons and azaleas (*Rhododendron*). Poison honey has been associated with bees feeding on nectar of mountain laurel and rhododendrons.

Dogbane family: Apocynaceae.   Herbs, shrubs, trees, or woody vines with opposite, simple, entire leaves; sometimes with milky juice. Local representatives (roadside weeds in the eastern United States) may have reddened stems. The corolla is sometimes seen to have a slight twist or rotation if viewed face on. The

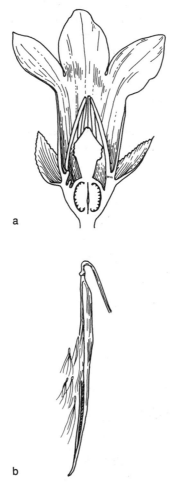

a

b

Figure 8–9 Apocynaceae (*Apocynum*): (a) flower; (b) follicle

style or stigma of the pistil is often enlarged, or clavate, and closely surrounded by the stamens. In fruit, two (or one through abortion) elongated follicles (containing seeds that are in some cases hair-tufted) arise from each flower. Potentially toxic or medicinal chemicals are either glycosides (often affecting the heart) or else alkaloids altering the blood, blood pressure, or central nervous system function. Dogbane or Indian hemp (*Apocynum*) is a common and poisonous roadside weed, flowering in mid- to late summer. *Strophanthus* (sawai) is the source of the heart medicine ouabain; species of periwinkle (*Catharanthus*, or by some authors *Vinca*) and snakeroot (*Rauwolfia*) have also found substantial medicinal use. Oleander (*Nerium*) is a highly toxic ornamental shrub.

Milkweed family: Asclepiadaceae.   Similar in appearance to some members of the dogbane family, these plants often contain abundant milky latex. Flowers commonly occur in umbellike inflorescences (but these umbels bloom from the inside or center outward, and hence in a direction opposite those of the carrot family; see Umbelliferae). In flowers of milkweeds, the anthers are often fused to the stigma head, forming a unit structure (the gynostegium); large (and sometimes hoodlike) nectaries are commonly present in the flowers. Fruits are somewhat expanded or inflated follicles containing numerous seeds. Seeds of milkweeds typically have a fluff, or tuft of hair on one end (that is, the seeds are comose). Some species of milkweeds (*Asclepias* spp.) are considered to be significantly toxic, and others perhaps less so or not so; however, increasing evidence indicates that all species are best treated with caution as items of human consumption. Toxic milkweeds contain glycosides causing emesis and potentially affecting the heart (cardiac glycosides) and, possibly, poorly characterized, toxic resinoids as well.

a

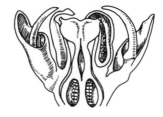

b

Figure 8–10 Asclepiadaceae (*Asclepias*): (a) flower; (b) flower in longitudinal section

Morning-glory family: Convolvulaceae.   Most commonly seen as twining, herbaceous vines (lacking tendrils), with simple, hastate or saggitate (arrowhead shaped), alternate leaves. Petals are almost completely united into a large, funnel-shaped corolla. The fruit is capsular. Seeds of various species of both *Ipomoea* (morning-glories) and *Convolvulus* (bindweeds) are known to contain (or suspected of containing) LSD-like substances, which are to be regarded as both potentially toxic and hallucinogenic.

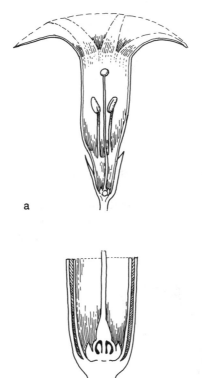

a

b

Figure 8–11   Convolvulaceae (*Ipomoea*): (a) flower; (b) enlargement of ovary portion of flower

Nightshade family: Solanaceae.   Mostly herbaceous and highly variable in appearance; however, the leaves frequently have a ragged, that is, unevenly toothed or lobed, margin. Petals are often fused into either a long, tubelike or else a smaller, saucer-shaped corolla (in which the lobes may exceed the tubular portion). Fruit is a berry (which can be quite toxic). In some of the local nightshades (*Solanum* spp.), the inflorescence occupies an internodal position, instead of the usual terminal or axillary position. Several distinct types of toxic alkaloids are to be found in the family, causing, variously, digestive upset, nervous system dysfunction, and even hallucinations. A large number (in relative terms) of poisonous and/or medicinal plant species belong to this family, including belladonna (*Atropa*), jimson weed (*Datura*), henbane (*Hyoscyamus*), tomato (*Lycopersicon*), mandrake (*Mandragora*), tobacco (*Nicotiana*), ground cherry (*Physalis*), Irish potato (*Solanum tuberosum*), and various nightshades (*Solanum* spp.).

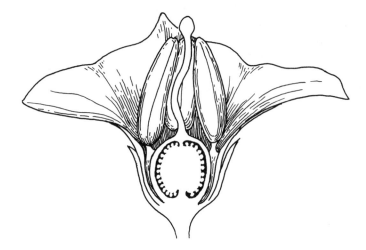

Figure 8–12 Solanaceae (*Solanum*): flower

Mint family: Labiatae or Lamiaceae.   Herbs with square stems, opposite leaves, and aromatic fragrance. The corolla of the flower is often strikingly two-lipped (bilabiate). Flowers often occur in pseudo-whorls at the stem nodes (verticillate inflorescence).   The fruit is characteristically four nutlets, remaining for a time in the persistent calyx. Not noted for their toxicity (although ground ivy, *Glechoma*, is known

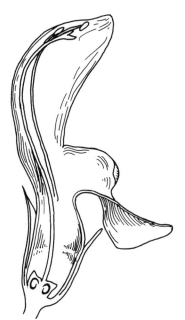

Figure 8–13 Labiatae: diagrammatic flower

to be toxic), certain of the mints have found substantial medicinal use historically. The mint-oils (actually terpenoids), found for example in various mints (*Mentha*) and in thyme (*Thymus*), are soothing to the digestive tract and are an aid to controlling intestinal gas or flatulence (that is, they act as carminatives). Another major use of mint oils has been as ingredients in cough drops and as inhalants in the treatment of colds and respiratory congestion.

   Foxglove (figwort) family: Scrophulariaceae.   Although most "scrophs" are nontoxic, inclusion of the foxglove (*Digitalis*) itself in the family is alone enough to merit inclusion of this family in our listing. Historically and presently, *Digitalis* has found a significant place in the treatment of certain types of heart disease, due to the particular type of cardiac glycoside present in the leaves (and other parts); in medicinal

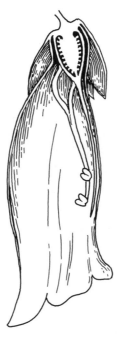

Figure 8–14 Scrophulariaceae (*Digitalis*): flower

overdose, digitalis is very toxic, causing cardiac arrhythmias. Scrophs resemble mints but may be distinguished by a capsular fruit and the lack of aromaticity characteristic of many mints.

C. Flowers Perigynous or Epigynous; Petals Free or Lacking

   Rose family: Rosaceae.   Alternate (sometimes compound) leaves, often with stipules (little flaps of tissue at the leaf base), are characteristic of the rose family; thorns, spines, or prickles are sometimes present on the stems. Flowers are actinomorphic, either perigynous or epigynous, and may have a distinct floral cup (hypanthium). The type of fruit is variably a pome, a drupe, or an aggregate of fleshy or dry, simple fruits; however, the type of fruit is always something other than a legume (a help in distinguishing this family from the following one). A number of members of the family contain a substance (amygdalin or a similar compound), found in the seeds (or the pits or stones of the fruit), which releases cyanide following ingestion. When extracted from pits of the apricot and commercialized, this substance is known as laetrile (an *alleged* cure for certain types of cancer). Wild (black) cherry (*Prunus*) is a rather common cyanide-containing tree (in this case, the cyanide-releasing compound is also present in the leaves). Peach pits and apple seeds also contain amygdalin. Fruits (stones) of some species of *Cotoneaster* possess a limited cyanide content. Roses per se (members of the genus *Rosa*) do not contain cyanogenic compounds.

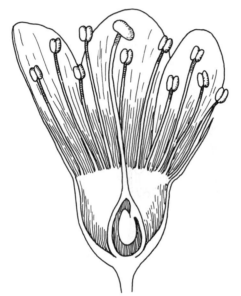

Figure 8–15 Rosaceae (*Prunus*): flower

Legume family: Leguminosae or Fabaceae.   A large and highly variable group of plants (herbs, shrubs, trees, vines). However, the usually perigynous flowers are often characteristically bilaterally symmetrical (zygomorphic). Of the five petals per flower, the upper petal, which tends to be more or less erect, is the *flag* (banner or standard), and the lowest two petals form a boat-shaped structure known as the *keel*; the two lateral petals are the *wings*. The stipulate leaves are typically compound (either pinnately or palmately compound, depending on the species). The fruit is a legume. The toxic substance varies, but is often either a particular type of toxic alkaloid (causing digestive upset, and perhaps affecting the nervous system as well) or else is a poisonous protein adversely affecting the blood and the cell machinery of various organs of the body. Toxic representatives of the family include precatory bean or rosary pea (*Abrus*),

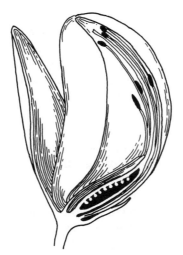

Figure 8–16 Leguminosae (*Lupinus*): flower

locoweeds (*Astragalus*), false indigo (*Baptisia*), senna (*Cassia*), Kentucky coffee tree (*Gymnocladus*), golden chain (*Laburnum*), vetchlings and sweet peas (*Lathyrus*), lupines (*Lupinus*), black locust (*Robinia*), and wisteria (*Wisteria*).

Carrot family: Umbelliferae or Apiaceae.   A sizable and predominantly harmless family; however, two toxic representatives, poison hemlock (*Conium*) and water hemlock (*Cicuta*), are so well known and potentially dangerous that these should not be omitted. The small, epigynous flowers of the carrot family are arranged in (indeterminate) umbels or compound umbels that bloom from the outside of the inflorescence in (toward the center). The often sheathing leaves are compound or decompound (more than once compound). Stems are hollow in the internodes. The toxic substance is either a simple alkaloid (in poison hemlock) or a long-chain alcohol (in water hemlock), both affecting the nervous system but producing quite different symptoms. It seems strange that closely related genera such as these two hemlocks

Figure 8–17 Umbelliferae (*Cicuta*): inflorescence

should contain radically different kinds of toxic substances. The hemlocks are partic- ularly dangerous plants, because both can be common in a given area, and both are readily mistaken for wild edible plants (such as wild carrot, *Daucus*). Additionally in the family, wild parsnip (*Pastinaca*), which is yellow-flowered (not white flowered as are the hemlocks and wild carrot), contains yet a different type of substance, which may cause an increase in the sensitivity of the skin to sunlight (that is, may contribute to photodermatitis).

D. Flowers Epigynous; Petals Fused through Part of Their Length to Form a Corolla Tube

Bellflower family: Campanulaceae.   The members of this herbaceous family that one is most likely to see in North America would belong either to the genus *Campanula* or the genus *Lobelia*. Species of both genera often have bluish flowers. However, in contrast to campanulas, lobelias have strongly zygomorphic flowers that are bilabiate (the upper lip of the corolla is erect and composed of

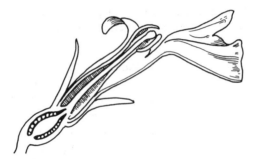

Figure 8–18   Campanulaceae (*Lobelia*): flower

two lobes; the lower, composed of three lobes, is downward pointing). Addi- tionally, lobelias have a characteristic dorsal slit in the corolla through which the stamens, surrounding the pistil, may be visible. Only lobelias (not cam- panulas) are likely to be toxic. Various species of *Lobelia* (*L. inflata*, Indian tobacco; *L. siphilitica*, great blue lobelia; and *L. cardinalis*, cardinal flower) may contain the emetic lobelia alkaloids, with effects similar to nicotine or to poison hemlock on the central nervous system.

Sunflower (aster, daisy) family: Compositae or Asteraceae.   The sun- flower family is possibly the largest family of flowering plants in terms of number of species (between 20,000 and 30,000 species are estimated to exist in the family). Predominantly herbaceous, this family is readily recognized by the inflorescence, which is a head (capitulum). The small flowers or florets (sometimes of two types, ray and disc florets) are sessile on an enlarged, compound receptacle. The inflorescence (head) as a whole resembles a single flower. Fruits are achenes (for example, sunflower

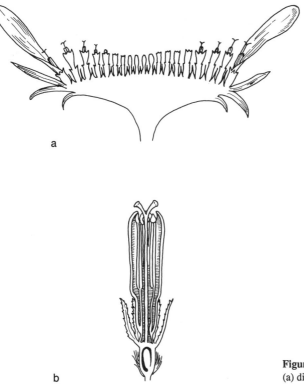

a

b

Figure 8–19 Compositae:
(a) diagrammatic head; (b) disc floret

"seeds"). Relatively few members of the sunflower family are poisonous; however, white snakeroot (*Eupatorium*), containing a toxic alcohol affecting the nervous system, and groundsel (*Senecio*), with a liver-damaging alkaloid, are well-known poisonous plants. Cocklebur (*Xanthium*) is considered to be toxic in the seedling stage. Other members of the family, especially the ragweeds (*Ambrosia*), are notorious for their role in the induction of respiratory or hay-fever allergy. Members of the sagebrush tribe, for example, sagebrush and mugwort (*Artemisia*), have been implicated in dermatitis (skin) allergy. Some members of the thistle tribe, such as species of *Cirsium*, cause mechanical injury (perhaps leading to secondary infection) in the oral passages of livestock because of spines on the leaves and seed heads.

MONOCOT CHARACTERISTICS

In monocotyledonous plants, the stem vascular bundles are scattered, that is, more or less evenly and apparently randomly distributed when the stem is viewed in cross section. The leaves are typically parallel veined, and although cross-connecting veins may be seen, an ultimate network of tiny veins is usually not apparent (as it often is in dicots). Flower parts of monocots frequently occur in whorls of three or multiples of three, although, rarely, a large number of parts may be present. The embryo in the seed possesses but a single cotyledon. Monocots, lacking the vascular cambium typical of dicots, are generally relatively small, herbaceous plants. Most typically, leaves of monocots are simple and either alternate or basal.

MONOCOT FAMILIES

Lily family: Liliaceae.   The lily family constitutes one of the large and classic groups of monocots. In addition to being 3-merous, lily flowers have a superior ovary; six stamens are present per flower. Sepals and petals are often similar in appearance (both are usually petalloid) in this family and are called

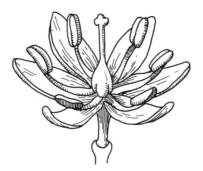

Figure 8–20   Liliaceae: diagrammatic flower

tepals. The leaves are typically alternate-basal and entire (common among monocots). Toxic substances in the family range from glycosides affecting the heart to alkaloids causing gastric distress, arresting cell division, lowering blood pressure, and even inducing birth defects. Poisonous and/or medicinal members include aloe (*Aloe*), autumn crocus (*Colchicum*), lily-of-the-valley (*Convallaria*), garden hyacinth (*Hyacinthus*), bunch flower (*Melanthium*), squill (*Scilla* and *Urginea*), star-of-Bethlehem (*Ornithogalum*), false hellebore (*Veratrum*), and death camus (*Zigadenus*).

Amaryllis family: Amaryllidaceae.   This family is similar in appearance to members of the lily family. The only consistent difference separating the two families is that in the amaryllis family the ovary is inferior rather than superior. Underground parts (bulbs, and the like) of various members of the family are suspected of containing alkaloidal substances that are at a minimum capable of causing digestive upset. Potentially toxic representatives include amaryllis (*Amaryllis*), snowdrops (*Galanthus*), and daffodil (*Narcissus*).

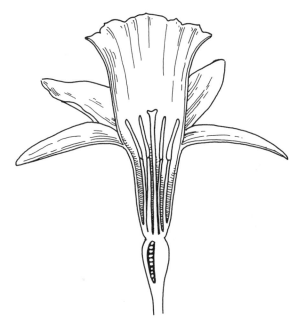

Figure 8–21 Amaryllidaceae
(*Narcissus*): flower

Iris family: Iridaceae.   The iris family also resembles the lily family. The Iridaceae differ from the Liliaceae by two consistent features; in the iris family the ovary is inferior, and there are but three (rather than six) stamens per flower. In *Iris*, as in a number of members of the lily and amaryllis family, underground parts (rhizomes or bulbs in the case of *Iris*) should be considered potentially toxic (possibly containing alkaloids causing gastric disturbance). The genus *Crocus*, with its predominantly spring-flowering species, is also a member of the Iridaceae; species of spring-flowering crocus are not known to be toxic, in contrast to autumn crocus (*Colchicum*, a member of the Liliaceae). Nonetheless, *Crocus* should be avoided as a food item, as should any member of the three look-alike families (lily, amaryllis, and iris families), unless edibility is known for certain. It has been recently pointed out in the literature that even the condiment saffron (from stigmas of *Crocus sativus*) may be deleterious if consumed in excess.

Aroid family: Araceae.   The aroids are recognized by a characteristic inflorescence, the spadix (a fleshy spike), surrounded by a spathe (hoodlike bract). Leaves of aroids are broader than in most monocots. Sharp, needlelike crystals of calcium oxalate are frequently found throughout the tissues of aroids. Upon chewing various parts of aroids (leaves, corms, and so on), these sharp crystals (raphides) may become lodged in the lining of the mouth, tongue, and throat, causing temporary burning, irritation, swelling, and even loss of speech. Members of the family include *Anthurium*, *Arisaema* (jack-in-the-pulpit), *Caladium*, *Dieffenbachia* (dumbcane),

Figure 8–22   Iridaceae (*Crocus*)

Philodendron, and *Symplocarpus* (skunk cabbage). In contrast to soluble oxalates, the solid (insoluble) oxalates of this family usually do not cause potentially life threatening illness because they are not absorbed from the digestive tract into the bloodstream.

Figure 8–23   Araceae (*Arisaema*): inflorescence

SELECTED REFERENCES

BENSON, LYMAN. 1957. *Plant Classification*. D. C. Heath and Company, Boston. Although a later edition of this book exists, this first edition is selected because of its clear adaptation of and reference to the system of classification of Charles Bessey (1915), the system fundamentally followed in this chapter; pages 110 to 114 of Benson's text provide a comprehensive family listing.

HEYWOOD, V. H. (consultant editor). 1978. *Flowering Plants of the World*. Oxford University Press. First U.S. edition published by Prentice-Hall, Inc., Englewood Cliffs, N.J. An excellent color-illustrated coverage of angiosperm families; good information on the geographic distribution of families is presented.

HICKEY, MICHAEL, AND CLIVE KING. 1981. *100 Families of Flowering Plants*. Cambridge University Press, Cambridge. Presents major families of flowering plants in a detailed fashion, focusing on variation within families and relationships between families; economic and ornamental representatives of families are also stressed; well illustrated.

JONES, S. B., JR., AND A. E. LUCHSINGER. 1986. *Plant Systematics*, 2nd ed. McGraw-Hill Book Co., New York. Chapter 14 constitutes an extensive coverage of flowering plant families using a modern system of classification.

SMITH, JAMES P., JR. 1977. *Vascular Plant Families*. Mad River Press, Eureka, Calif. Similar to book by Hickey and King, but presented in a more abbreviated manner; family recognition characteristics are stressed.

Common Questions Concerning Poisonous Plants

This chapter deals with ten common or at least frequently asked questions about poisonous plants and is presented in that format (that is, as numbered questions). As the reader will see, some questions are readily answerable, and others are indeed less so. Regardless of answerability, these questions are deemed worthy of consideration. The subsequent chapter is devoted solely to the question of the possible toxicity of common plant foods, and hence that topic will not be specifically considered in this chapter.

1. *How many kinds of poisonous plants are there?* Once during a lecture this writer was asked, are there any kinds of poisonous plants other than poison ivy? Clearly, there are many more; in fact, poison ivy is by some definitions not actually considered to be a poisonous plant (see question 2), although that viewpoint is not adopted in this book. However, reliable estimates as to the true number of poisonous plants in the world are nonexistent. In his excellent paperback *Deadly Harvest*, John Kingsbury indicates that "somewhat more than 700" species of plants in the western hemisphere "have caused loss of life or serious illness in man or animals." Although doubtless accurate based on information documentable at the time, an estimate of about 700 poisonous species is decidedly too low. There are most certainly many additional potentially toxic New World species (especially in the tropics) of which we simply have no record of a toxicity. Also, a considerable literature has developed since Kingsbury's statement that is indicative of the toxicity of hundreds of kinds of plants indigenous to the Old World (for example, B. Verdcourt, and E. C. Trump, *Common Poisonous Plants of East Africa*, Collins Clear-Type Press, London, 1969.) An accurate estimate of the actual number of poisonous plants in the world is probably decades away, if it is indeed ever knowable. As a serious complication to a future estimate, destruction of the tropical rain forest (at the astounding rate of 100 acres per minute) may result, or perhaps already has in some cases resulted, in elimination of the rarer of these species before we ever know about them. This impending elimination of species in the tropics (of the New and Old World) is especially tragic because certain exotic toxic species, for example, those yielding curare (*Chondrodendron tomentosum* and *Strychnos toxifera*), quinine (*Cinchona* spp.), ouabain (*Strophanthus gratus*), and physostigmine (*Physostigma venenosum*), have proved so valuable to formal medicine. We can only wonder how many kinds of plants of potential medical benefit may never "see the light of modern medicine," as a result of their extirpation before the possibility of discovery.

    2. *How do we define what a poisonous plant is?* Where do we draw the line in determining (that is, on what basis do we establish) whether a given plant is to be considered poisonous or not? Part of the problem of providing a reliable estimate of the number of poisonous plants in the world is that of deriving a meaningful definition of what actually constitutes a poisonous plant. Providing a truly adequate definition is a difficult matter indeed. If we consider a poisonous plant to be only one that is known to "have caused loss of life or serious illness in man or animals," then (as indicated under question 1) we will surely arrive at estimates of numbers of poisonous plants that are markedly on the low side. Such a definition will not only delete from the listing potentially internally toxic plants lacking a record of toxicity, but will also exclude well-known plant species associated with annoyances such as allergy (poison ivy, ragweed) and mechanical injury (thistles). To avoid controversy, this book begs the question of precise definition and treats the subject much more broadly, that is, without hard and fast definition, by consideration of plants that are *potentially harmful* in any manner. For the sake of dissemination of information on the topic of harmful plants, it is considered far better to err on the side of inclusiveness rather than exclusiveness.

    3. *How much toxin must a plant have to be considered internally poisonous?* This varies greatly with the particular poisonous principle contained by a plant species (and also by the mode of intake into the body). Estimates of toxic levels of chemicals in plants are not necessarily common in the literature, and when found are often expressed in different units or measurements from one publication to another. However, the following estimates (gleaned and interpreted by this writer and perhaps to be taken with a "small grain of salt") will at least provide an idea of the great variability of toxic level per type of toxin. The toxic protein (ricin) in castor bean (*Ricinus communis*) is one of the most powerful plant toxins known. If injected, a toxic level of only 0.0001 mg/kg of plant material may prove fatal; a greater concentration is required if ricin-containing material is ingested. In wild cherry (leaves) containing cyanide (HCN), the danger level is more on the order of 0.2 g (200 mg) of cyanide per kilogram of plant tissue. Concerning the much less toxic oxalates (soluble salts of oxalic acid), found for example in rhubarb leaf blades, toxic levels are on the order of 20 to 100 g of soluble oxalate per kilogram of plant tissue, depending on the type of animal and the speed of consumption. Even though the preceding examples constitute

Figure 9–1 *Ricinus communis.* Castor bean

only rough comparisons, it is an easy conclusion that differing amounts of plant materials must be consumed to reach the danger level, depending on the particular toxic substance contained. Also, mitigating circumstances come to bear in determining the degree of toxic response (for example, the type, size, and age of the animal, and rapidity and manner of "administration" of the toxin). Regardless, it should be understood that intake of any amount of a significantly toxic plant should be avoided; human (or animal) responsiveness to a given amount of toxin may vary from individual to individual and even within the life span of one individual.

4. *Which part or parts of a plant might be poisonous?* This varies substantially. In certain plants, such as mountain laurel (*Kalmia*), jimson weed (*Datura*), monkshood (*Aconitum*), and oleander (*Nerium*), the entire plant is to be considered dangerous, even perhaps the nectar of the flowers. In other species, localization of the toxin in specific portions of the plant is encountered. In water hemlock (*Cicuta*), the roots and lower portions of the stems are toxic. In poison hemlock (*Conium*), the roots are the least toxic part, and toxin appears to accumulate in the stem, leaves, and fruits (seeds). In the yew (*Taxus*), greatest concentrations are found in the foliage and the seed (but not in the fruitlike covering of the seed). In precatory bean (*Abrus*) and castor bean (*Ricinus*), the seeds are decidedly the most toxic part. In rhubarb (*Rheum*), it is the leaf that is toxic, but not all of the leaf; just the blade is toxic, not the leaf stalk. In nightshades (*Solanum*), the fruit (especially if unripe) is the deadliest component; however, in their relative the tomato

Figure 9–2 *Lycopersicon esculentum.*
Tomato

(*Lycopersicon*), the fruit is generally nontoxic, but the "green parts" (that is, the vines) are. In the peach and apricot (*Prunus*), toxin is confined within the stone of the fruit. In marijuana (*Cannabis*), the female flowers contain the greatest

Figure 9–3 *Cannabis sativa.* Marijuana, hemp

concentration of toxic resin, although other parts of the plant may be considered poisonous as well. Hence, the poisonous (or most poisonous) parts (structures) of plants must be learned essentially on a case-by-case (species-by-species) basis.

5. *Do toxins exhibit a botanical relationship?* If one is dealing with a flowering plant family (as in Chapter 8) containing poisonous representatives, should toxicity be expected from all members of that family? The answer to this question is no; in none of the major toxic families are all representatives of that family poisonous. In fact, in some of these families only a relatively few members are thought to be toxic. In essence, there is no way to ascertain which members of a given family are poisonous except to learn the toxic representatives, case by case.

Of those members of a given family that are toxic, is the same or a similar poisonous substance to be expected among them? In certain families, all (or at least the decided majority) of the toxic representatives seemingly contain a similar or identical toxic substance; for example, toxic members of the rose family contain cyanide (a component of the compound amygdalin, or a very similar substance, occurring among members of the genus *Prunus* such as cherries, peach, and apricot), and a number of poisonous representatives of the heath family uniformly possess the toxic resinoid andromedotoxin (also known as grayanotoxin). In the nightshade family, however, although the various toxic members contain, broadly speaking, alkaloidal substances, at least three distinct types of toxic alkaloids are to be found in the family: tropane type,

Figure 9–4 *Prunus persica.* Peach

found in *Atropa*; nicotine type, found in *Nicotiana*; and a steroidal type, occurring in *Solanum* (see Chapter 3).   In yet other families, even more distinct types of toxic substances are to be found, comparing one member of the family with another.   For example, in the carrot family, poison hemlock (*Conium*) contains a simple poisonous alkaloid, and water hemlock (*Cicuta*) contains an entirely unrelated poisonous substance, a long-chain toxic alcohol.   Among legumes (members of the legume family), precatory bean (*Abrus*) contains a toxic protein, but lupines (*Lupinus*) and false indigo (*Baptisia*) possess a poisonous alkaloidal substance.   In summary, thus, it is not necessarily possible to generalize about the nature of the toxic principle in a given family of flowering plants.

6. *Does the toxic nature of a poisonous plant change with time, that is, with the age of a plant?*   Indeed, it can!   Nightshades (*Solanum*) are known to increase in toxicity as the season progresses (accumulating toxic alkaloid in the unripe fruit). Marijuana plants (*Cannabis*) likewise may build up toxicity as they age.   In larkspurs (*Delphinium*), however, young growth (fresh foliage) is most poisonous, the plants becoming somewhat less toxic later in the season.   Cockleburs (*Xanthium*) are

Figure 9–5 *Delphinium.* Larkspur

considered to be poisonous only in the seed and seedling stage, the adult plant becoming nontoxic. The toxicity of the opium poppy (*Papaver*) often varies daily, with greatest concentrations of milky latex (opium) being produced in the morning. By contrast, the resin in poison ivy (*Rhus*) is active throughout the day and throughout the season, even after the leaves have fallen; both fresh and apparently dry specimens of poison ivy should be avoided by individuals susceptible to poison ivy allergy.

7. *Are different kinds of animals affected the same way by a given poisonous plant?* Certainly not in all cases. Insects (and perhaps invertebrate animals in general) are often not affected by chemicals having a deleterious effect on mammals, birds, and other vertebrate animals. The larvae (caterpillars) of monarch butterflies feed on certain species of milkweed (*Asclepias*) and accumulate cardiac glycosides from the milkweeds, these compounds being subsequently passed on to the adult butterfly. Although there is no apparent harm to the butterfly, birds such as bluejays, feeding on the adult monarchs, are sensitive to the glycosides and become rapidly ill (as evidenced by emesis). Bluejays soon learn to avoid the monarchs (and their nontoxic mimics, viceroy butterflies, which derive a benefit from their resemblance to monarchs). The milkweed–monarch–viceroy–bluejay story (admirably told by L. P. Brower, *Scientific American*, February, 1969, pp. 2–9) is indicative not only of the difference in the effect of a given plant toxin on different kinds of animals, but also of the potentially complex ecochemical interactions of various organisms in nature. Such nonnutritional effects of compounds produced by one organism upon another organism are part of a broad spectrum of biochemical phenomena occurring in the environment known as allelochemical interactions.

A simpler example of the differential effect of plant toxins on animals is that of the commercial rat poison known as red squill, prepared from bulbs of Mediterranean (red) squill (*Urginea maritima*, = *Scilla* of some authors), a member of the lily family. If consumed by human beings, red squill (which contains cardiac glycosides) affects the vomiting reflex in the brain, resulting in rapid emesis (and thereby serious poisoning does not usually occur). However, rats cannot vomit, and as a consequence of the inability to eliminate ingested squill in this way, the cardioactive substances become absorbed into the bloodstream and take their toll on the rat's cardiovascular system. This difference in the effect of red squill on animals having the capability to vomit and those that do not was the basis for the selection of red squill for use as a rodenticide.

8. *Will a given poisonous plant always affect a human being in the same way?* As indicated elsewhere in the book, a particular plant toxin may have multiple effects in the body, involving a variety of symptoms; and, often, not all symptoms will be observed in a given case of poisoning. Poisoning by the ergot fungus (*Claviceps*), ergotism, can be manifested in several ways, including a tingling or perhaps a burning sensation, hallucinations, convulsions, decrease of cranial capillary pressure (that is, actual relief of headache), abortion, and even possible gangrene (dry

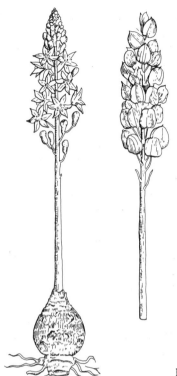

Figure 9–6 *Urginea (Scilla).* Squill

gangrene) of the extremities. Whether or not all symptoms are eventually experienced depends on the amount of ergot consumed, the time period over which it is consumed, and the susceptibility of the subject to the ergot toxins. The effects of a number of poisonous plants are at least somewhat unpredictable. This is true, for example, of jimson weed (*Datura*) in which the symptoms of poisoning are quite variable (hallucinations, drowsiness, coma, thirst, delerium, rapid heartbeat, mydriasis, bladder distension, and so on), as is the time interval in which the symptoms occur and the dose required to produce them; the unpredictability of the effects of jimson weed makes it a very dangerous plant to experiment with as a potential hallucinogenic agent. On the other hand, the effects of poisoning by other kinds of plants are more uniform and predictable; poison hemlock toxicosis is characterized by a dulling paralysis progressing from the legs upward to the respiratory muscles (diaphragm); poisoning from poison hemlock is very similar to that resulting from a nicotine overdose.

9. *Why are some plants poisonous, while others are not?* It is clear that the majority of plants in the world are not actually poisonous, and yet they survive as well perhaps as those that are. So, of what benefit is it for a given plant to be poisonous? Such a question could possibly be precisely answered in the context of the ecology of that particular species; that is, what is its special ecochemistry, what are its predators, are the predators affected by the plant's chemicals, and so on? The "answer" might simply turn out to be that there is no special reason that can be pinpointed for a plant's toxicity other than that the particular toxic compounds evolved as accidents of metabolism and result in no special harm or benefit to the plant (and hence are not likely to be either favored or eliminated by natural selection). However, speaking very generally, the toxic nature of many plants could be viewed as a survival mechanism; that is, if an animal is fatally poisoned by a plant belonging to a particular species, that animal will, of course, not eat any other individuals of that species (or of any other species, for that matter); also, animals may learn to avoid certain poisonous species. Hence, survival chances for a toxic plant species as a whole may be enhanced. There is no question that toxins (or, more broadly speaking, allelochemicals) present in a plant frequently help prevent "over-grazing" by insect (and other) predators; nicotine (from tobacco) and pyrethrin (obtained from a species of *Chrysanthemum*) are known to be potent insecticides, and there are a number of other such examples. Nonetheless, if plant toxicity is viewed as a survival adaptation of the plant, it is simply one of many. Toxicity may impart no greater survival potential (chance of survival) to a species than the presence of thorns or spines, or truly effective pollination mechanisms, or highly adaptive fruit/seed dispersal. It is the holism of all a plant's adaptations and its environment that determines its survival chances. Thus, as is often the case, "why" is an easy question to ask, but not necessarily an easy one to answer.

   10. *Where can information on poisonous plants be obtained?* In this writer's opinion, still the best general, albeit technical, reference on poisonous plants of North America is John Kingsbury's *Poisonous Plants of the United States and Canada*, published in 1964 by Prentice-Hall, Inc. However, many other publications, too numerous to list here, are available. Special attention as quick references (providing some insight into plants involved in poisoning, symptoms and treatment) might be accorded the following several book or journal publications: (1) *Handbook of Common Poisonings in Children*, HEW Publication No. (FDA) 76-7004; (2) "Common Poisonous Plants," published in *Family Safety*, Spring 1979, pp. 18–19; (3) "Plant-ingestion Poisoning from A to Z," published in *Patient Care*, June 30, 1979, beginning on p. 86; and (4) "The Peril in Plants" and "Poisonous Plants and What to Do about Them," both articles published together in *Emergency Medicine*, May 1970. Additionally, larger hospitals in major North American cities often have Poison Control Centers that will readily provide information upon request. Information on cases of poisoning is commonly funneled from these centers to the National Clearinghouse for Poison Control Centers, located in Washington, D.C.; case history information on toxic plants and other materials or substances commonly involved in human poisonings accumulates in this way. Certified regional poison control centers are listed in *Drug Topics Redbook* (1988, and probably years to come), the Annual Pharmacist's Reference.

SELECTED REFERENCES

ARENA, JAY M. (editor) Richard H. Drew (assoc. ed.). 1986. *Poisoning—Toxicology, Symptoms, Treatments*, 5th ed. Charles C Thomas, Publisher, Springfield, Ill. An excellent general reference on questions relating to toxicology; pages 719 to 727 summarize a considerable amount of information on symptoms and treatment of poisoning by plants.

HARBORNE, J. B. 1982. *Introduction to Ecological Biochemistry*, 2nd ed. Academic Press, London. Although technical, this book is must reading for anyone interested in the chemicals present in organisms that might affect or influence other organisms; a wealth of such information is presented, in ecological context; pertinent to questions 7 and 9 of my chapter, see especially Harborne's Chapter 3, "Plant Toxins and Their Effects on Animals."

KEELER, R. F., AND A. T. TU. (eds.). 1983. *Handbook of Natural Toxins*: Volume 1— *Plant and Fungal Toxins*. Marcel Dekker, Inc., New York. Chapter 20, "The Evolutionary and Ecological Significance of Plant Toxins," by John Kingsbury, discusses the possibilities of the origins of secondary compounds as evolutionary accidents or waste, and the certain role of many of these compounds in defense against predation by herbivores.

KINGSBURY, JOHN M. 1964. *Poisonous Plants of the United States and Canada*. Prentice-Hall, Inc., Englewood Cliffs, N.J. As indicated under question 10 of this chapter, still probably the best compendium of information on poisonous plants available.

———. 1965. (paperback edition, 1972). *Deadly Harvest*. Holt, Rinehart and Winston, New York. Addresses, one way or another, several of the questions posed in this chapter, including, in Chapter 1, the definition of a poisonous plant; entertaining reading presented in a nontechnical manner.

See also specific informational references referred to as a part of question 10, this chapter.

Potential Toxicants
in Common Plant Foods

Are there potential toxins in or associated with common plant foods? Perhaps surprisingly, there are indeed. In *Deadly Harvest* (1965), John Kingsbury makes the point that we perhaps worry too much about artificial additives in the foods we eat (admittedly a debatable issue), and not enough about potentially harmful natural chemicals contained in these foods. At least to an extent, this point is well taken. However, if food plants are toxic, it is often a part other than that customarily eaten that contains the poisonous substance. In other cases, the toxic substance may be present in the edible parts, but in such low levels as to cause no harm if these parts are consumed in reasonable quantities. Regardless, it is a good idea to be aware of the potential toxicity associated with certain plant foods and products. An itemization of some of the more significant of these is as follows.

Pits (stones) and/or seeds of peaches, cherries, apricots, almonds, apples, and certain other members of the rose family contain amygdalin, a substance (type of glycoside) that will release cyanide during the process of human or animal digestion. As discussed in Chapters 3 and 11, cyanide is a potent respiratory inhibitor. Kingsbury (*Deadly Harvest*) alludes to a case of human death from eating a cupful of apple seeds. Ground apricot pits are the commercial source of laetrile (trade name for amygdalin), of alleged (not proven) use in cancer chemotherapy. Laetrile is generally illegal in the United States, and yet in a sense is available in the produce section of the grocery store. In addition to members of the rose family, tropical lima beans (legume family) may also contain a cyanide-releasing substance (linamarin) in potentially unhealthy amounts. Shipments of such beans are now federally tested for cyanide content. Actually, a perhaps surprising number of potential food plants may contain cyanogenic compounds (see the articles by Eric Conn in *Toxicants Occurring Naturally in Foods* and by J. E.

Figure 10–1 *Malus sylvestris.* Apple

Poulton in Keeler and Tu, selected references, for a more comprehensive survey of plants containing cyanogenic glycosides).

Beans (legumes) are probably better known for another category of potentially harmful chemical, proteins (some are carbohydrate-containing proteins or glycoproteins) known as hemagglutinins or lectins. Discussed in Chapter 3, these are large seed protein molecules that can bind to cell surfaces and, in the case of red blood cells, cause agglutination or clumping. Experimentally (mostly using rats), certain of these lectins have been demonstrated to have antinutritional effects, at least in part through interference with intestinal absorption (by their adsorption to cells lining the intestine), suppressing growth and even resulting in death. Soybeans and kidney beans are among those legume products showing the most potent bean agglutinins. However, as proteins, these lectins are heat labile, and their precise molecular architecture and activity are destroyed by normal cooking. Edible beans thus are a potential hazard only if eaten raw.

Beans have also been associated, as is doubtless well known, with the generation of flatulence (flatus formation), probably more of a social than a clinical

Figure 10–2 *Phaseolus*. Bean

problem. However, if anyone doubted the connection between beans and flatulence, it has been demonstrated clinically in human beings (see page 488, *Toxicants Occurring Naturally in Foods*, selected references). Although the majority of gastrointestinal gas may come from swallowed air, diets rich in various types of beans cause significant increase in the quantity of gas produced, as well as changes in gas composition (for example, gas resulting from bean intake is generally richer in methane than under normal circumstances). Boston baked beans, pork and beans, and especially green lima beans proved to be effective in increasing gas volume and/or methane content, although several other types of beans could be expected to have similar effects. The effectiveness of beans in generating flatus is apparently the synergism between types of intestinal gas-forming bacteria (especially anaerobic bacteria) and the special mixture of sugars (oligosaccharides such as raffinose and stachyose) present in the beans.

  Also potentially causing digestive upset are various mustards (members of the mustard family). Edible, commercially available representatives of the family include cabbage, turnips, rutabaga, horseradish, and the mustards themselves (for example, black, white, and brown mustard). A number of mustards (including all the preceding) contain mustard-oil glycosides (glucosinolates). Glucosinolates, although often inactive as intact molecules, are hydrolyzed rather rapidly (in the oral cavity) during digestion to release glucose, sulfate ions, and mustard oils (thiocyanates or isothiocyanates). The sulfur-containing mustard oils (accounting for the pungent taste of mustards, for example, horseradish) can be severe irritants and vesicants of the lining of the digestive tract. Concentrations of mustard-oil glycosides in wild mustard (*Brassica*) seed may be such as to cause (if consumed in quantity) severe gastric irritation, colic, and even death in cattle. Eaten only as condiments (that is, in small quantities), commercial mustards and horseradish cause little trouble and add to the flavor and even the nutritional value of food.

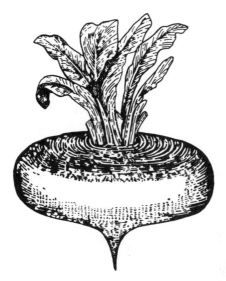

Figure 10–3 *Brassica rapa.* Turnip

Compounds also found in some members of the mustard family (for example, cabbage, turnips, kale, and rutabaga) very closely related to the mustard oils are the goitrins. These are appropriately named because they may contribute to an enlargement of the thyroid gland (goiter). This is likely to be a problem only if cabbage, turnips, or other mustards containing goitrin constitute a substantial part of the diet, and then only if the diet is deficient in iodine. Goitrins interfere with iodine uptake by the thyroid gland and consequently with production of the thyroid hormone; thyroid enlargement is the expected result. If a person uses salt on foods, then a simple measure that will in all likelihood prevent the onset of goiter is selection of iodinized salt for use as table salt.

Figure 10–4 *Brassica oleracea.* var. *capitata.* Cabbage

Sulfur-containing compounds, somewhat similar to the mustard oils, are to be found in garlic and onions (which belong to the lily, not the mustard, family). These oils are responsible for the flavor, odor, and (in the case of onions) the lacrimatory properties of the bulbs when cut. Once thought to contribute to conditions of anemia, these substances are now recognized as being largely beneficial. There is substantial evidence that compounds accounting for the smell of onions and garlic act as mild but effective anticoagulants or antithrombotics in the bloodstream. Hence, the very old notion that garlic benefits the heart and circulation (traceable to the medicine of ancient Egypt) appears to have merit (see "The Chemistry of Garlic and Onions," by Eric Block selected references). Stems of another member of the lily family, asparagus, are suspected of causing contact dermatitis; berries of aspar-

Figure 10–5 *Asparagus officinalis.*
Asparagus

agus are thought to have caused internal poisoning in animals, although precise details are lacking. The potential toxicity of older asparagus plants (so-called "asparagus fern") should be investigated.

Some plants contain compounds affecting blood pressure (vasoactive compounds). Substances (in this case, types of amines) capable of substantially raising blood pressure (if injected) are of special interest. Examples of such hypertensive amines are tyramine, dopamine, and norepinephrine (all phenethylamine derivatives). All three amines listed are commonly found in bananas, but, fortunately, mostly in the peels, and not the edible pulp. Lower concentrations of vasoactive amines are found in tomatoes, among other plants. Usually, intake of such amines orally, at least in average quantities, does not present a problem, as they are detoxified (deaminated) by the body prior to any potential hypertensive effect.

Although tomatoes (*Lycopersicon esculentum*) may have low concentrations of amines potentially altering blood pressure, they are perhaps better known for their possible alkaloid (glycoalkaloid) content. This solanine-type (steroidal) alkaloid (see Chapter 3) may cause acute digestive upset (vomiting, diarrhea, and so on) and/or nervous disorders, including trembling and weakness, paralysis, coma, and even death. Little or no solanine is present in the ripe tomato fruit. Small but usually inconsequential amounts are to be expected in green tomatoes; the eating of these typically results in no more than a slight belly-ache. On the other hand, the green vines of tomato can have a much higher alkaloid content and are potentially dangerous if consumed. Farm animals are occasionally poisoned as a consequence of the tossing of tomato vines "over the fence" from the garden. Irish potatoes (*Solanum tuberosum*) contain similar or identical toxic alkaloidal substances (that is, solanine, named, obviously, after *Solanum*). A fresh weight of 20 mg of solanine per 100 g of plant material borders on the danger level. Market potatoes usually have only 3 to 6 mg/100 g and are not dangerous at all unless

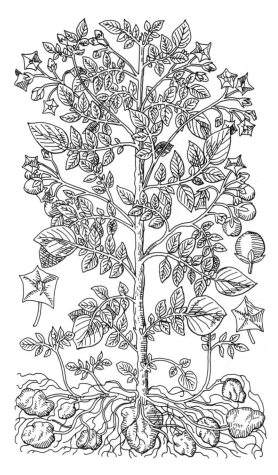

Figure 10–6 *Solanum tuberosum.* Irish potato

consumed in unbelievable quantity. However, small, greening, unpeeled tubers may have much higher levels of solanine (80 to 100 mg/100 gm) and do pose a potential health hazard; cases of human illness, and even death, from eating such potatoes have been recorded. The vines of potatoes are dangerous, in a manner similar to tomato vines. The article by Whitaker and Feeney (cited under *Toxicants Occurring Naturally in Foods*, selected references) provides useful information about the potential toxicity of Irish potatoes.

A variety of plants contains a simple organic acid (oxalic acid) or soluble (sodium or potassium) salts of this acid (soluble oxalates). Oxalic acid or soluble oxalates ingested in quantity cause blood ionic imbalance (by reaction with serum calcium), problems in proper clotting action of the blood, and potential kidney damage (and failure) as the result of accumulation of the solid (calcium) salt of oxalic acid. Food and beverage plants or products containing soluble oxalates include spinach, chard, beets, rhubarb, cocoa, and tea. These plants, or at least the parts or products consumed, generally contain levels of oxalate (usually less than 2 percent of plant weight) well below the danger level if average quantities are ingested. However, substantially higher levels (as much as 12 percent) are occasionally encountered in beet leaves (beet "tops"), which are known to have caused loss of life of livestock. In rhubarb, the leaf blade (generally not eaten) may have much

Figure 10–7 *Beta vulgaris.* Beet

Figure 10–8 *Capsicum.* Chili pepper

higher (dangerous) levels of oxalate than the harmless leaf stalks, in which a different, nontoxic, and tangy-tasting acid (malic acid) predominates. Human death (as in England during World War I, in an effort to conserve food) has been the consequence of consumption of rhubarb leaf blades.

Red peppers or chili peppers (the elongated berry of *Capsicum* spp.), used to spice food in Mexican cooking, are important in the tropics as a source of vitamin C and in the preservation of food (in the absence of refrigeration). Chili peppers contain the irritant resinoid (actually an amide), capsaicin, which can be detected by taste in any concentrations exceeding one part per million (of water). Acting on the pain receptors in the mouth, capsaicin can trigger the autonomic nervous system responses of both salivation and sweating, as well as digestive upset (gastric flow).

There is sketchy evidence that consumption of cultivated lettuce that has bolted, or gone to seed (developing milky latex at this stage), may affect the nervous system adversely (so-called "lettuce opium poisoning"). A similar syndrome has been observed in cattle feeding on wild lettuce in quantity.

True opium is the whitish latex obtained from green (unripe) capsules of the opium poppy (*Papaver somniferum*). Certain of the opium alkaloids (for example, morphine) are well known for their depressant, narcotic effect on the central nervous system (see Chapter 13). Interestingly, poppy seeds (containing no more than traces of alkaloid and having little or no effect on the nervous system), obtained from the mature (dry, brownish) capsules of *Papaver somniferum*, are commonly used in flavoring bakery goods (for example, poppy-seed rolls); poppy-seed oil is occasionally used in cooking.

Of unquestioned potential effect on the nervous system are nutmeg and mace. Nutmeg is the grated seed of the tropical tree *Myristica fragrans*, and mace is the ground aril of this seed; both are used as spices and condiments. Volatile oils from nutmeg and mace, in overdose, are intoxicant and potentially hallucinogenic. Large doses (for example, the equivalent of two whole nutmegs) are required to produce narcotic effects, and side effects are reputedly quite unpleasant, even severe.

In the baling of cotton (*Gossypium*), large quantities of cotton seed are produced as a by-product. Cotton-seed meal has found use as a feed for livestock, as a flour or extender for human consumption (especially in underdeveloped countries), and in the production of cotton-seed oil, used in cooking. There is only one problem. If un-

Figure 10–9 *Gossypium*. Cotton

treated, cotton seed is often poisonous. Roots, stems, and seeds of cotton plants may contain significant levels of gossypol, a phenolic substance produced by internal glands in the cotton plant. Gossypol is toxic and cumulatively may cause anorexia and weight loss, diarrhea, circulatory problems and buildup of edematous fluids, hair discoloration, and reduced sperm counts (in terms of viable, motile sperm). In spite of potential hazardous side effects, the fact that gossypol blocks or decreases spermatogenesis has led to serious investigation of this compound as a male contraceptive (see T. H. Maugh, "Male 'Pill' Blocks Sperm Enzyme," selected references). Because gossypol is a toxin, the level of free gossypol in cotton-seed products intended for consumption is now regulated.

It would be assumed that peanut meal is harmless, and it is unless allowed to become moldy. Strains of two species of black mold (*Aspergillus flavus* and *A. parasiticus*) that attack storage grains produce a phenolic toxin known as aflatoxin (named after *Aspergillus flavus*). In southern and eastern England, in 1960, 100,000 young turkeys died as a consequence of consumption of peanut meal contaminated with aflatoxin. The disease, then called "turkey X disease," is characterized by acute liver degeneration. Aflatoxin, a type of coumarin (furanocoumarin), is now considered to be one of the most (if not the most) potent liver carcinogens known to science, possibly affecting all grades of livestock as well as human beings. The aflatoxin-producing molds actually infect a variety of grains, including wheat, barley, rice, sorghum, and corn. Although it is possible (but not easy) to detoxify grain containing this type of coumarin substance, the best solution is prevention, that is, employment of grain-storage practices designed to prevent the development of moldy conditions (see Chapter 5).

Compounds related to coumarins, furans, are known to be produced under certain stress conditions, especially moldiness, by sweet potato (*Ipomoea batatus*) roots. Although liver-toxic compounds may be isolated from molded sweet potatoes, the most significant furan (in terms of disease) apt to be present causes a severe pulmonary disorder (lung toxicosis), resembling a type of pneumonia, in cattle; this was well documented by an outbreak in the southeastern United States in 1969 (see Wilson and Burka in Keeler and Tu, selected references).

What about honey (nectar regurgitated by honey bees and other bees)? Surely one could be sure that honey is safe. After all, honey is not only valued as a food, but is often prescribed in various accounts of folk medicine as being a substance that, if consumed, will help secure the path to holistic health. Unfortunately, poison honey, especially in the Appalachian region of the United States, is not all that uncommon. There, in the foothills and the mountains, shrubs belonging to the heath family (especially mountain laurel, rhododendrons, and azaleas) are common in the forest understory. All parts of these plants (including the floral nectar) are toxic (containing the resinoid andromedotoxin, mentioned in Chapter 9). Andromedotoxin can cause serious nervous system dysfunction, altered blood pressure and heart rate, and perhaps death. So, what is to stop bees (which are not affected by andromedotoxin) from feeding on these heath-shrub flowers before returning to the hive? The answer is, nothing, unless, through good bee-keeping practices, the bees are initially trained to other more appropriate nectar sources (such as a field of planted buckwheat). There are apparently no formal testing programs to screen out potentially toxic honey.

The question of food allergy is a topic related to food toxicity and should be given brief comment before concluding the chapter. As discussed by Werner Jaffe in *Toxicants Occurring Naturally in Foods*, selected references, allergy is a common phenomenon; estimates exist that roughly 20 percent of American schoolchildren suffer some kind of allergy. Foodstuffs associated with allergy include a variety of animal and plant products; frequently included in the list are grains, milk, eggs, fish, crustaceans, tomatoes, strawberries, nuts, and chocolate. The topic of allergenic foods is important and could well stand the light of further investigation, since the exact nature of the allergen(s) present in most foods remains unknown. However, as Jaffe points out, these allergens are probably proteins, and the allergic response is probably triggered by a specific type of antibody in sensitive individuals.

Related to food allergy is a syndrome known as celiac disease, a condition in which an abnormal sensitivity to a food protein (specifically, gluten from wheat, barley, or rye flour) occurs. In celiac disease, the enzyme reacting with gluten in

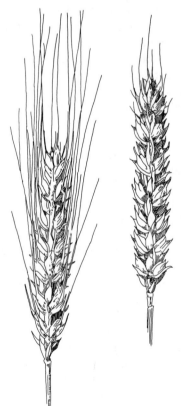

Figure 10–10 *Triticum.* Wheat

the intestine may be deficient in sensitive individuals (in addition to the article by Jaffe just cited, see Roy Hartenstein, *Human Anatomy and Physiology*, Van Nostrand Reinhold, New York, 1976, p. 411). The intestinal mucosa develops histological abnormalities in response to gluten, absorption is impaired, and malnutrition and abnormal stool are consequences. A gluten-free diet is typically essential to the patient's recovery, although other measures and complications may be involved. The entire spectrum of the topic of food allergies and comparable syndromes is significant and complicated, and is clearly deserving of more scientific research than in the past.

We should close this chapter by emphasizing that the standard plant foods, available from the garden, farm, or, secondarily, the grocery store, represent nothing that one should fear (unless specific allergies are known to exist in sensitive individuals); to the contrary, they are really the basis for the sustenance of the human race. However, there is potential benefit from the development of an awareness of potential health hazards in or associated with such foods; in part at least, that is what this chapter has attempted to accomplish.

SELECTED REFERENCES

BLOCK, ERIC. 1985. The Chemistry of Garlic and Onions. *Scientific American* 252(3): 114–119. An interesting account of the fact that the centuries-old belief in the efficacy of garlic and onions for the heart and circulation has indeed a real chemical basis.

COMMITTEE ON FOOD PROTECTION. 1973. *Toxicants Occurring Naturally in Foods.* National Academy of Sciences, Washington, D.C. Excellent, scientific coverage of a number of topics concerning potentially poisonous substances in foods; see particularly the following chapters: "Toxic Proteins and Peptides," by Werner Jaffe; "Some Vaso- and Psychoactive Substances in Food...," by Walter Lovenberg; "Natural Sulfur Compounds," by C. H. VanEtten and I. A. Wolff; "Cyanogenetic Glycosides," by Eric Conn; "Oxalates," by David W. Fassett; "Plant Phenolics," by V. L. Singleton and F. H. Kratzer; "Enzyme Inhibitors in Foods," by J. R. Whitaker and R. E. Feeney; "Toxicants Occurring Naturally in Spices and Flavors," by Richard Hall; and "Problems Associated with Particular Foods," by V. N. Patwardhan and J. W. White, Jr.

KEELER, R. F., AND A. T. TU (eds.) 1983. *Handbook of Natural Toxins*: Volume 1—*Plant and Fungal Toxins.* Marcel Dekker, Inc., New York. See especially Chapter 1, "Sweet Potato Toxins and Related Toxic Furans," by B. J. Wilson and L. T. Burka, and Chapter 4, "Cyanogenic Compounds in Plants and Their Toxic Effects," by J. E. Poulton.

KINGSBURY, JOHN M. 1965 (paperback edition, 1972). *Deadly Harvest.* Holt, Rinehart and Winston, New York. Pages 22–25 deal with the topic of "poisons and food."

LIENER, IRVIN E. 1984. "Natural Toxins in Plant Foods," pp. 113–114 in *Nutrition and Health*, Vol. 3, AB Academic Publishers, Great Britain. Brief but useful overview of potential toxins in plant foods, including tropical produce; a valuable list of references is provided.

MAUGH, THOMAS H., II. 1981. Male "Pill" Blocks Sperm Enzyme. *Science* 212: 314. A brief discussion of clinical trials and research into the contraceptive action of cottonseed oil.

WERTHEIM, ALFRED H. 1974. *The Natural Poisons in Natural Foods*. Lyle Stuart, Inc., Secaucus, N.J. Written in a popular vein, but similar in intent of content to the National Academy book on toxicants in foods, 1973, cited previously.

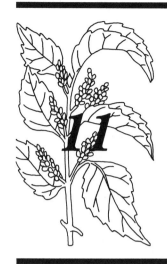

Effects of Poisonous or Harmful Plants

11

An outline of the effects of poisonous or, more broadly speaking, harmful plants on people and animals is offered in this chapter. Information on the natural chemicals generating a number of these effects is to be found in Chapter 3. The reader should bear in mind that the major categories or types of toxic effects and responses covered in the present chapter will not encompass every situation. For example, distinctions between dermatitis allergy and nonallergenic dermatitis can be particularly difficult to make, and disagreement on this topic exists in the literature. Additionally, regarding plant toxins that are internally toxic in the animal body, it is common to find that a particular plant (and its toxin), although best known for one type of effect, may in actuality have more than one effect in the body (as mentioned in Chapter 9), making categorization difficult. Nonetheless, an effort to systematize the complex topic of potentially harmful effects of plants, in a relatively simple matter, follows.

OUTLINE OF HARMFUL EFFECTS BY CATEGORY

A. Allergy

    1. Respiratory allergy

    2. Dermatitis allergy

        a. Contact dermatitis

        b. Phytophotodermatitis (photosensitivity)

B. Nonallergenic dermatitis

C. Internal poisoning
  1. Blood
  2. Nerve
  3. Muscle
  4. Digestive tract
  5. Heart
  6. Liver
  7. Kidney
  8. Enzyme
  9. Skeleton
  10. Teratogenic (birth defects)
D. Mechanical injury
  1. External
  2. Internal

The order of the following discussion is patterned after this outline. The more inclusive category of harmful (as opposed to purely toxic) effects permits broader parameters of discussion, as for example the license to include not only truly (internally) poisonous plants, but those responsible for allergy or causing mechanical injury, as well.

ALLERGY

To consider the broad category of allergy first, it should be pointed out that what is meant by allergy is that a person has (and manifests) an unusual sensitivity to an ordinarily harmless substance or material. Basic concepts in the study of allergy are that a person suffering allergy has the genetic capability of developing allergy (that is, the individual is atopic) and that a particular sensitivity developed prior to the manifestation of allergic response or symptoms of allergy. Hence, one should realize that an allergic individual had a preexisting sensitivity, and thus that allergy is in effect a preconditioned response.

The topic of allergy is often not included in discussions of poisonous and medicinal plants for various reasons, one being that allergy is not necessarily considered a serious disorder; another is the notion that normal people are not affected by allergy and that it is the exception rather than the rule. Whereas it is probably true that allergy typically is not serious (not life-threatening), it indeed can be; but even if the condition is not really serious, the level of discomfort from allergy may be substantial nonetheless. Also, it may well be the case that virtually anyone can develop a sensitivity based on repeated exposures to particular allergy-inducing materials. Since allergy commonly represents an immune reaction of the body, it is logical to speculate that a person's immune responsiveness may change with age or conditions and that sensitivities to allergenic materials or substances may increase (or decrease) with the passage of time. It is estimated that well over one-half of the present population exhibits some reactivity to plant allergens. At a minimum, allergy is a commercially significant topic, in that treatment of allergy is literally a billion dollar business annually in the United States alone.

Respiratory Allergy

A major subcategory of allergy is respiratory allergy, otherwise known as hay fever. In hay-fever allergy, the usual effect is on the nasal and, in general, the upper respiratory passages, although the lungs may be affected as well. Respiratory allergy is most typically due to windblown plant particles (microstructures). Allergenic particles and associated substances transported by the wind are generally known as aeroallergens. In the main these aeroallergenic particles are pollen and spores, especially pollen. It should be realized that, overwhelmingly, it is wind-pollinated plants that should receive attention in connection with respiratory allergy. If a plant is pollinated by insects (or other animals), its pollen would typically not be blown up into the air and transmitted to the nasal passages. Among other differences, pollen having an insect vector is sticky in comparison to pollen carried by the wind and is not readily dislodged from the anther of a flower by wind currents. Although a great many kinds of plants are insect pollinated (entomophilous), a number of major groups of plants are pollinated by the wind (anemophilous). Most of our deciduous trees, grasses, pines and other conifers, and a number of weed species are wind pollinated. However, we cannot make the assumption that all or even the majority of members of wind-pollinated groups are implicated in allergy; for example, the copious airborne pollen of most coniferous trees (evergreens) is apparently not allergenic. Spores of certain fungi, such as species of *Alternaria*, *Aspergillus* (black mold) and *Penicillium* (green mold), are also carried by the wind and may be involved in allergy (but, as with windborne pollen, one cannot generalize about the allergenicity of air-transmitted fungal spores).

    Pollen is present in the air at all times, even in the dead of winter over the middle of the ocean. But, of course, windblown pollen is much more prevalent at some times (and certain locations) than at others. In the eastern United States, there are three rather distinct seasonal pollen peaks, when concentrations of airborne pollen are much greater than at other times:

1. The midspring peak is dominated by pollen of our native deciduous trees; box elder, willow, and species of hickory are thought to cause the greatest reactivity in sensitive individuals, although a number of other species (oak, birch, sycamore, black walnut, and others) may also be involved. Cone-bearing trees (evergreens) produce windblown pollen in great abundance; however, as indicated, the pollen of most conifers is harmless (red cedar pollen, among a few others, is thought to cause some reactivity).

2. In early summer, another pollen peak is realized, due mainly to grass pollen. Although grass pollen was formerly considered highly and uniformly reactive

(essentially regardless of the species of grass in question), it is now known that certain species (for example, sweet vernal grass, orchard grass, June grass, redtop, and timothy) elicit higher levels of allergic reaction than other species.

3. The late-summer/early-fall peak occurs last. This early-fall peak is the greatest of the three peaks in quantity of airborne pollen (pollen rain) and the number of people showing reactivity. The main culprits eliciting fall pollen allergy are the ragweeds, both great (tall) and common (short) ragweed, which are different species of the genus *Ambrosia*. However, other species (not related to ragweed) are implicated as well; both lamb's quarters (*Chenopodium*), also known as goosefoot, and pigweed (*Amaranthus*) may contribute to fall allergy. Goldenrod (*Solidago*), often receiving major blame for late-summer/early-fall respiratory allergies, is predominantly (although loosely) entomophilous, and is probably at most only very occasionally and incidentally involved in hay-fever allergy.

It is logical to ask what happens when one develops respiratory allergy. To summarize, protein substances are present in the pollen grain walls; these substances leak out upon contact with a moist surface. The natural function of these recognition proteins is to identify (chemically) the stigma of flowers of the correct (same)

Figure 11–1 *Ambrosia trifida.* Great ragweed

species, thereby helping to ensure the integrity of interbreeding and continuance of that particular species. However, when allergenic pollen is inhaled, the recognition proteins leak out in the mucous lining of the nasal passages, often eliciting an immune response. The body recognizes these (actually harmless) substances as invaders (much as if they were harmful bacteria or viruses). Antibodies are produced by a particular kind of white blood cell (specifically, a type of lymphocyte) to counteract these foreign "antigens." Subsequent (future) inhalings may result in antibody attack of (reactions with) the plant antigen; histamine is released as a by-product of this reaction, and nasal secretion is increased. Inflammation (perhaps due to substances produced by types of white blood cells) and swelling may occur. Rhinitis, or irritation of the nasal passages, is the result. Rhinitis is generally not serious, but may become so in persons suffering asthma; in this case, the irritation may serve to trigger an asthmatic attack. Why some species of wind-pollinated plants (like the ragweeds) cause allergy and others (like cattails) do not is somewhat of a mystery, but may relate to minor but specific differences in the makeup of the recognition protein (antigen) molecules. Over-the-counter antihistamines are commonly used to control the symptoms of mild to moderate cases of allergic rhinitis.

Allergenic Dermatitis

Contact dermatitis.   The next broad category of allergy to be considered is that of dermatitis allergy, or allergic skin rash. The simplest category of allergenic dermatitis to explain is that of contact dermatitis. In contact dermatitis, a substance (allergen) is transferred directly from the plant surface to the skin, resulting in a delayed allergic reaction. The classic example of simple contact dermatitis is that induced by poison ivy (*Rhus radicans*). The allergenic substance in poison ivy is a resin known as urushiol. A phenolic type of molecule (actually a type of catechol), urushiol is chemically similar to lacquer. It is nonvolatile and readily bonded to the skin (cross-linked to proteins in the skin); hence, washing with warm, soapy water as soon as possible is probably in order if the plant is known to have been contacted. It should be pointed out, however, that some are of the opinion that washing, especially if not done thoroughly, may actually spread the urshiol around to parts of the body not contacted. Regardless, there is no question that urushiol can be spread by rubbing (especially scratching) other parts of the body if hand contact was made with poison ivy or with areas of the body where the allergen was already present.

Evidence exists that urushiol is absorbed by the skin; however, there is little or no evidence that it is spread significantly in the bloodstream to other areas of the body and/or that the immune response (resulting in the rash) is triggered on areas of the skin that have not contacted the toxin in one way or another.

Typically, it is one or two days before the skin reaction to the *Rhus* catechols will appear. This delayed hypersensitivity in susceptible individuals is brought about by the reaction of components of the body's immune system to the combined plant catechols and skin proteins (that is, to the complete antigen). The reaction is cell-mediated (by types of lymphocytes) and does not involve antibodies. Fluid-filled blisters will appear in a matter of another day or so. Poison ivy rash is possibly further spread by scratching blisters; these vesiculations, although containing mostly serum produced by the body, may still have some catechol present. Poison ivy dermatitis is usually self-limiting within one to two weeks. Treatment with topical cortisone compounds is often prescribed to relieve itching. On a yearly basis, potentially tens of millions of people are affected, at least to a degree, with poison ivy rash. Repeated exposure to poison ivy is known to increase the likelihood of developing a sensitivity (that is, to increase allergy potential).

A number of other kinds of plants can cause contact dermatitis allergy. For example, certain members of the sunflower family (belonging in particular to one tribe of the family, including sagebrush, mugwort, chamomile, and chrysanthemum) contain a different type of compound (sesquiterpene lactones) that can result in allergenic alterations (darkening) of the skin. Additionally, several unrelated plants, such as tree-of-heaven (*Ailanthus*) and trumpet vine (*Campsis*), are suspected of causing dermatitis (in these latter two examples, the rash is similar to that induced by poison ivy); tree-of-heaven and trumpet vine should be investigated further in connection with dermatitis.

Phytophotodermatitis.   A second and more complicated category of allergenic dermatitis is that of phytophotodermatitis (or photosensitization of the skin by plants). In this type of reaction, it is difficult to separate allergenic and nonallergenic aspects. Regardless, at least three components are involved in this type of reaction. In addition to the skin and a substance from the plant, sunlight (especially ultraviolet radiation) comes into play.

Several members of the carrot family (for example, wild parsnip, *Pastinaca*) contain psoralens (technically, furanocoumarin molecules—see Chapter 3), which may be directly (externally) transferred to the skin and increase the sensitivity of the skin to ultraviolet radiation. This allergic reaction, although perhaps involving a rash, is more burnlike than that caused by poison ivy and may last for a longer period of time. The reaction is sometimes referred to as false or artificial sunburn.

In more complicated examples of photodermatitis, as that involving St. John's wort (*Hypericum perforatum*), the plant is consumed, and the photosensitizing chemical (a type of phenolic molecule) is absorbed from the digestive tract into the bloodstream and distributed to tiny blood vessels present in the skin (once again increasing sensitivity to sunlight). Certain types of fair-skinned sheep are particularly sensitive to St. John's wort. Sensitive sheep, which have eaten a quantity of St. John's wort, develop burns and swellings in exposed, pale-skinned areas of the body, particularly the face (the bighead condition). Buckwheat (*Fagopyrum*) contains a type of photosensitizing pigment similar to that of St. John's wort.

In still other cases of hyperphotosensitivity, an excess of chlorophyll in the diet of an animal may result in an overload to the liver, which does not screen out all the light-absorbing pigment (phylloerythrin) from the bloodstream (also, a damaged liver may fail to screen out the usual amount of light-absorbing pigment);

Figure 11–2 *Hypericum.* St. John's wort

the light-trapping compound once again is distributed via the circulatory system to the skin's capillary beds (increasing susceptibility to ultraviolet radiation burns).

Photodermatitis is placed under allergenic, rather than nonallergenic dermatitis, in part because of the considerable variation among animals in their light sensitivity induced by light-absorbing molecules transferred from plants.

NONALLERGENIC DERMATITIS

Finally, under dermatitis, the category tentatively labeled as nonallergenic dermatitis (that is, potentially affecting everyone or a wide variety of animals, as the case may be) should be considered. However, even in these instances in which allergy is allegedly not involved, some people (or certain types of animals) are clearly more reactive than others to the plant materials and substances in question. Perhaps it is better to hedge the bet and simply call this category "irritant dermatitis." Included here would be the plants that transfer toxic substances to animals by means of stinging hairs, including stinging nettle (*Urtica dioica*), wood nettle (*Laportea canadensis*), and tread-softly *Cnidoscolus stimulosus*). Toxins (a variety may be involved) from these plants are injected into the skin of the subject upon contact. Also fitting in the category of irritant

Figure 11–3 *Urtica dioica*. Stinging nettle

dermatitis are the burns caused by the milky latex of some members of the spurge family (for example, snow-on-the-mountain, manchineel, and wartweed). The acrid latex of snow-on-the-mountain (*Euphorbia*) is such a potent irritant that it was once used to brand cattle; that from the manchineel (*Hippomane*) is corrosive to the conjuctiva and cornea of the eye and is alleged to cause temporary blindness. During the Middle Ages, beggars applied the caustic latex of certain spurges to their skin to fake leprosy and solicit pity (and money).

INTERNAL POISONING BY PLANTS

Under this topic, discussion is restricted to plants containing chemicals that, if eaten (or injected), cause death or serious illness in human beings or animals. Indeed, discussions or coverages of poisonous plants are often limited to this category; however, such an approach seems too restrictive. Although the discussion of internal poisoning by plants is outlined by targeted organ, system, or effect, it should be reemphasized that a given toxin may have more than a single effect. For example, virtually any toxin affecting the nervous system could, thereby, potentially affect almost any other organ (system) of the body. In the following discussion, for each category of internal toxin or toxic effect, only one or a few examples are provided; the reader should realize that there are certainly more. Once again, the reader is referred to Chapter 3 for more details on the plant chemicals involved in various effects.

Blood toxins.   Seeds of *Abrus precatorius* (known variously as rosary pea, precatory bean, prayer vine, jequirity, and crab's eyes), a tropical, vining member of the legume family, possess a powerful toxin potentially affecting the blood. The hard, glossy seeds are sharply two-toned, part scarlet-red and part (about one-third) shiny black; the hilum or seed-stalk scar occurs in the black portion. The poisonous substance (protein) in the seeds of *Abrus* is one of the most powerful plant toxins known. It is estimated that one seed, if thoroughly chewed, is capable of killing an adult human being. The toxic seed protein is a severe irritant of the mucous lining of the digestive tract, causing lesions, ulceration, and bleeding. The toxin may be absorbed through the digestive tract and reach the bloodstream, where it can cause clotting, perhaps with fatal results. The attractive seeds of precatory bean were formerly employed in making rosary necklaces and even other costume jewelry. This practice is now illegal in the United States. However, *Abrus* presently occurs in the

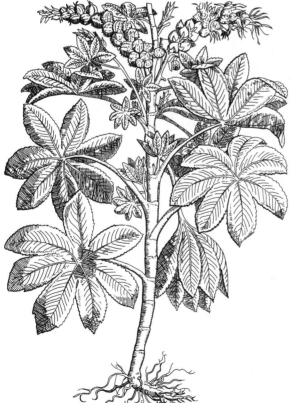

Figure 11–4 *Ricinus communis.* Castor bean

United States, having become naturalized in parts of southern Florida (for example, as a vine sometimes found in citrus groves or along fence rows).

It is interesting that certain other similar tropical vines (for example, *Rhynchosia phaseoloides*, coral berry), although perhaps harmless, have developed seeds similar in appearance to those of *Abrus precatorius*; this would seem to represent a case of mimicry among plants and an adaptation possibly enhancing survival of the mimic species. Seeds of *Rhynchosia* and *Abrus* may be distinguished, however. In *Rhynchosia*, the seed-stalk scar is in the red portion of the seed.

A toxin (ricin) quite similar to that in precatory bean is found in castor bean, *Ricinus communis*. In addition to affecting the blood (causing blood cells to stick together), kidney failure (and the failure of other organs as well) can be the ultimate consequence of castor bean poisoning (indicating the possible complex results of various toxicoses). Blood replacement and cleansing therapy has proved, in one case at least, an effective treatment for ricin poisoning (*Cleveland Plain Dealer*, August 1 and August 9, 1980).

Nerve toxins.   A wide variety of examples could be cited here, because the majority of plants with a significant alkaloid content might be expected to have some effect on the nervous system. A well-known example is thornapple or jimsonweed

Figure 11–5 *Datura*. Thornapple, jimsonweed

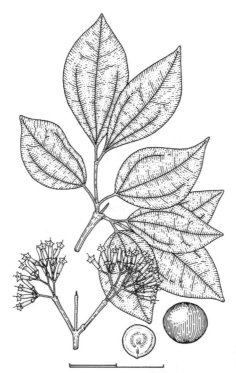

Figure 11–6   *Strychnos nux-vomica.*
Dogbutton, strychnine tree

(*Datura*), possessing a rather simple type of alkaloid substance that is hallucinogenic (obviously, any truly hallucinogenic substance is perforce affecting the nervous system). It is now hard to believe jimsonweed was marketed commercially in the nineteenth century and smoked as "Spanish Herbal Cigarettes." Although (through its antihistamine and bronchodilating properties) jimsonweed has proved of value in the relief of asthma, the smoking of jimsonweed is not only potentially hallucinogenic, but very dangerous as well. Effects of jimsonweed are unpredictable, and its use may result in delirium, convulsions, coma, and even death.

Another significant nerve toxin is the alkaloid strychnine (from seeds of the Asian-Indian tree *Strychnos nux-vomica*). Although scarcely used in the practice of medicine today, strychnine, a spinal stimulant, is commonly used in neurologic studies to stimulate (demonstrate) convulsions in animals (for research or teaching purposes). Strychnine is unusual in its ability to enhance sensations of sight, smell, touch, and hearing; in the past, strychnine was employed to overcome sexual impotence, as well as alcohol overdose. Strychnine is still used commercially in the preparation of pellets used as a poison for moles ("mole nots" or so-called "poison peanuts").

Muscle toxins.   Separation of a discussion of muscle and nerve toxins is difficult because toxins affecting the muscles typically act through the nerve innervations of musculature. *Strychnos toxifera*, a vine-forming, South and Central American relative of the strychnine tree (discussed above), is one of the sources of curare (a mixture of alkaloids). Explained more fully in Chapter 13 (see under *Chondrodendron*), the action of curare is to block the impulse from nerve to muscle, rendering the muscle flaccid and unusable. Initially used as an arrow poison by native peoples, curare has found substantial use in surgery, especially as a relaxant of abdominal muscles.

Digestive (gastrointestinal) tract.   Any plant that contains substances known as saponins (sapogenic glycosides) in sufficient amounts (for example, soapwort or bouncing bet, *Saponaria officinalis* and English ivy, *Hedera helix*) may be predicted as one that will cause severe gastroenteritis and irritation or even disruption of the intestinal mucosa. Although often not readily absorbed into the bloodstream, saponins may induce bursting (lysis) of red blood cells, underscoring the fact that toxins may often have more than a single effect in the body.

Wild mustards (*Brassica* spp.) may contain sufficient quantities of mustard oil (mustard oil glycoside) to cause digestive upset or irritation. Mustard seed can be a troublesome contaminant of grain fed to cattle, sometimes resulting in colic.

Figure 11–7 *Saponaria officinalis.*
Soapwort, bouncing bet

Figure 11–8 *Hedera helix.* English ivy

Heart.   Plants containing substances known as cardiac glycosides (dealt with more fully in Chapter 3) may be expected to affect the heart. Foxglove (*Digitalis purpurea*), considered in detail in Chapter 13, contains cardioactive substances that have found a substantial use in medical practice in the United States. Lily-of-the-valley (*Convallaria majalis*) is used in a similar fashion in Soviet medicine. Other species of plants possessing cardiac glycosides include oleander (*Nerium oleander*), which is much too toxic for medical use, dogbane (*Apocynum cannabinum*), and species of milkweeds (*Asclepias* spp.). Acting through the nervous system, cardiotonic substances in these plants initially have the effect of slowing and strengthening the heartbeat. Correspondingly, alterations in blood pressure and peripheral circulation may occur. In overdose, these substances lead to cardiac arrhythmias or even cardiac arrest.

Liver.   Two unrelated plants, groundsel (*Senecio* spp.) and blue devil (*Echium vulgare*), contain similar substances (an unusual type of alkaloid) capable of inducing cumulative liver damage in animals (often horses). Better studied than blue devil, species of *Senecio* have been implicated in various diseases of horses, for example, stomach staggers and walking disease, in which progressive and chronic liver damage (revealed postmortem), not unlike cirrhosis, results from continued feeding on these particular plants.

Two fungi (*Amanita* and *Aspergillus*) can be cited in connection with liver damage (these are dealt with more fully in Chapter 5). Toxins in *Amanita* are known to cause a degeneration of liver (and kidney) cells in a rather complex way (interfering with the genetic message of the cells). The very different type of toxic compound (known as aflatoxin) produced by species of *Aspergillus* alters the genetic message of liver cells, in this case very possibly resulting in liver cancer.

Kidney.   In transport through the bloodstream, an array of toxic substances may ultimately affect the kidneys and their normal function of urine production. As an example, any plant material such as rhubarb (*Rheum rhaponticum*) leaf blades, containing high concentrations of a simple organic acid, oxalic acid (or soluble salts of oxalic acid), has the potential to cause kidney damage. Reacting with calcium of the blood, solid crystalline particles form and accumulate in the tubules of the kidney, resulting in blockage. *Halogeton*, an introduced weed of western rangelands, may possess greater than 30 percent (dry body weight) of soluble oxalates; it has been determined as the cause of death of literally thousands of sheep on rangelands in the western United States.

Enzymes.   It might be argued that a number of toxins in plants have the capability of altering animal enzymes (biochemical helpers in the cell) in one way or another. A very specific example, however, is that of wild or black cherry (*Prunus serotina*), the foliage, young bark, and seeds of which may contain a compound (in dangerous concentrations) potentially releasing cyanide into the body. Distributed by the bloodstream, cyanide can have its effect throughout the body at the cell level. In particular, cyanide attacks one of the terminal enzymes of respiration (housed in particular organelles of the cell known as mitochondria), the result being that the cell does not properly uptake oxygen. Hence, an organism suffering cyanide poisoning, regardless of the source of the cyanide, will suffer an internal asphyxiation (cyanosis usually being a symptom). Several members of the rose family, in addition to wild cherry, contain this cyanide-releasing compound.

Skeleton.   Strange as it may seem, compounds are present in certain plants that can alter the adult skeleton of an animal or human being. Seeds of certain species belonging to the leguminous genus *Lathyrus* (vetchlings, winter peas, chick peas, sweet peas) contain such a substance, the lathyrus factor. This factor, known to be an amine type of molecule, will, through continued consumption in quantity, cause a progression of symptoms, including lameness, paralysis, skeletal lesions, and overgrowth of bone by cartilage resulting in skeletal deformity (scoliosis). In this disease (lathyrism), the skeletal disorder most commonly affects the lower legs or in animals the hindquarters. The overgrowth of cartilage that occurs in lathyrism bears some resemblance to the genetic disorder in humans known as premature ageing; the similarity in symptoms to premature ageing generated some medical interest in unraveling the secrets of lathyr-

Figure 11–9 *Lathyrus.* Vetchling

ism. At least part of the explanation of lathyrism is that substances from the seeds of *Lathyrus* may interfere with proper collagen formation, as well as contribute to degeneration of motor tracts of the spinal cord. Horses have typically been the animals most prone to lathyrism. Historically, human lathyrism is known, particularly when, driven by poverty, these types of peas have become a major component of the diet. With improved diet, some aspects of lathyrism are reversible; however, the paralysis is usually permanent.

Birth defects.   Substances that cause birth defects are referred to as mutagenic (mutation producing) or teratogenic ("monster" producing). Plant species causing mutations in humans or animals belong primarily to two families of flowering plants, the lily family and the nightshade family. Among members of the lily family, western false hellebore (*Veratrum californicum*), a rather common plant at mid- to higher-elevation rangelands in a number of western states, has received the most attention. Western false hellebore is, unfortunately, readily consumed by cattle and sheep and is decidedly teratogenic. Well studied in sheep, the effects on fetal lambs are greatest if the mother animal (dam) grazes western false hellebore on approximately the fourteenth day of gestation. Extreme congenital defects induced by western false hellebore include cyclopian malformations in which a single large eyesocket is formed, along with several other cranial and facial abnormalities (including upper and lower jaws of unmatched lengths). Lambs exhibiting congenital cyclopia are referred to, inappropriately, as monkey-face lambs. Lesser defects may be observed if ingestion of the teratogenic agent (*Veratrum* alkaloids) occurs substantially before or after the fourteenth day following conception.

In the nightshade family, both the Irish potato (*Solanum tuberosum*) and the tomato (*Lycopersicon esculentum*) contain types of alkaloid substances (potentially teratogenic) similar to those in western false hellebore. Green potato sprouts (not potato tubers!) have been demonstrated to be teratogenic in feeding experiments with hamsters, although the precise teratogen involved has evaded discovery. Much more attention has been accorded the teratogenicity of tobacco (*Nicotiana tabacum*). For a time, warning on tobacco products (cigarettes) only said something like "may be hazardous to your health." However, statements on cigarette packs currently admonish pregnant women not to smoke. Tobacco is now known to contain teratogens and to cause birth defects in animals and

Figure 11–10 *Nicotiana tabacum.*
Tobacco

human beings. The danger point for tobacco intake during gestation is imprecise, and smoking at any time during pregnancy should be considered a most unwise practice. In addition to the rather simple alkaloid nicotine (and the closely related and, based on animal experimentation, the more teratogenic alkaloid anabasine), tobacco contains (or, when smoked, generates) yet other types of mutagenic agents such as benzopyrene. And, of course, tobacco smoke contains carbon monoxide (which will reduce oxygen in the fetal blood supply). Of the various unfortunate consequences related to use of cigarettes, most definitively associated with smoking during pregnancy is low infant birth weight (and increased abortion rate). However, a variety of birth defects, including mental deficiency, are correlated with tobacco use during gestation.

MECHANICAL INJURY

This topic is included since we are considering the effects of plants that are potentially harmful in any way. Under *external mechanical injury*, we might cite the simple cases of cocklebur (*Xanthium*) and thistles (*Cirsium*), which possess spines surrounding their seed heads or on their leaves that can readily puncture flesh. Such a plant adaptation as

Figure 11–11 *Cirsium.* Thistle

spinyness is no doubt of survival value in dispersal and/or in helping to prevent predation by animals. Cacti would fit into the general category of external mechanical injury. However, in addition to the large, evident spines of cacti, much smaller, often unseen spines (glochids) occur, which may become lodged in the lining of the oral cavity of a feeding animal (causing internal mechanical injury). Perhaps as significant as any other plant with regard to *internal mechanical injury* is wild barley (or squirrel-tail grass), *Hordeum jubatum*. Wild barley occurs as a weed throughout much of the United States. Copious wiry bristles on the flowering spikes possess backwardly pointing (retrorse) barbs or teeth that, upon ingestion, become lodged in the lining of the upper digestive tract, potentially resulting in inflammation, swelling, inability to feed, and possible infections. Sheep are apparently most susceptible to damage from wild barley, and deaths are occasionally reported.

SELECTED REFERENCES

ANNALS OF ALLERGY. This periodical contains in its various issues a wealth of information on plants and allergy. See especially articles in the July, August, and September issues, 1975, by Walter H. Lewis and Wayne E. Imber dealing with allergenic grasses, trees, and weeds of the St. Louis, Missouri, area.

ARENA, JAY M. (editor) Richard H. Drew (assoc. ed.). 1986. *Poisoning—Toxicology, Symptoms, Treatment*, 5th ed. Charles C Thomas, Springfield, Ill. An excellent and detailed introduction to toxicology. Pages 719–727 contain a concise synopsis of symptoms or effects induced by common poisonous plants.

BUISSERET, P. D. 1982. Allergy. *Scientific American* 247(2): 86–95. A good explanation of respiratory allergy in terms of the responses of the body's immune system.

KINGHORN, A. DOUGLAS (ed.). 1979. *Toxic Plants*. Columbia University Press, New York. All chapters are meaningful; however, Chapter 3, by Richard F. Keeler, provides a good account of potential teratogenic substances in plants; Chapters 6 and 7, by A. D. Kinghorn and H. Baer, respectively, dealing with aspects of dermatitis, are especially instructive in regard to the irritation of skin by plants.

LEWIS, WALTER H., PRATHIBHA VINAY, AND VINCENT E. ZENGER. 1983. *Airborne and Allergenic Pollen of North America*. Johns Hopkins University Press, Baltimore, Md. Up-to-date and extremely well-illustrated information on the types of pollen involved in respiratory allergy.

MITCHELL, JOHN, AND ARTHUR ROOK. 1979. *Botanical Dermatology*. Greenglass Ltd., Vancouver, British Columbia. A well-referenced account, primarily alphabetical, of many plants suspected of involvement in dermatitis.

SELL, STEWART. 1980. *Immunology, Immunopathology and Immunity*, 3rd ed. Harper & Row, Publishers, New York. Pages 313–316 present a concise account of the mechanism of the development of poison ivy dermatitis, including a diagrammatic illustration.

WODEHOUSE, ROGER P. 1971. *Hayfever Plants*, 2nd ed. Hafner Publishing Co., New York. A standard reference on plants involved in respiratory allergy; page 7 contains a nice summary of families of plants playing a major role in hay fever.

Poisonous Plants
of the Eastern United States

Chapter 12 constitutes a listing of poisonous flowering plants encountered in the eastern United States, either as native, naturalized, or commonly cultivated plants (including a few grown in houses or greenhouses). The area of tropical Florida is not included in this listing. For an account of the poisonous plants of Florida, see the work of Julia F. Morton, selected references. It should be understood that no coverage of a region (eastern United States or otherwise) may be regarded as complete. No plant encountered should be considered safe simply because it does not appear in the following list, especially if the identity of the plant is uncertain. For information on toxic substances mentioned in this chapter, reference should be made specifically to Chapter 3. Additional information on the toxic effects of plants is to be found in Chapter 11. Major toxic families of flowering plants (families to which the majority of plants enumerated below are members) are covered in Chapter 8. In this presentation, for the sake of reference (especially to other books, such as state or regional floras), the scientific name of the family to which each toxic representative belongs is given in parentheses following the common name or names. Each plant in the following enumeration is illustrated; the shorter (or single) scale line on each illustration equates to 1 inch (actual size), and the longer scale to 2 inches.

***Aconitum* spp.: Monkshood, wolfsbane (Ranunculaceae).** Rather common garden ornamentals easily recognized by the humplike or hoodlike upper petal of the flower and a palmately lobed or divided, crowfoot type of leaf. Toxicity is due to a complex alkaloid, aconitine (a diterpenoid alkaloid), causing a burning

Figure 12–1 *Aconitum.* Monkshood, wolfsbane

sensation in the mouth and throat, intense abdominal pain, numbness (and a feeling of being chilled), and irregularities of heartbeat. Symptoms appear rapidly, and fatal poisoning can occur in a matter of a few hours time. All parts of the plant should be considered toxic.

Actaea spp.: Baneberry, doll's-eyes (Ranunculaceae). Woodland herbs with a ternately decompound leaf and striking red or white fruits projecting at right angles to the main stalk on elongated pedicels; each fruit contains a conspicuous dark spot (resembling a doll's eye). The poisonous principle is poorly known, but reputedly causes severe inflammation of the digestive tract.

Aesculus spp.: Buckeyes, horsechestnuts (Hippocastanaceae). Native and introduced trees with opposite, palmately compound leaves (variously

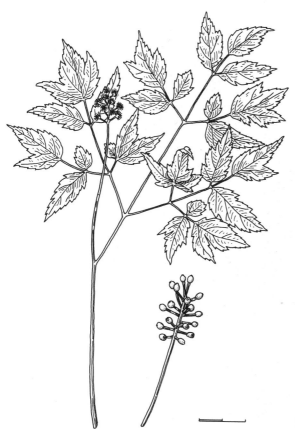

Figure 12–2 *Actaea.* Baneberry

with five or seven leaflets each). The fruit is a leathery capsule with one to three large shiny-brown seeds, each seed bearing a sizable pale spot (said to resemble the eye of a male deer or buck; hence, the common name derivation, from buck's-eye). Various parts of the plant reportedly contain the coumarin glycoside aesculin (esculin) and/or the saponin glycoside or glycoside mixture aescin. Intake of *Aesculus* seeds (or perhaps other parts) may result in digestive upset, possibly followed by some dysfunction of the nervous system (incoordination, twitching, and the like). Poisoning is more common in cattle than human beings, in that consumption of a quantity of seed is generally required to induce significant symptoms. Native species include *Aesculus glabra* (Ohio buckeye) and *A. octandra* (sweet or yellow buckeye); the European horsechestnut (*Aesculus hippocastanum*) is rather commonly planted.

Agrostemma githago: Corn cockle (Caryophyllaceae).

A relatively tall, opposite-leaved, winter annual with striking red-, pink- or purple-petalled

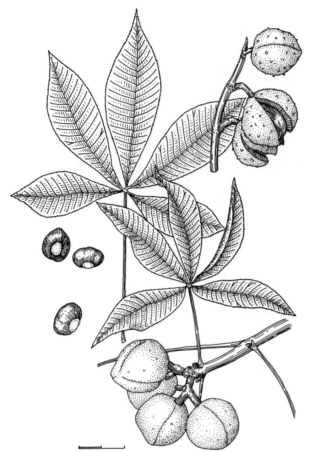

Figure 12–3 *Aesculus*. Buckeye

flowers having a very noticeable calyx, the lobes of which are perhaps longer than the tubular base. Corn cockle is a European weed often found in fields of winter wheat and rye. The warty, black seeds are about the same size as a grain of wheat, and, in the past (prior to good commercial seed screening practices), *Agrostemma* seed was a common contaminant of wheat sold at market; there is still a potential hazard in grain that never goes to market. Seeds contain a sapogenic glycoside, and, characteristic of this type of substance, severe gastroenteritis (irritation of the intestinal mucosa) is possible following ingestion; damage to red blood cells may occur if the sapogenin is absorbed into the bloodstream. Human and animal poisoning from *Agrostemma* seed is documented.

***Ailanthus altissima:* Tree-of-heaven (Simarubaceae).** Introduced tree thriving under the worst city (polluted) conditions. Recognized by large pinnately compound leaves, each leaflet bearing coarse, glandular (ill-smelling if

Figure 12–4 *Agrostemma githago*. Corn cockle

Figure 12–5 *Ailanthus altissima*. Tree-of-heaven

crushed) teeth at their base. Cases of contact dermatitis, similar to poison ivy rash, have been attributed to tree-of-heaven, but precise details seem lacking.

Aleurites fordii: **Tung-oil tree, tung nut (Euphorbiaceae).**   Not native, tung-oil trees are nonetheless occasionally planted in the Gulf South, sometimes in large orchards. Tung nuts are small trees with heart-shaped leaves and rather large, spherical, pendulous brownish fruits. Tung oil, extracted from the seeds, is commercially valuable and is used in paint thinners. Parts of the plant, especially the seeds, reputedly contain distinct toxins—a saponin (sapogenic glycoside) and possibly a toxic protein. A digestive and skin irritant (diterpenoid) found in certain other members of the spurge family may also occur. Symptoms of tung-nut poisoning include digestive upset and dyspnea.

Amaryllis **spp.:   Amaryllis and many other common names (Amaryllidaceae).**   Underground parts (bulbs) of various species of these cultivated

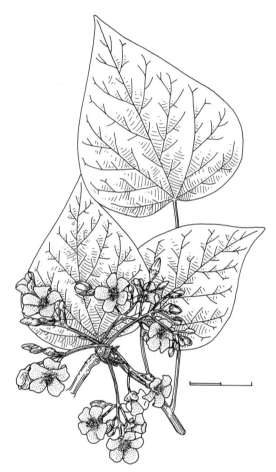

Figure 12–6 *Aleurites fordii.* Tung-oil tree

flowers apparently contain toxic substances (probably alkaloids) and are to be considered potentially dangerous if ingested. Digestive upset is the expected result. Amaryllis is distinguished from lilies by the inferior rather than superior ovary of the flower.

Anemone spp.: Windflowers (Ranunculaceae). Anemones are often included in lists of poisonous plants, and reportedly contain a toxic substance, protoanemonin, of glycosidic origin. Protoanemonin apparently has an irritant and corrosive action on mucous membranes, as those of the upper digestive tract, and may irritate the skin as well. Given that a number of members of the family to which anemones belong (the Ranunculaceae) are indeed toxic, these plants should be treated with caution. Anemones are recognized by their thimble-shaped flowers and by the fact that flowering peduncles are subtended (albeit remotely) by whorled or paired (and often palmately lobed) leaves (bracts).

Figure 12–7 *Amaryllis*. Amaryllis   **Figure 12–8** *Anemone canadensis*. Windflower

Apocynum cannabinum: Dogbane, Indian hemp (Apocynaceae).

A rather common weed of roadsides and fields, dogbane is recognized by milky latex (similar to that of milkweeds) and by often reddish stems. One or more commonly two long, slender follicles potentially appear at the position of each of the smallish, white flowers (the flowers borne in terminal cymes); each follicle contains a number of hair-tufted seeds. Dogbane is known to contain cardiac glycosides (having a digitalislike effect on the heart) and was employed in American medicine during the nineteenth century. Consumed in quantity, dogbane can cause cardiac arrest; it should be considered dangerous to livestock. In actuality, several closely related (and difficult to distinguish) species of *Apocynum* (*A. cannabinum*, *A. androsaemifolium*, and *A. sibiricum*) are thought to exist, with hybrid forms apparently occurring between them.

Figure 12–9 *Apocynum cannabinum.*
Dogbane, Indian hemp

***Aralia spinosa:* Hercules' club, devil's walking-stick (Araliaceae).**
Shrub or small tree with twice pinnately compound leaves and spiny branches. Black
berries follow the compound umbels of small, white flowers and may be poisonous if
eaten in quantity; the poisonous principle is uncertain. This plant is most common in
the southeastern United States.

***Arisaema triphyllum:* Jack-in-the-pulpit (Araceae).**   Contains sharp,
needlelike crystals of calcium oxalate (calcium salt of oxalic acid), which may become
lodged in the mucous lining of the mouth and throat. Considerable discomfort, but not
fatal poisoning, is typically the result. The large hoodlike bract (spathe) surrounding
the fleshy spikelike inflorescence (spadix) will aid in recognition of jack-in-the-pulpit
and other members of the aroid family.

***Asclepias* spp.: Milkweeds (Asclepiadaceae).**   Very similar in botan-
ical characteristics to dogbane (Apocynum), that is opposite leaves, milky juice,
development of follicles with hair-tufted seeds, and so on; in milkweeds, however,

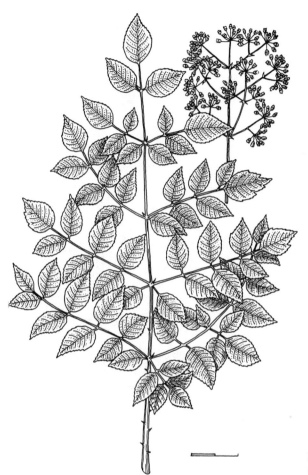

Figure 12–10 *Aralia spinosa.* Hercules' club

flowers usually occur in umbellike clusters. As with dogbane, milkweeds may contain significant cardioactive substances (cardiac glycosides). Although certain species of milkweeds have been considered edible and even sought after as wild or natural food, virtually all species examined chemically contain at least small quantities of potentially cardiotoxic substances (although some species contain much more than others); consequently, it is probably wise to avoid any species of *Asclepias* as a food item. *Asclepias syriaca* is a common roadside weed species in the East.

Atropa belladonna: Belladonna, deadly nightshade (Solanaceae).

Belladonna is a native of Eurasia, but is occasionally planted in American herb gardens. Atropine (a tranquilizing and potentially hallucinogenic alkaloid) and closely

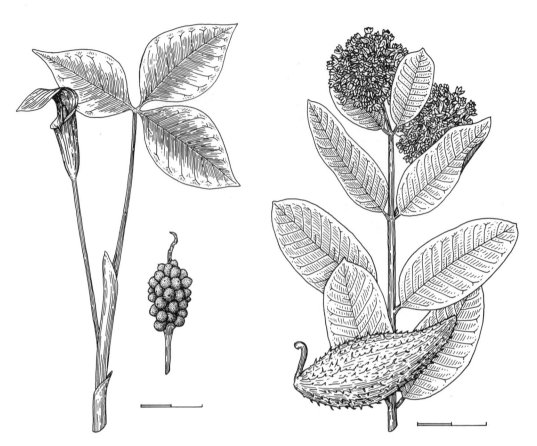

Figure 12–11 *Arisaema triphyllum.*
Jack-in-the-pulpit

Figure 12–12 *Asclepias syriaca.* Common milkweed

related alkaloids also occurring in the plant should be considered toxic and extremely dangerous. The medium-sized, tubular, red-purple or green-purple flowers are followed by shiny, black, marble-sized berries, a characteristic identification feature. The many medical uses of belladonna will be described in Chapter 13.

Baptisia **spp.: False indigo (Leguminosae).** Species of *Baptisia* are native in the eastern and western United States. They somewhat resemble lupines, but the leaves of false indigos are typically three foliate, and the terminal racemes often have a more open appearance. The general structure of the toxic alkaloid is similar to that of lupine. Symptoms expected in animals poisoned by *Baptisia* include nausea, diarrhea, and other manifestations of digestive upset.

Figure 12–13 *Atropa belladonna*. Belladonna, deadly nightshade

Figure 12–14 *Baptisia*. False indigo

Brassica spp.: Wild mustards (Cruciferae). Mustards typically are rather inconspicuously yellowish-flowered, annual herbs, bearing slender fruits below the flowers; the basal or lower cauline leaves are sometimes lyrate in appearance (lobed so as to resemble a lyre). Some of the wild mustards contain mustard oils (mustard oil glycosides) in sufficient quantity to cause colic (digestive upset) in cattle. Mustard seed is a common contaminant of grain fed to livestock.

Buxus sempervirens: Boxwood or common box (Buxaceae). Boxwood is an evergreen shrub with smallish, opposite, oval or elliptic leaves. Commonly planted around houses and buildings, it is to be considered a dangerous hedge plant because of the steroidal alkaloid (buxine or cyclobuxine) content of the leaves and bark. Animals are occasionally poisoned by hedge clippings involving this plant.

Figure 12–15 *Brassica nigra.* Wild (black) mustard   **Figure 12–16** *Buxus sempervirens.* Boxwood

Caltha palustris: Marsh marigold, cowslip (Ranunculaceae).

Growing along streams or in wet meadows, marsh marigold is recognized by its cordate (heart-shaped) basal leaves and relatively large, somewhat shiny, yellow flowers with numerous stamens. *Caltha* apparently contains a toxic substance (protoanemonin) similar to that occurring in *Anemone* and may be similarly irritating to the digestive tract.

Campsis radicans: Trumpet vine (Bignoniaceae).

Trumpet vine (or trumpet creeper as it is also known) is a rather large vine with opposite, pinnately compound leaves and sizable orange-red flowers. As with tree-of-heaven (*Ailanthus*), trumpet vine has been implicated in cases of contact dermatitis. However, more research on the actual effect of the plant would be helpful.

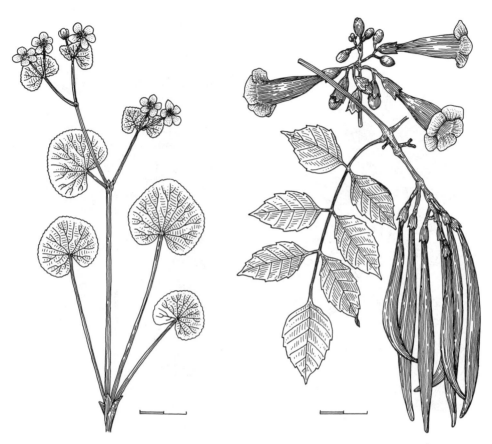

Figure 12–17 *Caltha palustris.* Marsh
marigold

Figure 12–18 *Campsis radicans.* Trumpet vine

> ### *Cannabis sativa:* **Marijuana, hemp (Cannabinaceae).** Originally
> introduced as a fiber plant, marijuana has fallen into disrepute as a conse-
> quence of other uses. Marijuana contains the mildly narcotic resinoid tetrahy-
> drocannabinol (THC), a phenolic type of substance. Although cases of actual
> poisoning from marijuana are supported by scant documentation, this plant
> should be considered at least potentially toxic to livestock. Marijuana is readily
> recognized by its characteristic palmately compound leaves, with slender, dis-
> tinctly serrate leaflets.

> ### *Cassia* spp:. **Senna (Leguminosae).** *Cassia* is a large and wide-rang-
> ing genus of herbs or shrubs. Several species may occur in the eastern United States.
> Cassias have pinnately compound leaves, usually with glands on the petiole or

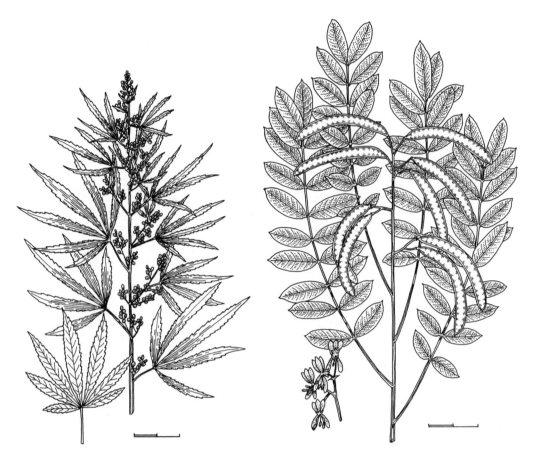

Figure 12–19 *Cannabis sativa.* Marijuana, hemp   **Figure 12–20** *Cassia.* Senna

rachis. Atypical of many legumes, the yellow flowers are almost regular, not showing marked differentiation in size and shape among the petals. Species of *Cassia* may contain one or more cathartic substances, which can be seriously purgative if the plant material (usually seeds) is consumed in excess. *Cassia fistulosa* (senna) has been used commercially as a cathartic.

***Caulophyllum thalictroides*: Blue cohosh, papoose root, squaw root (Berberidaceae).** *Caulophyllum thalictroides* and the closely related *C. giganteum* are herbaceous members of the barberry family characterized by fleshy, blue seeds (resembling fruit) and by a single, ternately decompound leaf (often resembling three separate compound leaves). Blue cohosh contains alkaloids and possibly other substances (saponins) causing gastroenteritis if consumed. Histori-

Figure 12–21   *Caulophyllum thalictroides.* Blue cohosh

Figure 12–22   *Celastrus scandens.* American bittersweet

cally, blue cohosh was employed medicinally as an oral, oxytocic drug (that is, to help induce childbirth).

Celastrus **spp.: Bittersweet (Celastraceae).**   Both the American and oriental bittersweet are reasonably common and very similar in appearance. Bittersweets are twining vines with alternate, simple, serrate-crenate leaves, and may occur along fencerows bordering pastures. The yellow- or red-orange capsules split open to reveal the fleshy, red covering (aril) of the seeds; stems bearing these capsules are often sold as ornamental material at Thanksgiving time. Although chemically poorly known, bittersweet is suspected of causing violent purgation in types of livestock.

Cicuta maculata: **Water hemlock (Umbelliferae).**   This plant is very similar in appearance to poison hemlock; however, the leaves of water hemlock are not as finely divided and there is little or no purple blotching on the lower stem. The

Figure 12-23 *Cicuta maculata.* Water hemlock

Figure 12-24 *Clematis virginiana.* Virgin's bower

inflorescence closely resembles wild carrot, and the root is similar to that of wild parsnip, hence the potential for mistaking this plant for certain wild edible plants. Sectioning of the root and lower stem reveals chambers (diaphragms); this feature distinguishes water hemlock from similar looking plants. The oily, yellowish fluid that exudes from the cut root contains a long-chain, toxic alcohol, cicutoxin (technically a polyacetylenic molecule). Violent convulsions and death may be the result of consumption of the roots of water hemlock. Because of its resemblance to particular edible plants, human poisoning is more common from water hemlock than from many other types of poisonous plants; it should be considered a very dangerous wild plant.

***Clematis* spp.: Clematis, virgin's bower (Ranunculaceae).**   A vining genus, various species are planted for their ornamental bracts subtending the flowers or for their unusual plumose fruit (cluster of achenes). *Clematis* may contain substances similar to those found in anemone or even larkspur and should be considered potentially dangerous.

Cnidoscolus stimulosus: **Tread-softly (Euphorbiaceae).** The majority of species of *Cnidoscolus* occur in southwestern North America or in tropical America. However, *C. stimulosus* occurs in sandy (coastal plain) areas as far north and east as Virginia. It is a herb with deeply palmately lobed leaves and unisexual flowers. The male flowers are highlighted by a white, trumpet-shaped calyx. All parts of the plant are prone to be armed with hairs that can inflict a painful sting or burning sensation resembling that of stinging nettle. The chemicals causing irritation and inflammation are not known with certainty.

Colchicum autumnale: **Autumn crocus (Liliaceae).** Planted for its crocuslike flowers (which appear in the fall, not spring when the leaves are present), autumn crocus is actually in a different family from the spring-flowering crocuses. The alkaloid, colchicine, known from experimentation to interfere with the cell division process, causes digestive irritation, capillary dilatation, and possible kidney damage. The cytotoxic effects of colchicine can be cumulative, as it is only slowly eliminated from the body.

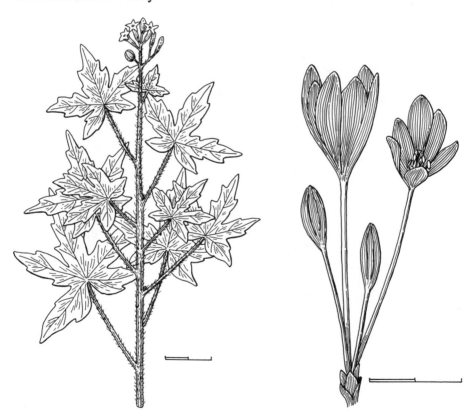

Figure 12–25 *Cnidoscolus stimulosus.* Tread-softly

Figure 12–26 *Colchicum autumnale.* Autumn crocus

***Conium maculatum:* Poison hemlock (Umbelliferae).**   Historically famous as a poisonous plant, poison hemlock contains the simple but quite toxic alkaloid, coniine, the first alkaloid made synthetically in the laboratory. The effect of coniine on the central nervous system is similar to that of an overdose of nicotine; coniine acts as a depressant on motor tracts in the brain and especially the spinal cord; symptoms include numbness and paralysis beginning with the lower limbs and progressing to the arms and chest; death may result from paralysis of the muscles involved in respiration (the diaphragm). Poison hemlock resembles wild carrot, but the compound umbel is less compact and purple blotching occurs toward the stem base. The foliage is sometimes mistaken for that of a fern. All parts of the plant should be considered potentially dangerous; however, the seedlike fruits and the foliage apparently contain the greatest concentration of alkaloid.

***Convallaria majalis:* Lily-of-the-valley (Liliaceae).**   Commonly planted, lily-of-the-valley contains the cardioactive glycoside convallarin (or convallatoxin), which has an effect on the heart similar to that of digitalis. In fact, lily-of-the-valley has been employed in Soviet medicine in much the way that

Figure 12–27 *Conium maculatum.* Poison hemlock

Figure 12–28 *Convallaria majalis.* Lily-of-the-valley

digitalis has in medicine of the United States. As with digitalis, the danger is in overdosage, leading to cardiac arrhythmias and possible cardiac arrest. The small, white, bell-shaped flowers with six petallike lobes are characteristic; the leaves of lily-of-the-valley are relatively broad in comparison to many monocotyledonous plants.

Convolvulus spp.: Bindweeds (Convolvulaceae).

Herbaceous vines with alternate, arrowhead-shaped leaves and large, funnellike flowers that are eventually replaced by capsular fruits. Various of these "wild morning-glories" may contain toxic or even hallucinogenic substances in the seeds and should be treated with caution.

Corydalis spp.: Fumatory (Fumariaceae).

Corydalis possesses finely dissected leaves and spurred corollas resembling *Dicentra* (squirrel corn and Dutchman's breeches). In *Corydalis*, however, there is only one nectar spur (not two as in *Dicentra*), this being at the base on the upper side, and the flowers are often more yellow than white. Species of both *Corydalis* and *Dicentra* possess alkaloids,

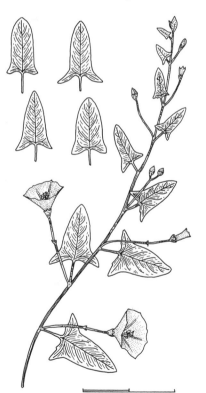

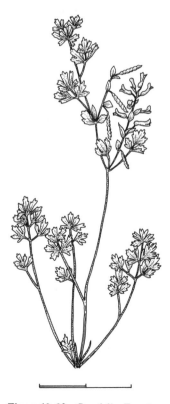

Figure 12–29 *Convolvulus arvensis.*
Field bindweed

Figure 12–30 *Corydalis.* Fumatory

similar to those found in the poppy family, that are depressants of the central nervous system. Twitching, loss of muscular control, and even convulsions may be expected following consumption.

Daphne mezereum: **Daphne, flowering mezereon (Thymelaeaceae).**   European shrub naturalized in parts of the northeastern United States (also in Canada). The red fruits are borne tightly on the stem, immediately below the leaves, and contain a diterpenoid substance (mezerein) that is corrosive to the lining of the upper and lower digestive tract, causing vesication, ulceration, and severe enteritis; mezerein may irritate the skin and even be cocarcinogenic, as in the case of certain substances isolated from spurges (see under *Euphorbia*).

Datura stramonium: **Jimsonweed, thornapple (Solanaceae).**   A common weed of barnyards or pastures; the uneven leaf-blade margins, the long, whitish to pale violet, tubular corollas, and the spiny or prickly fruits (capsules) are characteristic. Jimsonweed has an unpleasant odor (and presumably an unpleasant taste) and is usually avoided by livestock. Apparently all parts of the plant contain alkaloids similar to those found in belladonna (*Atropa*) and should be considered

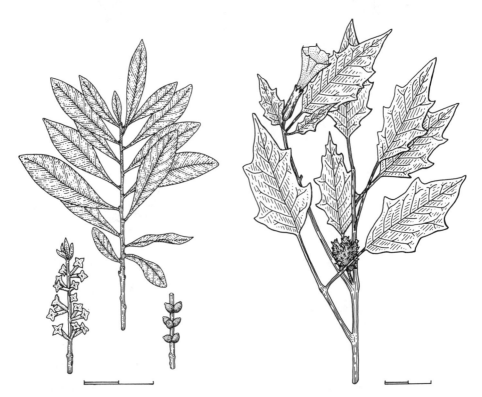

Figure 12–31 *Daphne mezereum.* Flowering mezereon

Figure 12–32 *Datura stramonium.* Jimsonweed

dangerous. The sedative effect of these atropinelike substances may be followed by rapid heartbeat, hallucinations, coma, and death. Although seeds have been smoked to get "high," fatal amounts are unpredictable, and any amount should be avoided. A by-product of the activity of these alkaloids is to decrease secretion by the nasal passages while dilating bronchial tubes; consequently, jimsonweed historically received some use in the treatment of asthma.

***Delphinium* spp.: Larkspurs (Ranunculaceae).**   Both native and culti-vated larkspurs may contain a complex type of alkaloid similar to that found in monkshood (*Aconitum*); in the case of larkspur, the concentration of toxin usually decreases with the age of the plant (hence, young growth is most dangerous). Various species of larkspur occur on western rangelands, and species of *Delphinium* may be frequently encountered in the East as well. Of the various classes of livestock, cattle seem most susceptible to larkspur poisoning. Both the digestive system and the nervous system may be affected (bloating and constipation are common symptoms, as is a stiff or rigid stance or gait), and fatalities of cattle are well known on western rangelands when the plant is eaten in quantity. Larkspurs are recognized by the deeply dissected,

Figure 12–33 *Delphinium tricorne.* Dwarf larkspur

crowfoot leaf (not unlike *Aconitum*) and the purplish flower with a backwardly projecting nectar spur (arising from the uppermost petallike structure).

Dicentra spp.: Dutchman's breeches, squirrel corn, bleeding heart (Fumariaceae).
Both native woodland and cultivated plants, members of the genus *Dicentra* contain the alkaloid protopine, which is related to alkaloids found among members of the poppy family. As with the poppy type of alkaloid, protopine affects the nervous system. Cattle venturing into woodlots in the spring may feed on Dutchman's breeches and squirrel corn, which are often found growing together. Such animals are seen to tremble and even stagger following consumption, indicating a nervous system dysfunction. The colloquial name staggerweed is applied collectively to native species of *Dicentra*. If the consumption of staggerweed by cattle is not great, usually recovery is complete. Species of *Dicentra* may be recognized by the double-spurred, white, yellowish-white, or red corollas that are closely pendulous on racemes or panicles and by the pinnately decompound (fernlike) foliage.

Dieffenbachia spp.: Dumbcane (Araceae).
These tropical plants, which are popular, ornamental herbs of houses and greenhouses, sometimes obtain the size of a small tree. Similar to jack-in-the-pulpit and other members of the aroid family (for

Figure 12-34 *Dicentra*. Dutchman's breeches   **Figure 12-35** *Dieffenbachia*. Dumbcane

example, *Philodendron*, *Colocasia*, *Caladium*), dumbcane contains sharp, needlelike crystals of calcium oxalate known as raphides. In dumbcane, these are often contained in special raphide ejector cells in the leaf's epidermis; pressure on these cells (as in biting or chewing) causes ejection of the sharp crystals (and perhaps free oxalic acid as well). The raphides may consequently become lodged in the lining of the mouth and throat of the unwitting victim. A severe burning sensation and swelling of tongue and other oral tissues may result, perhaps interfering with the ability to talk (hence the name dumbcane; that is, the plant can "strike you dumb"). Such poisoning is rarely serious, and total recovery usually occurs naturally within a few days. Varieties of at least two species of *Dieffenbachia* (*D. picta* and *D. seguine*) are cultivated under glass. Variegated (white-spotted) forms are perhaps most often *D. picta*.

Digitalis purpurea: Foxglove, deadman's bells, bloody fingers, witch's bells (Scrophulariaceae).

A well-known medicinal plant commonly and currently used in American medicine, *Digitalis* contains cardiac glycosides capable of altering the rate and force of the heartbeat. *Digitalis*, although native to Europe, is often planted in American herb gardens. A biennial (or occasionally perennial or even annual herb), it is recognized by the long, tubular flowers pendulous on terminal racemes. Although the flowers are typically red or purple, pale-flowered (sometimes speckled)

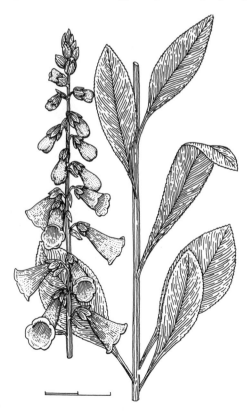

Figure 12–36 *Digitalis purpurea.* Foxglove

horticultural varieties are seen in gardens. Digitalis tea, prepared from the leaves, is sometimes sold in the herb trade, but should be avoided because an overdose of the cardioactive substances may cause dangerous cardiac arrhythmias. Other medicinal species of *Digitalis* (such as *D. lanata*, Greecian foxglove) are also occasionally cultivated in herb gardens (see Chapter 13).

Echium vulgare: Blue devil, blue thistle, viper's bugloss (Boraginaceae).

Blue devil is a biennial herb with rough, hispid pubescence and striking blue flowers; subunits of the inflorescence tend to curve downwardly. Native to Europe, this species is adventive in North America in dry meadows where limestone bedrock is close to the surface. Contact with the hairs can produce skin irritation and possible dermatitis. Also, blue devil contains a type of alkaloid (pyrrolizidine type) capable of causing liver damage if repeated ingestion occurs. Details of the toxicity of blue devil require further investigation.

Euonymus spp.:   Euonymus, and other common names (Celastraceae).

The genus *Euonymus* contains a number of species, ranging in form

Figure 12–37 *Echium vulgare.* Blue devil   **Figure 12–38** *Euonymus alatus.* Winged euonymus

from vines and ground-cover plants to shrubs and small trees. The leaves are typically opposite, simple, and bear small teeth; seeds are surrounded by a bright-colored aril and contained in a capsular fruit. Several parts of the plant, including the leaves, bark, and the attractive seeds, reputedly contain a poisonous principle (not completely identified) causing violent purging; recent evidence indicates that cardiotonic glycosides and alkaloids are present in the seeds of *E. europaeus*. It is not known with certainty whether or not the toxic substance(s) in *Euonymus* is similar to that found in bittersweet (*Celastrus*), another genus in the family. The most commonly encountered species of *Euonymus* are *E. atropurpureus* (burning bush or wahoo), *E. europaeus* (spindle tree), *E. alatus* (winged euonymus), *E. fortunei* var. *radicans* (winter creeper), *E. americanus* (strawberry bush), and *E. obovatus* (running strawberry bush).

Eupatorium rugosum: **White snakeroot (Compositae).**   This white-flowered member of the sunflower family has opposite, rather prominently three nerved leaves. It typically occurs in fields at the edges of woods or woodlots. White snakeroot contains an unusual toxin, tremetol, which is a rather large, alcohollike molecule, soluble in oil or fat. Tremetol can become concentrated in the milk of cows feeding (inadvertently) on white snakeroot and hence may be passed on to human beings. Tremetol affects the nervous system; the condition in cattle is known

Figure 12–39 *Eupatorium rugosum.*
White snakeroot

as trembles, and in human beings it is termed milk sickness. General weakness and prostration are typical symptoms; death may be the eventual result if continued consumption occurs. Milk sickness is for the most part now a historical disease because of the current practice of pooling milk from various dairy farms into large vats for commercial production, hence diluting any tremetol that might be present. However, milk sickness was apparently common and a matter of serious concern at various times during the nineteenth century in parts of the eastern United States.

***Euphorbia* spp.: Spurges (Euphorbiaceae).** Euphorbias vary greatly in form from large, cactuslike plants (of the Old World) to small, delicate herbs of lawn and garden. Characteristic species include *E. cyparissias* (cypress spurge), *E. marginata* (snow-on-the-mountain), *E. maculata* (wartweed), and *E. supina* (a small prostrate form commonly found in sidewalk cracks). Regardless of general differences in form, all share in common a peculiar and highly reduced inflorescence known as a cyathium (a cuplike structure surrounding tiny unisexual flowers; the female flower usually protrudes from the cyathial cup; see Figure 8–4). Abundant milky latex exudes from stems or leaves of many euphorbias when they are broken. This acrid latex can be very irritating to the skin, causing a burn, although dermal reactivity to the milky juice varies. The latex may also

Figure 12–40 *Euphorbia maculata.*
Wartweed

be harmful to the cornea of the eye. Diterpenoid substances, phorbol and ingenol, have been isolated (from various spurges) that are cocarcinogenic; that is, the substances are capable of inducing tumors, but the tumors are nonmalignant. At a minimum, direct skin contact with these plants should be avoided. Poinsettia (*Euphorbia pulcherrima*) does not possess milky latex and is probably no more than mildly toxic.

Galanthus nivalis: Snowdrops (Amaryllidaceae).

An early-flowering, introduced, garden ornamental, snowdrops is recognized by its green-tipped, white perianth, clearly subtended by a green ovary. As with a number of other members of the amaryllis family, the underground parts (in the case of snowdrops, the bulbs) are thought to contain toxic alkaloidal substances and should not be ingested.

Gelsemium sempervirens: Yellow jessamine, Carolina jessamine (Loganiaceae).

Occurring in the coastal and piedmont areas of the southeastern

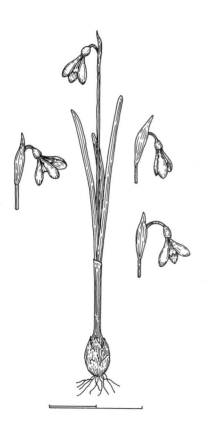

Figure 12–41 *Galanthus nivalis.* Snowdrops

Figure 12–42 *Gelsemium sempervirens.* Yellow jessamine

United States as far north as Virginia, yellow jessamine is an early-flowering, attractive evergreen vine with opposite leaves and striking, funnel-shaped, yellow flowers. Yellow jessamine contains several alkaloids similar to strychnine in their molecular structure. Historically, the powdered rhizome and roots of Gelsemium received a reasonably substantial use (as a motor nerve depressant) in treating migraine headache and types of neuralgia. However, all parts of the jessamine plant (even the flowers and the floral nectar) are poisonous. In addition to contractions and difficulties in the use of voluntary muscles, possible convulsions may be expected from jessamine poisoning.

Glechoma hederacea: Ground ivy, gill-over-the-ground, creeping charlie (Labiatae).

Ground ivy is a prostrate, spreading herb with technical features of flower and stem typical of the mint family. It is considered a lawn or field pest and reportedly has proven toxic to horses if ingested in quantity. The nature of the toxic substance in ground ivy is unclear.

Figure 12–43 *Glechoma hederacea.*
Ground ivy

Gymnocladus dioica: **Kentucky coffee tree (Leguminosae).**   A native tree in a number of areas of the eastern United States, Kentucky coffee tree is seldom abundant in natural settings, but is occasionally planted.   It is recognized by the twice pinnately compound leaves (which become only once pinnate at the base), by the rough, scaly bark, and by the large, fat seed pods.   Seeds and pulp between the seeds contain the alkaloid cytisine and are capable of causing substantial intestinal disorders (including vomiting and diarrhea).   Nonetheless, roasted seeds were at one time used as a coffee substitute (the heating process apparently driving off the toxin).

Hedera helix: **English ivy (Araliaceae).**   English ivy is probably toxic, at least in quantity, but more exact information on its toxicity would be helpful.   It is suspected of toxicity because of the presence of the steroid hederagenin, a component of a sapogenic glycoside (hederin).   Plants containing this type of glycoside (that is, saponins) are potential irritants of the lining of the digestive tract, having a purgative action.   English ivy

Figure 12–44   *Gymnocladus dioica*. Kentucky coffee tree   **Figure 12–45**   *Hedera helix*. English ivy

is doubtless familiar to most; it is a readily recognizable woody vine, with leathery, dark-green leaves possessing three to five shallow to medium-depth palmate lobes.

Helenium autumnale: Sneezeweed, bitterweed (Compositae).

Various species of *Helenium* have been implicated in cases of poisoning in animals due to the alleged presence of a glycoside causing vomiting and other aspects of digestive upset (spewing sickness). Actually, species of *Helenium* occurring on western rangelands (especially *H. hoopesii*) are more of a serious concern with regard to loss of livestock through poisoning than is the broadly distributed weed *H. autumnale*. A help in recognizing this genus of the sunflower family is the yellow-orange, convex heads, and the shallowly but distinctly three-lobed ray corollas.

Helleborus niger: Christmas rose (Ranunculaceae).

This often winter blooming, white- or purplish-flowered member of the crowfoot family is reasonably popular as a garden ornamental. Unlike some other toxic members of this family, it does not appear to contain a complex type of alkaloid; rather, Christmas rose apparently contains glycosides that may result in gastric disturbance; also, there is a possible effect on the heart. It is not clear how severely toxic this plant actually is.

Figure 12–46 *Helenium autumnale.* Sneezeweed   **Figure 12–47** *Helleborus niger.* Christmas rose

Hyacinthus orientalis: **Garden hyacinth (Liliaceae).**   Easily recognized by its terminal racemes of fragrant flowers (radiating from the raceme at all angles), garden hyacinth once again proves the point that there is much to learn about poisonous and medicinal plants.   Underground parts (for example, bulbs) of a number of members of the lily (including *Hyacinthus*), amaryllis, and iris families are suspected of at least mild toxicity (causing purgation, if nothing else).   However, in chemical terms, toxic compounds in members of these families are, often as not, poorly understood.

Hydrangea **spp.: Hydrangea (Saxifragaceae).**   Leaves and possibly other parts of some species of *Hydrangea* are known to contain a cyanogenic glycoside and should be avoided as items of human consumption.   Hyrangeas are generally shrubs, recognized by their opposite leaves with long petioles and by inflorescences that often contain a number of showy but sterile flowers in addition to the small, unattractive fertile flowers.   In some cultivated species (or varieties), the sterile flowers dominate and occur in ball-like clusters.   Both native and cultivated taxa should be considered potentially dangerous if consumed.   *Hydrangea arborescens* is the common native species.

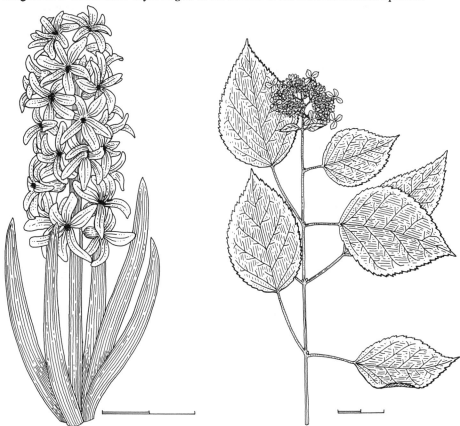

Figure 12–48 *Hyacinthus orientalis.*
Garden hyacinth

Figure 12–49 *Hydrangea arborescens.*
Wild hydrangea

***Hydrastis canadensis:* Golden seal (Ranunculaceae).**   Spring-flowering perennial with an unbranched stem bearing two cordate, three- to seven-lobed leaves and a single flower that, at maturity, lacks a perianth, but possesses numerous stamens and separate simple pistils. The pistils form a crimson, berrylike aggregate in fruit. The knotted rhizome yields a yellowish fluid when cut, the juice being used historically for irritations of the skin, eyes, and mucous membranes, and even taken internally. *Hydrastis* was a favorite of John Uri Lloyd and the late nineteenth-century school of eclectic medicine, centered in the Cincinnati, Ohio area. Lloyd was instrumental in the cultivation of golden seal (which was nearly exterminated in the wild because of medical interest) and the purification of alkaloids, hydrastine and berberine, extracted from the plant. These drugs have been used in the treatment of cutaneous and venereal disease. Being isoquinoline alkaloids, they have a potentially depressant action on the central nervous system. Also, they may cause ulceration of mucous membranes if applied in excess.

***Hyoscyamus niger:* Henbane (Solanaceae).**   Henbane is a European plant used for centuries as a sedative and for the relief of pain. It is noted for its potentially hallucinogenic alkaloids (tropane type of alkaloid, that is, belladonna type), and was doubtless employed in witchcraft during the Middle Ages because of its potential for inducing psychoactive states. Occasionally planted in American gardens

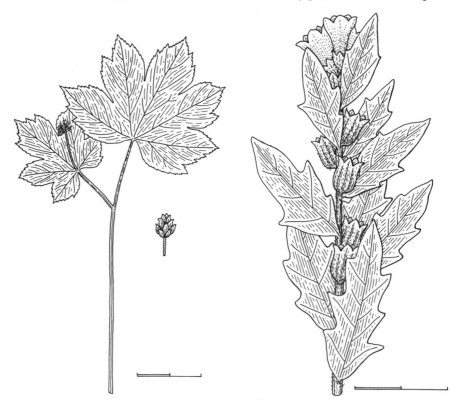

Figure 12–50 *Hydrastis canadensis.* Golden seal   **Figure 12–51** *Hyoscyamus niger.* Henbane

and even becoming naturalized, henbane is recognized by its funnel-shaped, yellowish, purple-veined flowers and by the characteristic nightshade type of leaf (with large and/or uneven toothing or lobing). Henbane should be considered very dangerous and should not be ingested.

Hypericum perforatum: **St. John's wort (Guttiferae).**

St. John's wort, recognized by its flowers with yellow, often dark-dotted petals subtending numerous stamens in several bundles and by its opposite, entire leaves with transparent glandular dots (when held up to the light), is among the plant species implicated in cases of phytophotodermatitis (or animal photosensitization by plants). Pale-skinned animals, such as particular breeds of sheep, upon eating this plant, run the risk of accumulation of a light-absorbing molecule (hypericin) near the skin surface following its absorption into the bloodstream. The skin is thereby rendered extra sensitive to sunlight (that is, to ultraviolet radiation), and exaggerated sunburnlike reactions may occur. Swelling (edema) of pale facial tissue may occur as well, resulting in a condition known as bighead.

Ilex **spp.: Hollies (Aquifoliaceae).**

Holly leaves and berries (technically, drupes) are popular as plant decorative materials and are probably not seriously toxic.

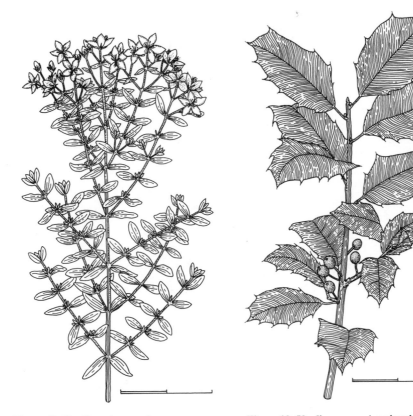

Figure 12–52 *Hypericum perforatum.*
St. John's wort

Figure 12–53 *Ilex opaca.* American holly

However, berries of various species of *Ilex* may contain purgative saponin glycosides and perhaps other types of irritant compounds (possibly triterpenoids), and are known to cause considerable digestive upset (diarrhea and emesis) if consumed in quantity. Children should be discouraged from eating any plant materials employed in decorations.

Ipomoea purpurea and tricolor: **Morning-glories (Convolvulaceae).**
Well-known vines with large, funnel-shaped flowers, morning-glories have achieved a sort of fame among cultivated plants because seeds of certain varieties are known to contain LSD-like substances, capable of inducing hallucinations. Varieties with potentially potent seeds include "Heavenly Blue," "Pearly Gates," and "Flying Saucer." One almost has to wonder if these cultivar names relate to the appearance of the plant (the probable explanation) or experiences encountered if the seeds are ingested. Regardless, various wild species of "morning-glory" (including species in the genus *Ipomoea* and the genus *Convolvulus*) may contain similar compounds as well.

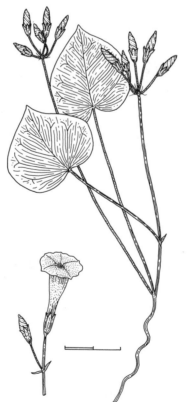

Figure 12–54 *Ipomoea purpurea.*
Common morning-glory

***Iris* spp.: Irises (Iridaceae).**   As in the case of a number of members of three potentially look-alike monocot families (lily, amaryllis, and iris families), underground parts should be viewed with caution when considering human consumption. The rootstock (rhizome or bulb) of *Iris* is probably toxic, but the poisonous principle is yet to be identified with certainty.

***Kalmia* spp.: Mountain laurel (Ericaceae).**   Common in the shrub layer of the vegetation of the Appalachian Mountains, mountain laurel is recognized by its evergreen foliage and saucerlike white to pink flowers. All parts of the plant contain a resinous (probably terpenoid) substance, andromedotoxin (grayanotoxin), which is incompletely characterized. Whether poorly known chemically or not, andromedotoxin is a serious toxin, and the effects on the nervous system are documented, including a tingling sensation, possible paralysis of the limbs, and eventual stoppage of the heart (via the nervous system). Poison honey is occasionally the result of bees working on these plants. Mountain laurel was used in a "suicide tea" by the Delaware Indians. Several species of mountain laurel (including *Kalmia latifolia* and *K. angustifolia*) are recognized botanically.

Figure 12–55 *Iris.* Iris

Figure 12–56 *Kalmia latifolia.*
Mountain laurel

***Laburnum anagyroides:* Golden chain (Leguminosae).**   The golden chain is a small, European tree of the legume family, with long, pendulous racemes of golden-yellow flowers and trifoliate leaves. It is occasionally planted in the United States. The beauty of this tree belies its toxic nature, as indeed it is poisonous and has been implicated in human death. All parts of the plant contain the toxic alkaloid cytisine. Initial symptoms include nervous excitement, incoordination, and considerable digestive upset. Respiratory paralysis may finally result.

***Lantana camara:* Lantana (Verbenaceae).**   Herbaceous, opposite-leaved shrub with flowers (in the same cluster) varying from yellow to pink to orange. Lantana contains substances that can have several possibly related effects, including acute gastrointestinal disturbance, liver dysfunction, and skin photosensitization. Exactly which compounds in the plant produce these effects is still a matter of debate, although triterpenoid substances are suspected. The green fruit is to be considered especially dangerous. Lantana is commonly cultivated in the southeastern United States and in houses or greenhouses farther north.

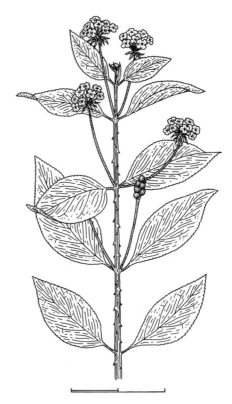

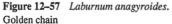

Figure 12–57   *Laburnum anagyroides.*
Golden chain

Figure 12–58   *Lantana camara.* Lantana

***Laportea canadensis:* Wood nettle (Urticaceae).**   Wood nettle is similar to stinging nettle but is a slightly larger plant with alternate rather than opposite leaves. As in stinging nettle, the stem hairs of wood nettle contain a reputed mixture of irritant chemicals (see under *Urtica dioica*). Portions of the hairs may break off in the skin, releasing the chemicals and resulting in a very unpleasant, burning sensation (much like the bite of an ant), which persists for some minutes.

***Lathyrus* spp.: Vetchlings, sweet peas, winter peas (Leguminosae).**
These are herbaceous vines with apparently compound leaves (possessing two or more leaflets) that terminate in tendrils. Seeds of several species of *Lathyrus* contain an amine type of substance known to cause lameness, paralysis, and even skeletal lesions and deformity in livestock, especially horses. Symptoms developing from ingestion of *Lathyrus* seeds are known collectively as lathyrism or, more specifically, osteolathyrism. Historically, cases of human lathyrism are known.

***Leucothoë* spp.: Dog laurel, sweet bells (Ericaceae).**   Leucothoes are evergreen or deciduous shrubs resembling *Pieris* (Japanese andromeda); however, in *Leucothoë*, the inflorescences are commonly axillary rather than terminal.

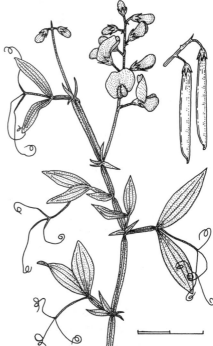

Figure 12–59 *Laportea canadensis.* Wood nettle

Figure 12–60 *Lathyrus latifolius.* Vetchling (everlasting pea)

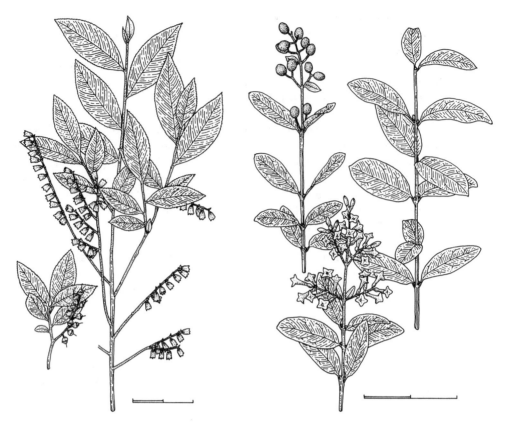

Figure 12–61 *Leucothoë*. Dog laurel   **Figure 12–62** *Ligustrum vulgare*. Privet

Similar to other members of the heath family, such as Japanese andromeda, rhododendrons, and mountain laurel, leucothoes contain andromedotoxin; and similar results are to be expected following ingestion (see under *Kalmia*).

***Ligustrum vulgare:* Privet (Oleaceae).**   Commonly planted as a hedge, privet is noted for its simple, opposite leaves and panicles of smallish white flowers, followed eventually by the blue-black, somewhat waxy berries. Although privet has long been known to cause digestive upset, including purgation, the toxic principle remained relatively unknown; however, berries and leaves are now believed to contain a glycoside irritating to the gastrointestinal tract.

***Linum usitatissimum:* Flax (Linaceae).**   Slender, erect annual with narrow leaves, pale blue flowers (the petals broadest and subtruncate at the apex), and capsular fruit. Flax (a European plant) is cultivated for its fiber (the source of linen) and for linseed oil, which is expressed from the seed; plants occasionally escape from cultivation in the United States. Flax contains varying (with environmental

Figure 12–63 *Linum usitatissimum.* Flax

Figure 12–64 *Lobelia siphilitica.*
Great blue lobelia

conditions) quantities of a cyanogenic glycoside, causing difficulties in breathing if consumed.   Additionally, linseed oil may induce contact dermatitis.

Lobelia spp.: Includes great blue lobelia, Indian tobacco, cardinal flower, and others (Campanulaceae).   Lobelias are herbaceous plants recognized by a two-lipped corolla that is split to the base on the upper side. The united stamens may be visible or even protrude through this dorsal slit. Lobelias have had a history of medicinal use, especially in nineteenth-century America, when the visionary Samuel Thomson selected *Lobelia inflata* (Indian tobacco) as his panacea to combat what he regarded as the "unity of disease." Indian tobacco received its common name from early settlers who observed the practice of smoking dried leaves by Indians for some type of "effect." Indeed, lobelias have pharmacologically active compounds, the lobelia alkaloids. These are rather simple alkaloids, resembling those found in tobacco and in poison hemlock. The effect of lobeline on the central nervous system

is similar to that of nicotine (emetic and depressant), but perhaps somewhat less intense; lobeline may actually stimulate respiration, but its effects are unpredictable. Because of chemical similarity to nicotine, lobeline found use for a time in various no-smoking aids or products. Root and leaf teas and poultices of great blue lobelia (*Lobelia siphilitica*) were used by Cherokee Indians for a variety of purposes, including treatment of hard-to-heal sores such as those associated with venereal disease (P. B. Hamel and M. U. Chiltoskey, *Cherokee Plants—Their Uses—A 400 Year History*, published by the authors, 1975).

Lupinus **spp.: Lupines (Leguminosae).** Although present in the eastern United States, lupine species become more prevalent in the western half of the country. They are recognized by terminal racemes (or spikes) of attractive, often bluish flowers (of the legume type) and by their typically palmate, multifoliate leaves. Although eastern representatives are toxic, lupines cause much more trouble westward, having been implicated as a leading cause of unnatural deaths of sheep on rangelands. The toxic alkaloid is a relatively simple (two-ringed) structure affecting the nervous system. Symptoms leading to death vary from relatively peaceful (sleepiness and coma) to convulsant.

Figure 12–65 *Lupinus.* Lupine

***Lycopersicon esculentum:* Tomato (Solanaceae).**   Green parts of the tomato (leaves, stems) and perhaps the roots are toxic and contain the solanine type of alkaloid (solanidine or tomatidine). This is not the structurally simpler, hallucinogenic type of alkaloid characteristic of some other members of the nightshade family (such as belladonna), but rather is a complex, steroidal type of alkaloid, causing digestive upset and eventual nervous system dysfunction (but not true hallucinations). Parts of the tomato plant other than the fruit should not be consumed in any form or fashion.

***Melanthium virginicum:* Bunch-flower (Liliaceae).**   Bunch-flower is a large herb with panicles of modest-sized, green-yellow flowers and sheathing leaves, the lower leaves being quite elongated. As with a number of members of the lily family, whose toxicity is indefinitely known, *Melanthium* is probably toxic and should be avoided; bunch-flower, mixed with hay, has been circumstantially implicated in poisoning of horses (see Kingsbury, 1964).

***Melia azedarach:* Chinaberry (Meliaceae).**   Although native to southwest Asia, chinaberry is widely naturalized in the southeastern United States. Many farmyards or lots in the Southeast have their in-resident chinaberry, a short to medium

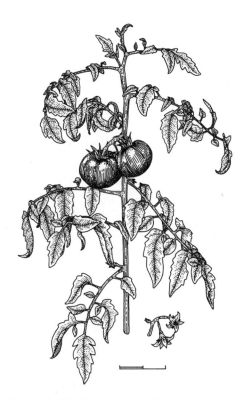

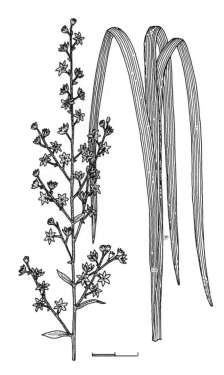

Figure 12–66 *Lycopersicon esculentum.*
Tomato

Figure 12–67 *Melanthium virginicum.*
Bunch-flower

height tree with bipinnately compound leaves bearing pointed leaflets; the thick trunk and low, spreading branches of chinaberry no doubt contribute to its popularity. Although perhaps fun to climb, the yellowish, smooth (eventually wrinkling), semipersistent drupes contain a poorly understood resin that is known to have caused human death through ingestion. Symptoms of poisoning include severe digestive irritation and manifestations of dysfunction of the nervous system; kidney malfunction and damage may eventually occur. More than one toxin may be present in chinaberry.

Menispermum canadense: **Canada moonseed (Menispermaceae).**
Moonseed vines resemble grape vines but the leaves have fewer lobes (and the lobes are generally more obtuse than those of grapevines). Moonseeds are less common than grapevines, and, unlike grapevines, moonseeds (including the fruit) are toxic. Although the toxin is poorly known, it is probably a type of alkaloid affecting the nervous system and heartbeat; convulsions are a possible consequence of moonseed poisoning.

Mirabilis jalapa: **Four-o'clock (Nyctaginaceae).**
An opposite-leaved herb, flowers of four-o'clock are known for their trumpetlike perianths, which usually

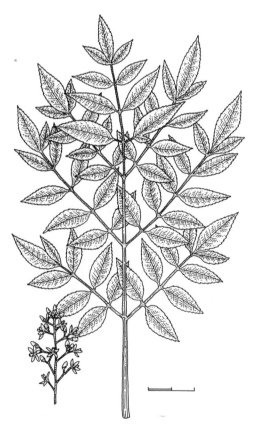

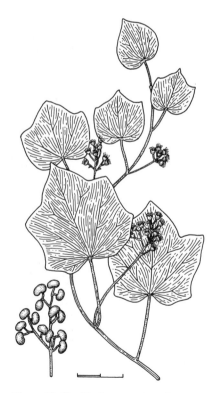

Figure 12–68 *Melia azedarach.* Chinaberry

Figure 12–69 *Menispermum canadense.* Canada moonseed

Figure 12–70 *Mirabilis jalapa.* Four-o'clock   **Figure 12–71** *Morus alba.* White mulberry

do not open until late afternoon. The chemical nature of the toxin is unknown, but seeds and perhaps other parts of the plant are considered capable of causing acute gastric distress.

Morus spp.: Mulberries (Moraceae).   Small- to medium-sized trees with ovate, sometimes irregularly lobed leaves. Although ripe mulberry fruit (a multiple fruit) is edible, the milky latex of unripe fruit and of leaves and young twigs reportedly causes digestive upset and stimulation of the nervous system (including possible hallucinations). Leaves of mulberry (and for that matter of osage orange, *Maclura pomifera*, also in the mulberry family) have been linked to dermatitis. It would appear that all the preceding "information" stands in need of confirmation.

Narcissus spp.: Daffodils, jonquils (Amaryllidaceae).   Bulbs of daffodils are thought to contain toxic alkaloidal substances capable of causing potentially serious digestive upset; excessive handling of daffodil bulbs may cause dermal irritation due to the presence of sharp crystals of calcium oxalate. Bulbs and other

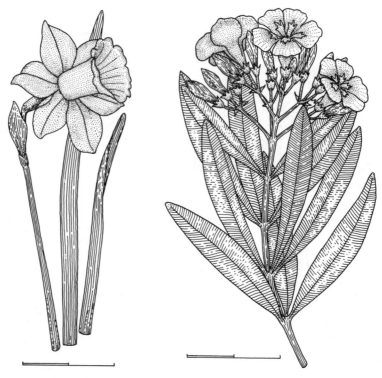

Figure 12–72 *Narcissus.*
Daffodil

Figure 12–73 *Nerium oleander.* Oleander

underground parts of members of the amaryllis (and lily and iris) family should not be consumed unless the plant is known to be edible, and identification is certain.

Nerium oleander: Oleander (Apocynaceae). Native to Mediterranean Europe, oleander is rather commonly planted in the southeastern United States and in California. Usually seen as a shrub, it is admired for its attractive, opposite or whorled, dark, moderately slender, evergreen leaves and its showy, red, pink, white, or even yellow flowers. Oleander contains various digitalislike cardiac glycosides, and all parts of the plant are considered toxic (although recent literature indicates that the leaves and flowers may be less toxic than the seeds). The cardioactive substances in oleander have an exaggerated digitalislike effect in unnaturally increasing the contractility of heart muscle; subsequently, the heartbeat may weaken and loss of heart function (cardiac arrest) may occur. Glycosides from oleander have generally proved too toxic for medical use.

Nicotiana tabacum: Tobacco (Solanaceae). Although tobacco is an introduced plant, it is widely cultivated in the mideast central and mid-Atlantic United States. In addition to its characteristic, large tobacco foliage, the plant is recognized by

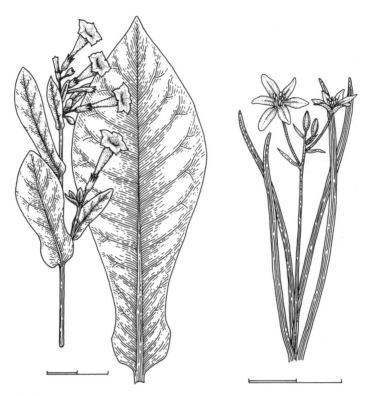

Figure 12–74 *Nicotiana tabacum.* Tobacco

Figure 12–75 *Ornithogalum umbellatum.* Star-of-Bethlehem

its terminal inflorescences of long, tubular, yellow to cream or pinkish flowers. Tobacco contains, among other potentially harmful substances, nicotine, a simple alkaloid with an action much like coniine (alkaloid from poison hemlock) if even low levels are absorbed (or injected) directly into the bloodstream. Nicotine, as well as coniine, is a central nervous system depressant; respiratory paralysis can be the ultimate result of nicotine overdose. Insects are generally sensitive to nicotine, which has been employed commercially as an insecticide.

Ornithogalum umbellatum: **Star-of-Bethlehem (Liliaceae).** This spring-flowering member of the lily family is a smallish, scapose herb with several erect, medium-sized, white flowers; the six petalloid structures of a flower each bear a broad, medial, green stripe. Bulbs and other parts are known to contain substances (possibly cardiac glycosides) adversely affecting the gastrointestinal system and the rhythm of the heart. In some countries it is customary to decorate the manger scene at Christmas time with this plant, perhaps increasing the likelihood of human consumption. Human and animal poisonings have been attributed to star-of-Bethlehem.

Papaver spp.: Poppies (Papaveraceae).   Poppies are easily recognized by the single, large, white to deep red, usually four-petaled flower terminating a stem. The ensuing capsule has a disclike apex (originating from the stigma of the flower), beneath which (when the fruit is mature) tiny openings occur that function in seed release. Various species of poppy, including especially *Papaver somniferum* (the opium poppy), contain the opium (isoquinoline) type of alkaloid.   In chemical structure, alkaloids of this type are relatively simple molecules and are depressant to the activity of the central nervous system. These alkaloids are present in the drug opium, which is the crude white latex exuding from the cut surfaces of green capsules. Refined or derivative drugs from opium (that is, from the raw latex), such as morphine, codeine, and heroin, are well known for their narcotic and anesthetic properties, as well as for their legal and illegal uses. It is illegal to grow the opium poppy in the United States.

Parthenocissus quinquefolia: Virginia creeper (Vitaceae).   Virginia creeper, an alternate-leaved vine belonging to the grape family, has five palmately

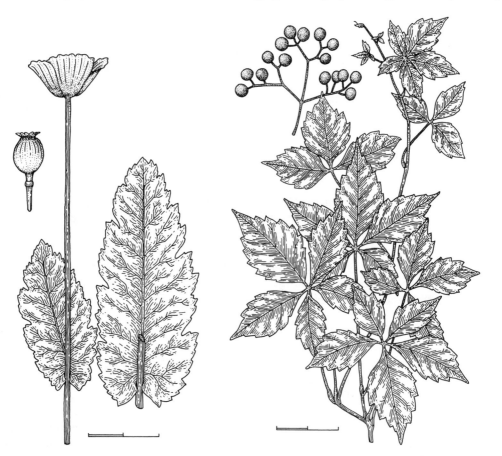

Figure 12–76 *Papaver somniferum.*
Opium poppy

Figure 12–77 *Parthenocissus quinquefolia.*
Virginia creeper

arranged leaflets per leaf and tendrils with small, disclike terminations. The smallish, dark-blue berries are suspected of having caused human poisoning, but there is little knowledge of the exact conditions under which this occurred or of the precise nature of the toxic substance. However, death of small laboratory animals as an apparent conse- quence of ingestion of berries of Virginia creeper has been reported. Available infor- mation, thus, suggests at least some level of toxicity of Virginia creeper.

***Pastinaca sativa:* Wild parsnip (Umbelliferae).**   This yellow-flowered member of the carrot family with once-pinnately compound leaves would not appear on most lists of toxic plants, as the roots are even considered to be edible. However, wild parsnip does contain a type of substance (furanocoumarin) that can cause the skin to gain an increased sensitivity to ultraviolet light. People swimming in ponds or lakes where wild parsnip is common around the edge may develop an unexpected, rashlike sunburn due to the combined effects of the substance, transferred in moisture from the plant, and sunlight. This dermatitis is referred to as parsnip poisoning or swimmer's rash.

***Phoradendron serotinum* (= *P. flavescens*): Mistletoe (Loran- thaceae).**   Mistletoe is a small, opposite-leaved, evergreen shrub, parasitic on

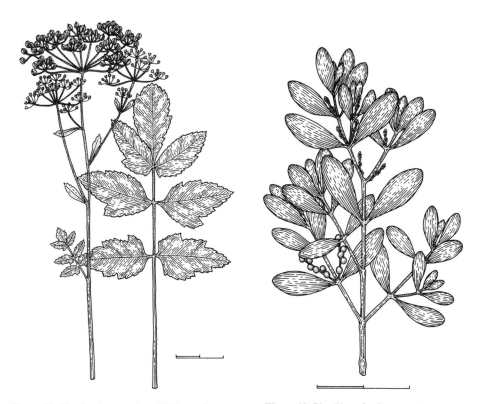

Figure 12–78 *Pastinaca sativa.* Wild parsnip

Figure 12–79 *Phoradendron serotinum.*
Mistletoe

branches of certain species of deciduous trees in the eastern United States (especially the Southeast). The whitish berries contain toxic substances (amines and perhaps also proteins) capable of inducing gastric distress and drastically lowering blood pressure, even to the point of cardiovascular collapse. Mistletoe should be considered a potentially dangerous Christmas decoration, especially if children are around.

Physalis spp.: Ground cherry, Chinese lantern (Solanaceae).

Vegetatively, and even florally, ground cherry resembles various of the common nightshades (*Solanum* spp.); however, the berry is surrounded by the persistent calyx, which becomes enlarged and papery (bladderlike). Similar to nightshades (and to green parts of the potato and the tomato), at least some ground cherry species contain the steroidal type (solanidine type) of alkaloid. In ground cherry, as in nightshades, the unripe fruit is considered more dangerous than the ripe fruit.

Phytolacca americana: Poke, pokeweed, pokeberry (Phytolaccaceae).

Pokeweed, a large, smooth, reddish-stemmed herb with sizable alternate leaves, develops racemes of modest white flowers, after which the smallish,

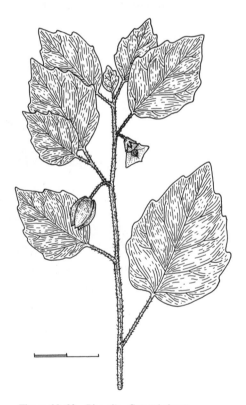

Figure 12–80 *Physalis.* Ground cherry

Figure 12–81 *Phytolacca americana.* Pokeweed

dark-purple berries (with crimson juice) appear. In America, historically, "poke root" has been used as a cathartic. Indeed, poke does contain a saponin with laxative properties; however, the substance is toxic and poke should be used medicinally only with knowledge and then with extreme caution. "Pickled poke" stems are eaten like celery; apparently, pickling or parboiling removes some or all of the toxin. If poke leaves are used in salad, younger leaves are considered safer than older ones. Actually, the ripe berry is probably the least toxic part of pokeweed, but should still be considered potentially dangerous to infants. In addition to the presence of sapogenic glycosides, *Phytolacca* has been found to contain types of proteins capable of stimulating certain kinds of cells, especially types of white blood cells (lymphocytes), to divide. These protein substances, of medical interest, have been termed mitogens (because of their stimulation of mitosis, the division of the cell's nucleus).

Pieris japonica: Japanese andromeda (Ericaceae).

This is an evergreen shrub with terminal, sometimes drooping, white panicles of bell-shaped flowers. Japanese andromeda is a common planting in zoological gardens, along with other evergreen shrubs such as rhododendron (a member of the same family), and is occasionally implicated in the poisoning of zoo animals. *Pieris, Rhododendron, Kalmia* (mountain laurel), and *Leucothoë* (dog laurel) contain the same resinoid toxin, andromedotoxin (see discussion under *Kalmia*).

Figure 12–82 *Pieris japonica.* Japanese andromeda

***Podophyllum peltatum:* Mayapple (Berberidaceae).**   The large, palmately lobed, umbrellalike leaf of mayapple is a common feature seen in the springtime herb layer of eastern deciduous forests. Older mayapples develop two leaves, a single, stalked, whitish flower occurring where the leaves are joined together; a green-yellow berry eventually occupies the position of the former flower; the berry when soft and yellow is considered scarcely toxic and, by some, even edible. A resinous material is rather easily extracted from the powdered rhizome of mayapple, usually by alcohol; this pale, yellowish-brown, resinous extract is called podophyllin. Although podophyllin has been employed as a cathartic, it is caustic to the gastrointestinal tract, causing severe purging. However, concerning external application, podophyllin has had a long history of largely beneficial use in the United States in the treatment of certain types of warts (especially soft, venereal warts) and even skin cancers; it is considered to have an antimitotic activity, similar to colchicine.

***Prunus serotina:* Wild cherry, black cherry (Rosaceae).**   This common, alternate-leaved native tree belonging to the rose family is recognized by the presence of one to three small glandular bumps on the petiole (near the leaf-blade) and by its showy racemes of white flowers appearing in late spring; the racemes are subsequently occupied by smallish, red-black drupes (cherries). The ripe fruit flesh is the least dangerous (probably harmless) part, although it is reputedly not very tasty. Seeds (pits),

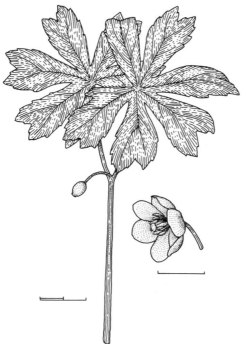

Figure 12–83 *Podophyllum peltatum.*
Mayapple

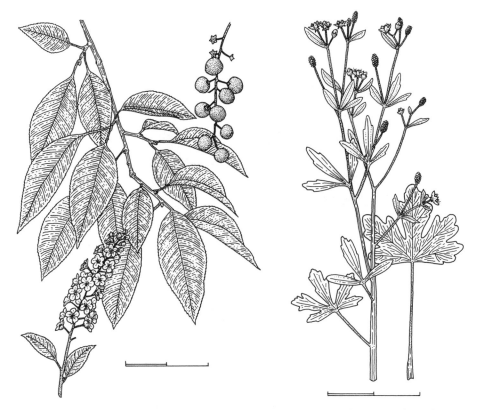

Figure 12–84 *Prunus serotina.* Wild cherry

Figure 12–85 *Ranunculus sceleratus.*
Cursed crowfoot

twigs, bark, and fresh leaves may contain levels of cyanide (HCN), a component of a larger molecule (amygdalin), well exceeding the danger point. Intake of cyanide can lead to internal asphyxiation (that is, asphyxiation at the cell level). Although *Prunus serotina* is perhaps the most dangerous of the wild cherries, other species (for example, choke cherry, *Prunus virginiana*) may have a relatively high cyanide content as well.

Ranunculus **spp.: Buttercup, crowfoot (Ranunculaceae).**   Buttercups are recognized by their small- to medium-sized, yellow, thimblelike, often metallically shiny flowers, and by the palmately lobed/compound, crowfoot leaf. They may contain a substance (protoanemonin), similar or identical to that found in *Anemone*, that can be irritating to the skin or, more importantly, corrosively irritating to the mucous lining of the digestive tract. The immediate precursor to this substance is an apparently harmless glycoside known as ranunculin. However, the potentially toxic protoanemonin is released from ranunculin during digestion.

Rhamnus cathartica: **Common or European buckthorn (Rhamnaceae).**   Common buckthorn is a shrub, recognized by its often spine-tipped

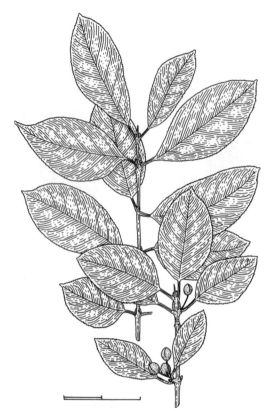

Figure 12–86 *Rhamnus cathartica.*
Common buckthorn

branches, subopposite leaves, and blackish, globose, berrylike drupes. Drupes of buckthorn contain anthraquinones (athraquinone or anthracene glycosides) that cause intestinal catharsis (and perhaps nausea). Typically, buckthorn poisoning is not serious; in fact, buckthorn fruit has been employed medicinally as a purgative. Alder buckthorn, *Rhamnus frangula*, contains similar purgative substances.

Rheum rhaponticum (= *R. rhabarbarum*): Rhubarb (Polygonaceae).
Rhubarb is recognized by its broad leaf blades, subtended by elongated, often reddish, celerylike petioles (leaf stalks). The petioles are edible (sold in grocery stores) and typically contain a concentration of the harmless acid, malic acid, which imparts the pleasant, tangy taste to rhubarb. However, the leaf blades, surprisingly, may be toxic, often containing substantial levels of oxalic acid (or soluble oxalate), which, upon absorption from the digestive tract, can interact with blood calcium, altering blood chemistry (and the clotting potential of the blood) and forming solid particles that may eventually collect in the kidney tubules. Rhubarb

may also contain cathartic anthraquinone glycosides, which perhaps contribute to the symptomology of rhubarb poisoning.

Rhododendron spp.:   Rhododendrons and azaleas (Ericaceae).

These are popular, native or introduced ornamental bushes with terminal clusters of showy, often somewhat irregular flowers. Generally, species known as rhododendrons are evergreen or semievergreen, and those referred to as azaleas are deciduous. Regardless, species of both categories contain the still poorly known resinoid toxin andromedotoxin. This toxin affects the nervous system, resulting in convulsions, limb paralysis, or both, and may eventually affect the heart. The toxin is similar or identical to that found in mountain laurel (*Kalmia*). Similar to Japanese andromeda (*Pieris*), rhododendrons and azaleas constitute a potential hazard to zoo animals because of their popularity as plantings.

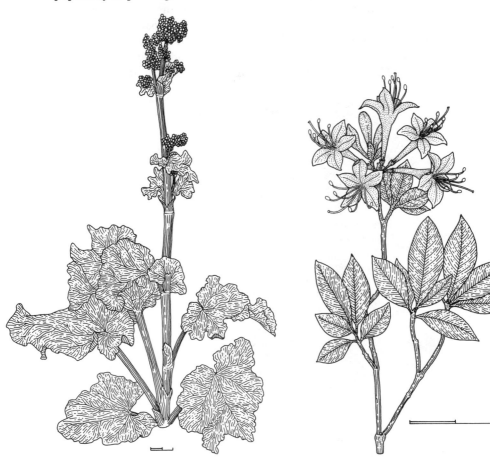

Figure 12–87 *Rheum rhaponticum*. Rhubarb

Figure 12–88 *Rhododendron*. Rhododendron, azalea

***Rhodotypos scandens (R. tetrapetala):* Jetbead (Rosaceae).**   Jetbead is an ornamental, opposite-leaved shrub characterized by usually four persistent, shiny-black drupes, deriving from each showy, white, four-petaled flower. A cyanide-releasing compound is thought to be contained within the drupes. This substance is probably similar or identical to that found in certain other members of the rose family, such as wild cherry (*Prunus*).

***Rhus (Toxicodendron)* spp.: Poison ivy, poison oak, poison sumac (Anacardiaceae).**   Contrary to the opinion of some, these are three different species. Poison sumac (*R. vernix*) has seven or more leaflets per leaf and is found in true swamps or bogs. Poison ivy (*R. radicans*) and poison oak (*R. toxicodendron* = *R. quercifolia* of some authors) both have three leaflets per leaf; in poison oak, the leaflets are more deeply lobed and the plants are generally more pubescent. Poison oak occurs in pine/scrub-oak savannas of the eastern coastal plain and is never a climbing plant. Poison ivy has a much broader distribution and often produces aerial roots by which it may climb on other vegetation (or other structures in general). All three species contain urushiol, a rather simple, lacquerlike phenolic compound. Careful analysis has revealed that urushiol is actually a mixture of very

Figure 12–89 *Rhodotypos scandens.*
Jetbead

Figure 12–90   *Rhus radicans*. Poison ivy   **Figure 12–91**   *Ricinus communis*. Castor bean

similar substances (varying by slight differences in the sidechain of the molecule). The exact composition of the urushiol mixture may vary among different toxic species of *Rhus*. Regardless, through skin contact with the plants, the familiar contact dermatitis (skin rash) may result. It is estimated that at least one-half of the population is sensitive to urushiol to some extent. The rash is usually self-limiting in a matter of days (or, in rarer instances, weeks); burning and itching are typically relieved with various topical creams. As a generality, harmless species of *Rhus* (good sumacs) have terminal, erect, pubescent, reddish fruit clusters; on the other hand, species causing dermatitis (bad sumacs, including poison ivy and poison oak) have axillary, more or less drooping clusters of glabrous or pubescent, whitish (green- or yellow-white) fruit.

Ricinus communis: Castor bean, palma christi (Euphorbiaceae).

This familiar herblike shrub or small tree is rather commonly planted around houses for the large, ornamental, palmately lobed foliage. Eventually, spiny capsules are produced containing attractive, brown- or gray-white, mottled seeds, reputedly (unfortunately) with a pleasant taste. The seeds contain a toxic protein (ricin) that attacks the lining of the digestive tract, the blood, and ultimately the kidneys. Seeds are to be considered hazardous if consumed; a very few seeds may cause serious poisoning or death in children, especially if well chewed. The toxic protein is water soluble and is not present in (not soluble in) the expressed oil fraction (castor oil), which, at least in the past, has been commonly used as a laxative.

Robinia pseudo-acacia: Black locust (Leguminosae).

A common and rapidly growing tree with odd-pinnately compound leaves, each leaf possessing a pair of spiny stipules at the base; pendulous, axillary racemes of fragrant, white flowers appear in late spring, followed by rather typical leguminous pods. Young foliage and the inner bark contain a phytotoxin (toxic protein) capable of causing digestive upset. Physiologically active proteins have been isolated from the seeds as well. It is not clear how severely toxic black locust is.

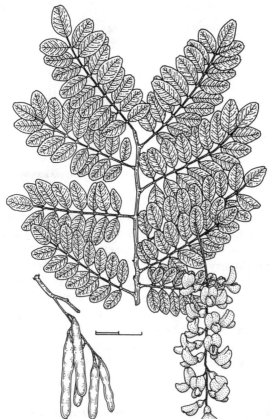

Figure 12–92 *Robinia pseudo-acacia.*
Black locust

***Sambucus canadensis:* Elderberry (Caprifoliaceae).**   Elderberry (or elder) is a herbaceous shrub with pithy stems and opposite, pinnately compound leaves. Not the ripe fruit (a source of wine), but green parts of elderberry, and apparently the root as well, contain a type of glycoside capable of releasing cyanide; a toxic alkaloid may also be present. Hollowed-out stems (pith removed) are apparently popular as pea-shooters or homemade blowguns; however, putting these in the mouth should be considered an unwise practice. Cathartic saponins may be present in various members of the honeysuckle family to which elderberry belongs.

***Sanguinaria canadensis:* Bloodroot (Papaveraceae).**   This plant is a common and attractive member of the perennial, herbaceous spring flora. The showy, solitary white flower on a leafless stalk is soon accompanied by a single, kidney-shaped, palmately lobed leaf. The underground stem (rhizome) yields a blood-red fluid when cut. Bloodroot juice was once widely (and is still occasionally) used in the treatment of skin (and other) cancers; the powdered rhizome has been employed as an expectorant. Bloodroot contains alkaloids, related to those in the

Figure 12–93 *Sambucus canadensis.*
Elderberry

Figure 12–94 *Sanguinaria canadensis.* Bloodroot

opium poppy (a member of the same family), that have a depressant action on the central nervous system; it is to be considered dangerous if eaten in quantity.

Saponaria officinalis: **Soapwort, bouncing bet (Caryophyllaceae).**

A common summer-flowering weed, soapwort is recognized by the opposite, palmately veined leaves and by the fused sepals of the flower, which provide a functional tube to the corolla (the petals themselves are not actually fused); each petal has an apical notch. Soapwort, at one time employed as a soap substitute, contains a substance (sapogenic glycoside) that generates a soaplike (frothing) action when mixed with water. This substance is very irritating to the lining of the digestive tract and, if absorbed into the bloodstream, is potentially destructive to red blood cells as well.

Scilla **spp.:** **Squill (Liliaceae).**

These plants resemble small hyacinths and are commonly planted in spring ornamental gardens. Species of *Scilla* and the closely related genus *Urginea* contain dangerous cardiac glycosides, potentially

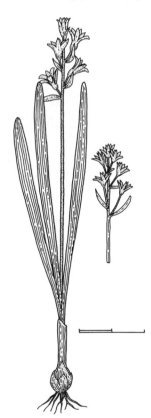

Figure 12–95 *Saponaria officinalis.*
Soapwort, bouncing bet

Figure 12–96 *Scilla.* Squill

affecting heart rhythm. The bulb of *Urginea maritima* (red squill) has been used in the preparation of a commercial rat poison.

Senecio spp.: Groundsels (Compositae).   Senecios are yellow-flowered members of the sunflower family, in some cases with lyrately lobed or compound leaves. Typically, a whorl of more or less equal, slender, valvate bracts surrounds the base of the flowering head. Mainly a problem with regard to livestock (especially horses) on rangelands, a number of species of *Senecio* (in various habitats) have been found to contain a particular category of alkaloid (pyrrolizidine alkaloids) capable of inducing cumulative and chronic liver damage, reminiscent of alcohol-induced cirrhosis, if continued consumption occurs. In North America, *Senecio* is of very little concern in human poisoning.

Solanum spp.: Nightshades (Solanaceae).   Various species of nightshade occur as weeds in eastern North America, including *S. dulcamara*, bittersweet nightshade; *Solanum nigrum* (*S. americanum* of some authors), black nightshade; and *Solanum*

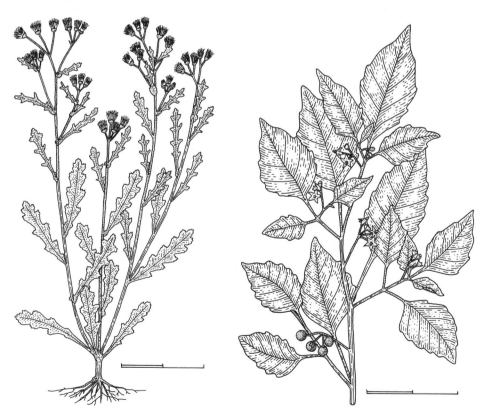

Figure 12–97 *Senecio vulgaris.* Common groundsel

Figure 12–98 *Solanum nigrum.* Black nightshade

carolinense, horse nettle. Bittersweet nightshade is a perennial vine, with purple flowers; black nightshade and horse nettle are white- or violet-flowered herbs, the latter being spiny. All contain the solanine type of alkaloid, a complex, steroidal type of alkaloid initially attached to a sugar molecule (technically, a glycoalkaloid). The alkaloid component (solanidine) is dangerous when released from the sugar moiety during animal digestion, and severe gastrointestinal irritation is to be anticipated, followed by nervous system dysfunctions such as dyspnea, trembling, restlessness, and possible convulsions. In these common nightshades, solanine content often increases as the season progresses (including the content in the unripe fruit). Even dried specimens are potentially toxic. The Irish potato, *Solanum tuberosum*, also contains solanine, but only the green parts are dangerous; the solanine content of the edible tuber of the potato is generally low, well below danger levels, unless considerable greening has taken place (see Chapter 10).

***Spigelia marilandica:* Pinkroot, Indian pink (Loganiaceae).**   Pinkroot is recognized by its simple, sessile, opposite leaves and terminal, tubular, red flowers in one-sided, spikelike racemes. The alkaloid spigiline is a potential convulsant. However, serious problems have typically been encountered only in medicinal overdose (pinkroot was at one time employed medicinally as a vermifuge).

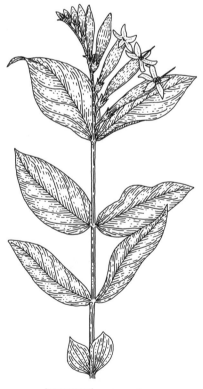

Figure 12–99 *Spigelia marilandica.*
Pinkroot

Symphoricarpos spp.:   Coralberry, snowberry (Caprifoliaceae).

Smallish, occasionally planted shrubs with opposite, ovate leaves, these plants develop axillary (or sometimes terminal) clusters of red-purple or white, berrylike drupes. If consumed in quantity, the berries may cause emesis and diarrhea; evidence is increasing that various members of this family (the honeysuckle family) contain saponins that are at least mildly cathartic.

Symplocarpus foetidus: Skunk cabbage (Araceae).

One of the earliest-flowering members of the spring flora, skunk cabbage is recognized by its purple-brown (or greenish), sometimes mottled spathe (hoodlike bract) surrounding a balllike spadix (fleshy spike) and by its fetid odor. As with jack-in-the-pulpit (*Arisaema*), skunk cabbage tissues contain sharp crystals of calcium oxalate, which may become lodged in the lining of the oral cavity, causing irritation and swelling.

Urtica dioica: Stinging or common nettle (Urticaceae).

Stinging nettles have prominently toothed, opposite leaves with subpalmate venation; dense

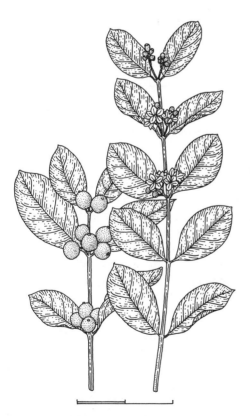

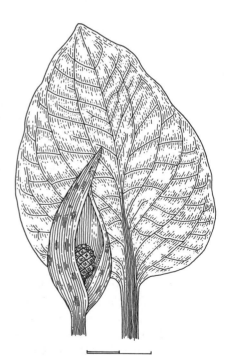

Figure 12–100 *Symphoricarpos*. Coralberry, snowberry

Figure 12–101 *Symplocarpus foetidus*. Skunk cabbage

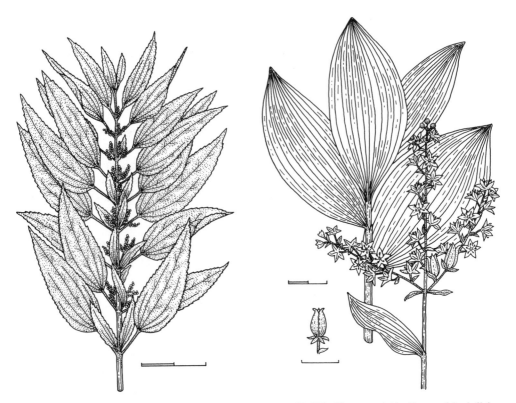

Figure 12–102 *Urtica dioica.* Stinging nettle   **Figure 12–103** *Veratrum viride.* Eastern false hellebore

clusters of small, greenish-white (to pinkish) flowers occur in the leaf axils. Nettles often occur in dense stands and can be a barrier difficult to walk through. Stinging hairs (like tiny hypodermic needles) become more concentrated toward the base of the plant. Each hair, examined microscopically, consists of a glandlike (secretory) base, a hollow (syringelike) tube, and a bulbous tip that readily breaks off in the skin, releasing what is apparently a mixture of chemicals; this injection results in a burning or stinging sensation that continues at least for a matter of minutes. Suggested chemical components of this still incompletely known stinging mixture have included histamine, acetylcholine, serotonin, and formic acid.

***Veratrum viride:* Eastern false hellebore (Liliaceae).** False hellebore is a tall, monocot herb of swamps or moist wooded areas, characterized by broad, parallel-veined, sheathing leaves and sizable terminal panicles of green-yellow flowers. A variety of complex, steroidal alkaloids (veratrum alkaloids) has been isolated from this species. *Veratrum* preparations were in the past occasionally used in medicine because of the ability of certain of these alkaloids, acting through the autonomic nervous system, to lower blood pressure. However, overdose results in severely depressed heart action and shallow respiration; hence, the plant is definitely to be considered toxic; its use in formal medicine was discontinued. Teratogenic (mutagenic) substances occur in *Veratrum viride*, but are better known from its western cousin, *V. californicum* (western false hellebore, common in high-elevation rangelands); documented cases of birth defects in livestock are attributed to *V. californicum* (see Chapter 11, under birth defects).

Vinca spp.: Periwinkles (Apocynaceae).

Several species of periwinkle have (or are suspected of having) a significant alkaloid content, involving more than one specific kind of alkaloid. Although often omitted from lists of poisonous plants, periwinkles are nonetheless probably not suitable items for human consumption. One species, *Vinca rosea* (now *Catharanthus roseus* according to most authors), has received considerable medical interest because of its particular alkaloid content (see Chapter 13 under *Catharanthus*). Periwinkles are herbs or trailing subshrubs with opposite (and in some cases evergreen) leaves. Flowers feature a salverform corolla that exhibits a slight twist or rotation if viewed face on. *Vinca minor* (common or lesser periwinkle) is frequently employed as an evergreen ground cover; it is known to contain the potentially pharmacologically active alkaloid vincamine.

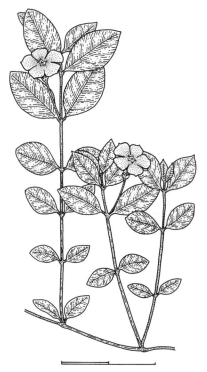

Figure 12–104 *Vinca minor.* Common periwinkle

Wisteria spp.: Wisteria (Leguminosae). Wisterias are familiar woody vines, sometimes shrub- or treelike, with alternate, odd-pinnately compound leaves; blue, purplish or white flowers (resembling in form those of black locust) occur in long, pendulous, fragrant racemes. Eventually, flattened pods (legumes) are seen to hang from the inflorescence branches. Reports of the chemical nature of the toxic substance or substances in wisteria vary in the literature (toxic glycosides and lectins have been suggested). Regardless, wisterias (notably the pods and seeds) are probably toxic and may, at a minimum, produce gastric distress if ingested.

Xanthium strumarium: Cocklebur (Compositae). A common, coarse, alternate-leaved herb; seeds of cocklebur are toxic, but are uncommonly consumed because they are contained in the burs (involucre of the female flower heads), which are typically too spiny to ingest. However, young seedlings retain a toxic content for a brief period, and these may indeed be eaten by livestock (especially pigs). The poisonous substance is hydroquinone, and effects of poison-

Figure 12–105 *Wisteria.* Wisteria   **Figure 12–106** *Xanthium strumarium.* Cocklebur

ing are generally manifest in various nervous system responses (including anorexia, depression, and possible spasms) and altered (weakened) heartbeat. Poisonings range from mild to severe.

Zigadenus (sometimes spelled *Zygadenus*) spp.: Death camas (Liliaceae).

Both eastern and western species of death camas (also known by other common names) occur. They resemble wild hyacinths, but may be distinguished from these and other related plants by the presence of shiny glands (one or two) toward the narrowed base of each petaloid perianth segment. Species of *Zigadenus* contain characteristic and complicated steroidal alkaloids (similar to those found in *Veratrum*), usually producing a specific progression of symptoms if ingested; this syndrome involves digestive upset, muscular weakness and loss of neuro-muscular control (ataxia), weakened heart action and lowered blood pressure, dyspnea, and perhaps coma and death. Species of *Zigadenus* have been responsible for the death of many head of sheep on western rangelands. Although perhaps "less famous," eastern species should probably be considered equally dangerous if consumed.

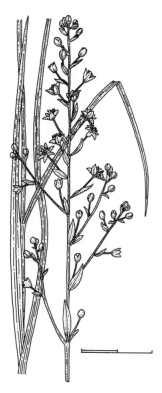

Figure 12–107 *Zigadenus.* Death camus

SELECTED REFERENCES

EVERS, R. A., AND R. P. LINK. 1972. *Poisonous Plants of the Midwest and Their Effects on Livestock.* Special publication 24, College of Agriculture, University of Illinois at Urbana-Champaign; distributed by the University of Illinois Press, Urbana. This book, focusing exclusively on poisonous plants and livestock, should prove very useful to the veterinarian, farmer, or anyone interested in animal husbandry; concise and readable information is presented on conditions of poisoning, toxic principles, clinical signs of poisoning, treatment, and even postmortem details.

FROHNE, D., AND H. J. PFANDER. 1983 (English translation 1984). *A Color Atlas of Poisonous Plants—A Handbook for Pharmacists, Doctors, Toxicologists, and Biologists.* English text translation, Wolfe Publishing Ltd., London. As subtitled, this is a handbook suitable for scientists interested in the topic of poisonous plants. The illustrations are excellent, including those of histological parts of the plant; good information on toxic chemicals is often given.

HARDIN, JAMES W., AND JAY M. ARENA. 1974. *Human Poisoning from Native and Cultivated Plants,* 2nd ed. Duke University Press, Durham, N.C. A descriptively precise and well-illustrated guide to common poisonous plants, arranged by botanical family.

KINGSBURY, JOHN M. 1964. *Poisonous Plants of the United States and Canada.* Prentice-Hall, Inc., Englewood Cliffs, N.J. Still the standard reference on North American poisonous plants; an indispensable resource for the serious student.

————. 1965 (paperback edition, 1972). *Deadly Harvest.* Holt, Rinehart and Winston, New York. A popularized and highly readable account of poisonous plants.

LAMPE, KENNETH F., AND MARY ANN MCCANN. 1985. *AMA Handbook of Poisonous and Injurious Plants.* American Medical Association, Chicago. Contains up-to-date references on a number of poisonous plants; includes specific information on toxins and symptoms.

LEVY, CHARLES K., AND RICHARD B. PRIMACK. 1984. *A Field Guide to Poisonous Plants and Mushrooms of North America.* Stephen Greene Press, Brattleboro, Vt. Contains surprisingly detailed information on toxic plants and fungi, including information on symptomology and first-aid treatment.

MORTON, JULIA F. 1982. *Plants Poisonous to People—in Florida and Other Warm Areas,* 2nd ed. Southeastern Printing Co., Inc., Stuart, Fla. A small but nicely color-illustrated and well-presented account of toxic plants more tropical in origin than those generally covered in this chapter.

MUENSCHER, W. C. 1951. *Poisonous Plants of the United States,* 2nd ed. Macmillan Inc., New York. Muenscher's work on poisonous plants in North America laid the foundation for a number of subsequent works, such as those of Kingsbury.

STEPHENS, HOMER A. 1980. *Poisonous Plants of the Central United States.* Regents Press of Kansas, Lawrence. Good information on poisonous plants occurring in the more westerly portions of eastern North America; excellent black and white photographs.

WESTBROOKS, RANDY G., AND JAMES W. PREACHER. 1986. *Poisonous Plants of Eastern North America*. University of South Carolina Press, Columbia. A color-illustrated account of common eastern North American toxic plants; information presented is relatively brief, but nonetheless precise; the same logical order of presentation is followed with regard to each plant.

Significant Medical Plants

In a way, this has been a difficult, though enjoyable, chapter to write. It is simply that it is hard to decide which plants to include and which to omit. A sliding scale exists between plants that are little known, perhaps rare woodland species, used occasionally in the art of healing by a backwoods practitioner or herb doctor, all the way to plants used presently, or in the recent past, in formal medicine for their precisely known chemical constituents. The latter category has been finally selected here because the use of these plants in medicine can be accurately documented, and their medicinally beneficial chemical constituents are generally clearly known. Even with these major medical plants, however, decision as to inclusion is difficult, because some species retain importance, no longer for the original chemicals they contain, but for the modern synthetic analogs based on these original chemicals. Regardless, the plants discussed here are those considered to have had, one way or another, a major impact in medicine throughout the twentieth century. It is hoped that the informational summaries presented for each will avoid the necessity of the reader having to thumb through the pages of many books, some very technical, to glean comparable information. By each illustration, the shorter (or single) scale line equals 1 inch of actual size; the longer equates to 2 inches.

ALOE spp.: Aloes (Liliaceae)

Predominantly of African descent, the aloes are relatively large, perennial members of the lily family with basal, more or less erect, succulent, swordlike leaves possessing sawtooth margins. The yellow-orange or red flowers are borne in racemes, often terminating an elongated scape. *Aloe ferox*, *A. perryi*, and *A. barbadensis* have proved

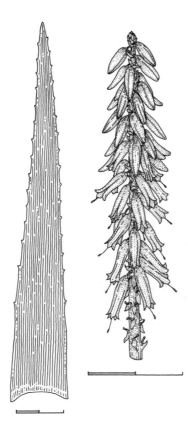

Figure 13–1 *Aloe barbadensis.*
Barbados aloe

to be medicinally useful species of aloe. *Aloe barbadensis*, Barbados aloe, is commonly cultivated in the Caribbean area.

If one considers the whole sweep and history of aloe use, including an unquestioned commercial success, these plants should definitely be included in a listing of medically important plants. Perhaps most significant is the use of aloe in treating burns, especially sunburn (ultraviolet radiation burns). Folk use long preceded the appearance of aloe in commercial products, and the raw plant is as effective as ever in soothing burns; the succulent leaf is simply slit open and the mucilaginous sap applied to the burned area. Commercial products of aloe often contain nothing more than the crude aloe latex. Aloe has proved particularly effective in treating certain types of dangerous burns, especially x-ray burns. Substances are apparently present in the aloe juice that have antibacterial properties and help prevent the infections that possibly follow a more severe type of burn. There is little question that aloe is in general good for the skin. A host of commercial skin creams, moisturizers, sun screens, and even shampoos contain aloe extract. Sap from the aloe leaf is mostly water; however, chrysophanic acid (technically, an anthraquinone molecule) has been detected, a substance that is believed to contribute to healing of the skin.

Another use of aloe leaf sap has been as a cathartic. Aloe juice contains various anthraquinone glycosides (collectively, aloin). One of these, barbaloin, yields the aglycone emodin (otherwise known as aloe-emodin). Emodin has an irritant action on the colon and can be effective as a purgative in relief of constipation. The action of emodin may, however, be drastic; so the drug should be used with caution or perhaps in combination with other drugs that will mollify the effect of emodin. Aloe cathartics are typically prepared from bitter aloes, which basically is the dried and hardened latex from the leaf.

ATROPA BELLADONNA: Belladonna, Deadly Nightshade (Solanaceae)

Belladonna is a shrublike, perennial, European herb with dull reddish to bluish- or greenish-purple, bell-shaped, axillary flowers, shiny black fruits (berries), and leaves that are more evenly margined than some of its solanaceous relatives. Belladonna and related genera and species in the nightshade family such as henbane (*Hyoscyamus niger*), mandrake (*Madragora officinarum*), and jimsonweed (*Datura stramonium*) have had a long and sometimes sordid history of human use, that is, in intentional poisoning or in black magic. In particular, belladonna, henbane, and mandrake were used in the practice of witchcraft and sorcery during the European

Figure 13–2 *Atropa belladonna.* Belladonna, deadly nightshade

Middle Ages. They were employed in witches' brews to induce hallucinogenic states for communing with the supernatural, particularly during witches' celebrations (known as sabbats). Through the use of these plants, witches could induce the desired visual, and sometimes frenzied, states in their subjects.

Belladonna and its botanical cousins contain atropinelike alkaloids, a relatively simple category of alkaloid (tropane type) consisting fundamentally of a single ring with nitrogen bonded across the molecule (see Chapter 3). In belladonna, three very similar, principal alkaloids may occur: hyoscyamine, scopolamine, and atropine itself. Hyoscyamine is usually most abundant in the plant, with scopolamine perhaps most effectively psychoactive. However, all three alkaloids are potentially present and hallucinogenic.

But all for belladonna is not a dark history, focusing on witchcraft and psychoactivity. To the contrary, belladonna has probably been put to as many different medicinal (and related) uses as has any other plant. The atropinelike alkaloids from belladonna (all loosely termed atropine) are powerful antispasmodics and anodynes. They are particularly effective in relaxation of smooth muscle, such as that lining the digestive tract, and are consequently useful in relieving intestinal cramps (whether due to diarrhea or spastic constipation). Stomach medicine containing belladonna extract is currently available (by prescription). Atropine can reduce mucous secretions, and it is utilized in some nasal sprays or decongestants (in which it acts as an antihistamine). Because of the bronchodilating properties of atropine (that is, its activity in relaxing constricted bronchial tubes), belladonna has been used to treat asthma. For years, belladonna extract was employed as "the drop" used by ophthamologists as a mydriatic agent, to dilate the pupil of the eye during examination. In a similar vein, belladonna was used by Italian women to brighten their eyes, the red sap of the plant also being employed as a cosmetic; the meaning of the common name belladonna, from the Italian language, is "beautiful lady." Belladonna has been used to control unwanted, nocturnal urination and also night sweating, as a treatment of symptoms in Parkinson's disease, as an aid in limiting epileptic seizure, for control of whooping-cough spasms, to treat bradycardia (atropine is used to stimulate the heart following cardiac arrest), and to counter the effects of opiate overdose. Indeed, the medical benefits of belladonna over time would seem to outweigh by far the less attractive features in the history of its use.

CATHARANTHUS ROSEUS (Vinca rosea): Madagascar Periwinkle (Apocynaceae)

The Madagascar periwinkle is thought in actuality to be native to the West Indies. A member of the dogbane family, Madagascar periwinkle is a perennial herb with smooth, opposite leaves and striking salverform corollas that are usually white or rose-tinted; a red or yellow circular nectar guide typically occurs at the mouth of the corolla tube. It is occasionally cultivated as an ornamental in the United States.

In the late 1950s, scientists in Canada and the United States (Eli Lilly Company) independently and essentially simultaneously discovered that extracts of

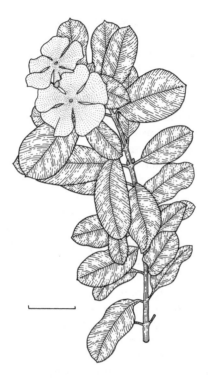

Figure 13–3 *Catharanthus roseus.*
Madagascar periwinkle

Madagascar periwinkle exhibit antitumor activity. This is all the more unusual because both groups of workers were initially pursuing the belief that periwinkle extract might be of benefit in the treatment of diabetes. As it turned out, the plant was of no use in treating diabetes. However, specific alkaloids were extracted that possessed antineoplastic activity; in particular, vincaleukoblastine (vinblastine, VLB) and leurocristine (vincristine, VCR) were found to be anticarcinogenic. Sulfates of the two alkaloids are marketed, respectively, as Velban and Oncovin (Vincovin). These alkaloids proved effective against certain types of abnormal white blood cell development. Although VLB and VCR are in chemical terms similar and closely related alkaloids, their effects in the human body (against cancer) are not identical. For example, after a blood cancer builds up resistance to VLB, VCR may then become effective as an agent of control. Also, VLB is particularly effective in achieving remissions in Hodgkin's disease (and related diseases), whereas VCR is often the medication of choice in types of acute, childhood leukemia. The percentage of remission achievable with these drugs is truly remarkable. Length of life may be considerably extended and life quality improved significantly as well. Of course, it may be years before the patient knows whether or not a cure has actually been accomplished, although apparent cures are recorded from use of these drugs. Of the tens of thousands of plants screened for antineoplastic activity by various agencies, extracts from *Catharanthus roseus* constitute the biggest success story to date. Perhaps surprisingly, other species of periwinkle have, so far at least, been of little or no benefit in the treatment of cancer.

CEPHAELIS IPECACUANHA: Brazilian Ipecac (Rubiaceae)

Native to moist forests of Brazil (and Bolivia), ipecac is a shade-loving, perennial herb with mostly opposite, stipulate leaves and smallish, white, funnelform flowers in headlike, bracteate clusters. It is valued for its medicinal underground stem (and horizontal roots). Ipecac is cultivated at various locations in the tropics; however, the need for shade restricts sites where the plant can be grown effectively.

The underground stem and roots contain several alkaloids: emetine, cephaeline, and psychotrine. Extracts from the underground parts of *Cephaelis* have long been used to treat amoebic dysentery in tropical America. Additionally, the emetine in *Cephaelis* extract has proved of substantial worth as an expectorant in cases of chronic respiratory congestion and viscid sputum. However, the main role of ipecac has been as an emetic agent. Syrup of Ipecac is commonly used by parents and physicians alike to induce vomiting in children, especially if poisoning is suspected. Reputedly, the alkaloid cephaeline has a direct action on the vagus nerve, prompting a rapid emptying of the stomach contents. Although perhaps unwise to use in a few

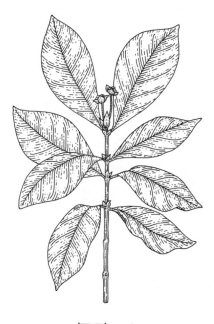

Figure 13–4 *Cephaelis ipecacuanha.*
Brazilian ipecac

types of poisonings (for example, lye poisoning), it would be impossible to estimate how many lives, especially of children, a valuable drug product like syrup of Ipecac (seemingly so ordinary) may have actually saved.

CHONDRODENDRON TOMENTOSUM: Pareira (Menispermaceae)

Chondrodendron tomentosum along with *Strychnos toxifera*, especially the former, are the chief sources of curare. Knowledge of curare is centuries old and is traceable, directly or indirectly, to a number of different South American Indian tribes, variously from Peru, Ecuador, Colombia, and Brazil. Both *Chondrodendron* and *Strychnos* grow wild as broad-leaved, woody vines in tropical American lowland forests. These and a number of other kinds of plants (and materials) were combined in various and often inscrutable ways by native peoples to make curare, used as an arrow poison. The vessel in which curare was prepared seemed for a time to have significance. In some cases, curare was prepared in an earthenware pot (pot curare), in other cases in a hollow, bamboolike stem (tube curare), and in still other instances in a gourd or calabash (gourd curare). The method of delivery of poison to the animal being hunted, that is, by blowgun, by bow and arrow, or by spear, also added some early mysticism to the story of curare. Regardless of the method of preparation and the weapon, curare was boiled down to a sticky mass and applied to a sharp projectile point. Apparently, the bark, stem, and roots were primarily used. Final elucidation

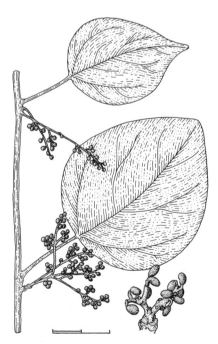

Figure 13–5 *Chondrodendron tomentosum.* Pareira

of the plant species actually contributing the active ingredients of curare required many years of investigation.

The action of curare is rapid and involves blocking of impulses from nerve to muscle. Such enervated muscles become quickly relaxed, flaccid, and useless. An animal well-lanced with curare will be unable to run any appreciable distance and, subsequent to muscular paralysis, may well die of asphyxiation (due to failure of the muscles of respiration to function). Knowledge of the rapid, relaxant action of curare led to its present application in medicine. Muscle rigidity is a major problem in certain types of surgeries. An injection of curare is particularly effective in relaxing rigid abdominal muscles during surgery (as, for example, during appendectomy). Although its use in surgery has been perhaps the main medical application, curare has also received significant use in treatment of spastic cerebral palsy, in rehabilitation therapy of patients stricken with poliomyelitis, in counteracting the effects of tetanus, in setting broken bones, and in diagnosis of myasthenia gravis. The active ingredients of curare consist of several different alkaloids; in particular, one of these, tubocurarine, is effective in upsetting the chemical mechanism of nerve impulse transmission. These natural drugs (curare alkaloids) have now been replaced partially (not totally!) by synthetic drugs. Regardless, it is amazing that a tropical arrow poison would eventually find its way to major medical use in the United States.

CINCHONA spp.:   Peruvian Bark, Fever Tree, Jesuit's Bark, Quinine Tree (Rubiaceae)

Species of *Cinchona* that have been utilized commercially to obtain quinine are usually rather large trees, perhaps rarely common, occurring at medium to higher elevations in the Andes (Peru, Bolivia, Ecuador, and Colombia). Leaves are large, opposite, and evergreen, and the flowers are tubular, pink or white, and occur in terminal panicles. The bark is corky and bitter to the taste. It is the bark that is of commercial (medicinal) importance.

Popular legend has it that the Countess of Chinchon, wife of the Viceroy of Peru, was cured (of malaria) in the early to mid-1600s by "fever bark." Thereafter, she allegedly returned to Spain and distributed the powdered bark to many others in need of treatment. This legend is now regarded as untrue. What is true, apparently, is that Catholic missionaries (Jesuit priests) working in Peru in the mid-seventeenth century became aware of the effectiveness of the powdered bark of the tree against malaria and did indeed make it known in Spain and Italy. Linnaeus (1753) nonetheless named the Peruvian fever tree *Cinchona*, apparently accepting the legend of the Countess of Chinchon. Use of *Cinchona* bark was readily adopted by some European physicians as an antimalarial agent, and *Cinchona* eventually became the object of an intense Dutch trade monopoly (persisting into the twentieth century) with plantations established in Java and India.

Bark of such species as *Cinchona calisaya*, *C. ledgeriana*, *C. officinalis*, and *C. succirubra* contain quinoline alkaloids, in particularly quinine; these and even

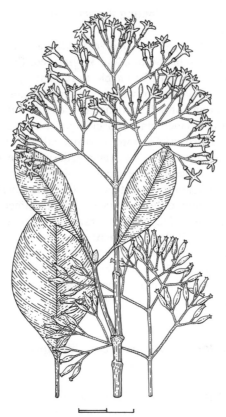

Figure 13–6 *Cinchona officinalis.*
Fever tree

other species of *Cinchona* have been utilized as quinine sources. Quinine is highly effective against the multiplication of certain protozoa, such as the genus *Plasmodium*, the cause of malaria. *Plasmodium*, a unicellular parasite, is transmitted by the *Anopheles* mosquito (the host of the sexual stage of the parasite). Human beings are the host for the asexual stage of *Plasmodium*, which undergoes its initial phase in the liver; the next phase of the parasite enters the bloodstream and invades red blood cells, in which *Plasmodium* cells multiply, to be released again into the bloodstream (to invade additional erythrocytes). The rupturing of erythrocytes every 48 to 72 hours, releasing their metabolic products (and new parasite cells), is thought to account for the intermittent paroxyms (fevers and other symptoms) associated with malaria. Quinine was found to be particularly effective against the parasite at the red blood cell stage. Although synthetic quinoline alkaloids (based on the molecular structure of quinine) have largely replaced quinine since about 1930, quinine has relieved great suffering and prevented death in the case of literally millions of people suffering the scourge of malaria. Discovered incidentally in the treatment of malaria, the quinine type of alkaloid (especially quinidine) has also proved of some use in controlling cardiac arrhythmias.

COLCHICUM AUTUMNALE: Autumn Crocus (Liliaceae)

Although a similar plant to true crocus, autumn crocus (*Colchicum*) is actually in a different family (lily, not iris family), and flowering occurs in the fall, rather than the spring (as in a number of *Crocus* spp.). Leaves and fruit of autumn crocus, which do appear in the spring, are not present during the fall-flowering episode. Flowers of *Colchicum autumnale* are long and tubular, terminating in large perianth lobes, and are superficially similar in form to *Crocus* spp.

Autumn crocus has apparently been used medicinally for the treatment of gout since the time of the ancient Egyptians. It was also used for the same condition in Europe during the Middle Ages. Modern medicine was relatively slow to adopt autumn crocus extract for this purpose. However, with the extraction of the alkaloid colchicine from the corm, coupled with the awareness of experimental use of this drug, which occurred during the late 1930s, interest increased.

Colchicine, specifically, is a treatment for the condition of gout (allegedly a disease of cranky, middle-aged men, who are sometimes said to behave in a "gouty" manner—doubtless due to the intense pain they may feel!). Gout is, loosely speaking, a type of rheumatism or arthritis in which something has gone awry in the metabolism of uric acid. Uric acid is secreted in excess and/or not properly excreted;

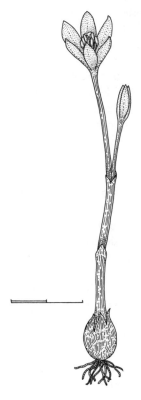

Figure 13–7 *Colchicum autumnale.*
Autumn crocus

it accumulates as crystals of monosodium urate in joints of the toes, ankles, and eventually even the knees, resulting in pain (sometimes severe), inflammation, and swelling. Much of the inflammation (and pain) of gout is caused by types of white blood cells that attack the foreign material (urate crystals) and are in the process themselves ruptured, emptying their cell contents. Colchicine does not cure gout; rather, it alleviates the symptoms through direct inhibition of the activity of the leucocytes (which are simply trying to do their job). As a consequence, pain and swelling diminish. Colchicine is very toxic; hence the physician must be careful in adjusting a toxic versus a medicinal dosage.

Colchicine has also found a use in experimental botany. Similar to the activity of colchicine in halting the division and activity of white blood cells, colchicine can arrest or delay the division of plant cells. It was found that injection of colchicine into the ovary of a plant can block spindle formation (the mitotic spindle) in the dividing fertilized egg cell. This means that the chromosomes will be duplicated, but the cell does not divide. Hence, a doubling of the chromosome number in the fertilized egg, and consequently in the new plant, can be achieved. Such laboratory or greenhouse manipulations of plant chromosomes can be very useful in studying the origin of plant polyploids (plants with multiple sets of chromosomes) in nature. Polyploidy is naturally a common phenomenon among angiosperms (flowering plants); colchicine provides the investigator a chemical tool with which to analyze the development and meaning of this phenomenon in particular cases.

Because of its activity in halting cell division (as of plant cells or, more pertinently, of leucocytes), it was hoped that colchicine would be of benefit in situations involving abnormal cell division, as in treatment of various blood cancers. Unfortunately, colchicine proved to be too toxic for use in chemotherapy. However, an alkaloid (similar to colchicine, but less toxic) from a related species of *Colchicum*, *C. speciosum*, has shown cytotoxic activity against a type of leukemia in mice (by arresting lymphocyte division) and has found limited use in the treatment of forms of cancer in human beings.

DIGITALIS spp.:   Foxgloves (Scrophulariaceae)

Several species of foxglove have been utilized medicinally. However, *Digitalis purpurea* (purple foxglove, dead-man's bells) and *D. lanata* (Grecian foxglove) have been the two main species employed in formal medicine. *Digitalis purpurea* is distinguished from *D. lanata* by generally longer, more tubular corollas and by broader leaves (relative to the length). Both species are herbs (variously annual, biennial, or perennial) with alternately placed leaves and flowers in terminal, sometimes one-sided racemes.

Spanning a period of 10 years (1775–1785) of careful, clinical experiments with powdered digitalis leaf, the English physician William Withering worked diligently to put foxglove (*D. purpurea*) "on the map" (and in so doing greatly enhanced the field of pharmacognosy). Knowledge of digitalis came to Withering

Figure 13-8 *Digitalis purpurea.*
Foxglove

initially as a component of a Shropshire folk remedy for dropsy, an accumulation of fluid in the extremities (due to weakened heart action); we would now refer to the general condition known as dropsy as congestive heart failure. Use of *Digitalis* in English folk medicine is in fact traceable back to the practice of witchcraft during the Middle Ages. However, regardless of the initial source of knowledge of the medicinal value of digitalis, it was Withering's subsequent controlled experiments on preparation and dosage that did so much for the future of heart medicine; this work was published in his monograph on the medicinal use of digitalis in 1785: *An Account of the Foxglove, and Some of Its Medical Uses, with Practical Remarks on Dropsy, and Other Diseases.*

The active constituents extracted from the crude (powdered leaf) preparations of digitalis are a number of related cardiac glycosides, including digoxin, digitoxin, deslanoside, and lanatoside. Perhaps most commonly used (by several million patients a year in the United States) is digoxin (from *D. lanata*). Digitalis preparations are most useful in treating progressive heart failure caused by atherosclerosis (or, more generally, by hypertension). The force of the heartbeat (the contraction of heart muscle) is increased and at the same time the beat is slowed (making the drug valuable in treating tachycardia). The upshot of digitalis therapy is increased cardiac output, decreased fluid accumulation or edema (in the extremities and the lungs) due to improved circulation, and increased renal output (also a consequence of better circulation). The action of the cardiac glycoside on the heart is actually through the nervous system, specifically through the nerve innervation of the heart (that is, the atrioventricular node).   A secondary, but significant, benefit of digitalis is the reduction of peripheral venous blood pressure in patients that are hypertensive.

As is a problem with many drugs, there is not a great difference between a therapeutic dose of digitalis and a toxic dose. Dosage must be monitored carefully and adjusted on a patient-by-patient basis by the cardiologist. As a result of overdose of digitalis glycosides or through chronic use and accumulation of these glycosides in the system, digitalis poisoning or intoxication can occur and indeed is a serious consideration in the treatment of heart patients. Such patients may develop dangerous cardiac arrhythmias due to digitalis; however, the November 1982 issue of the *New England Journal of Medicine* (Smith and others, pp. 1357–1362) reports a potentially effective antidote (involving digoxin-specific antibodies obtained from immunized sheep) that is useful in cases of life-threatening digitalis intoxication.

DIOSCOREA COMPOSITA: Mexican Yam, Barbasco (Dioscoreaceae)

Native to southern Mexico, this plant is a monocotyledonous vine with rather large, heart-shaped leaves possessing parallel-palmate veins and long petioles. The smallish male and female flowers are borne on separate plants (in certain other species of *Dioscorea* the two sexes may occur on the same plant). The fruit is a winged or strongly

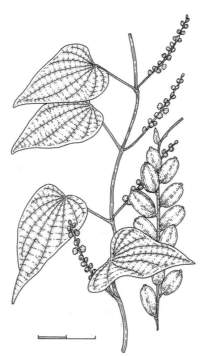

Figure 13–9 *Dioscorea composita.* Mexican yam

angled capsule. Barbasco is cultivated for its large, brownish, fluted, white-fleshed tubers.   Other species of Mexican yam, such as *Dioscorea floribunda* and *D. spiculiflora*, are also cultivated for their valuable underground stems or roots.

The discovery and appreciation of the chemical content of tubers of Mexican yam, about 1940, has had a truly profound influence on the steroid industry. It was formerly assumed that steroid products and medicines suitable for human use could be obtained only from animal sources and then only in small quantities. However, in Mexican yam, a relatively abundant saponin (sapogenic glycoside), dioscin, was found that yielded a steroidal aglycone (sapogenin) called diosgenin. Diosgenin proved suitable to serve as the starting steroid nucleus from which a variety of valuable steroid compounds could be manufactured in a relatively few steps, some steps involving rather inexpensive and readily available microbial transformation processes. Diosgenin thus alleviated the difficult or impossible task of synthesis of complex steroids from scratch and/or the hideous expense and waste of extraction of finished steroid products from animal sources. In other words, in the Mexican yams, a reasonably plentiful and cost-efficient resource for the production of commercially valuable, derivative steroids was found. Semisynthetic commercial steroids, now based largely on diosgenin or diosgeninlike starting material, include antiinflammatory compounds such as cortisone and hydrocortisone and sex hormones such as androgens, progestogens (progestins), and estrogens, employed in oral contraceptives. The commercial-medical success of diosgenin as a plant product would now seem undeniable.

ERYTHROXYLUM COCA: Coca, Divine Coca (Erythroxylaceae)

Coca is a shrub or small tree found in uplands on the Amazonian side of the Andes Mountain Chain. Its simple alternate, evergreen leaves, often clustered toward the branch tips, show a characteristic veining pattern (nerves paralleling the midrib on each side). Flowers are white or yellow-white, five-parted, pedicillate, and solitary or fascicled in the leaf axils. Smallish, oblong, drupaceous berries (scarlet when ripe) may be seen on lower axils of a branch. Occurring naturally in parts of Peru, Bolivia, Colombia, and Ecuador, *Erythroxylum coca* is also cultivated in small, sometimes terraced plantations, known as *cocals*.

For centuries, leaves of coca have been chewed (by the Incas, their descendants, conquering Spainards, and others) as a combatant against fatigue encountered while working in the high elevations of the Andes. However, knowledge of the effects of coca did not really affect Europe and the United States until the mid- to late nineteenth century. It was approximately 1860 before the active ingredient, cocaine (a tropane alkaloid), was isolated (in German laboratories) from the leaves. During the 1880s, awareness developed of the value of cocaine as a local anesthetic. To appreciate what cocaine meant as an anesthetic, one has only to contemplate having even minor surgery without the benefit of such a drug.

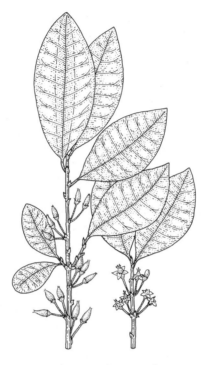

Figure 13–10 *Erythroxylum coca.* Coca

In the latter nineteenth and very early twentieth centuries, cocaine appeared in a variety of popular products, including wines, snuff powders, throat lozenges, and, yes, even Coca Cola (hence the origin of the name of the popular soft drink). Such uses of the drug in commercial products have, of course, long since been banned. As is well known though, the partaking of cocaine continues in a major way in the illicit drug trade. It is the drug of choice for many because of the feeling of exhilaration and well-being produced, apparently without hallucination or significant intoxication—and hence the perceived value in the workplace. Cocaine is less physically addictive (it should not be considered nonaddictive!) than certain other hard drugs, such as heroin. However, mental addiction is another question entirely, and psychological dependence on cocaine is readily developed. Additionally, no one should minimize the danger of cocaine overdose, resulting in possible respiratory or heart failure. The death rate from cocaine has risen sharply during the last few years. The amount of cocaine that has proved fatal has been found to vary considerably on a virtually individual basis.

Cocaine per se finds limited use today in formal medicine, at least in the United States; cocaine or cocaine hydrochloride is used as an ingredient of a "cocktail," also often containing morphine, given to certain individuals for pain associated with terminal cancer. Perhaps the main value of cocaine to medicine (and dentistry) of the present is that its molecular structure served as a model for the creation of its replacement drugs, novocaine (procaine) and xylocaine. Novocaine and xylocaine are entirely synthetically produced, but their existence has to be credited to knowledge gained from the initial natural product extract (cocaine). Novocaine and xylocaine have the anesthetic value of cocaine, without the undesired feature of central nervous system stimulation. Also, they can be administered to have a more prolonged effect, as when one has a trip to the dentist. It is only a shame that a drug such as cocaine, which has provided the human race with so much relief of pain (and insight into the development of synthetic pain-relieving or pain-numbing drugs), and which has had such a rich history (once being held sacred by the Incas), should have its image so tarnished by misuse in the illegal drug market of the latter twentieth century.

PAPAVER SOMNIFERUM: Opium Poppy (Papaveraceae)

The opium poppy is a rather large, annual herb with simple, toothed, clasping leaves, and a single, terminal flower (per stem) possessing large, showy petals (that range from white or pinkish to red or purple) and numerous stamens. The flower is followed by a green capsule, the fused stigmas of the pistil persisting as a disclike structure on the fruit apex; the capsule eventually dries and turns brown; small apertures that function in seed release form underneath the persistent stigma disc.

Opium is a crude drug; specifically, it is the white latex (browning when dried) that exudes from the shallowly cut sides of a green (immature) capsule. As might be suspected, knowledge of opium constitutes a long history. The manuscript of Dioscorides in the first century A.D. contains an accurate account of the extraction of opium (that is, by slitting of the unripe capsule), outlining the basic way that it is extracted today. An appreciation of opium as an analgesic and an aid to sleep (narcotic) goes back many centuries indeed. It was no accident that Linnaeus applied the epithet *somniferum* to the opium poppy in 1753, indicating his awareness of its past history in relation to humankind.

From opium latex, more than 20 different alkaloids have been isolated. Perhaps the most famous of these, both in and out of medicine, is morphine, sometimes utilized, in some cases along with cocaine, in the "death and dying cocktail" (more appropriately, Brompton's cocktail) to bring relief of pain to many thousands suffering catastrophic illness, especially forms of terminal cancer. Morphine is a type of alkaloid having a strong depressant action on parts of the brain involved in the sensation of pain and also of fear and anxiety; morphine thus offers both pain relief and some sense of contentment to the terminally ill. Codeine basically is methylated morphine; it is a milder narcotic than morphine, causing less of a sensation of dull euphoria. Codeine is particularly effective in suppressing the coughing reflex center in the brain and is widely distributed as an antitussive. Medically, codeine is the most commonly used opium alkaloid. Thebaine (technically, dimethylmorphine), another alkaloid extractable from opium, is often used to make codeine. Thebaine is a convulsant, rather than a narcotic or depressant like

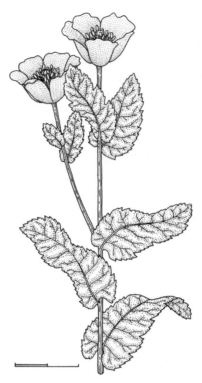

Figure 13–11 *Papaver somniferum.*
Opium poppy

morphine or codeine, indicating the profound difference in effect sometimes possible between even closely related alkaloids. Heroin (a synthetic drug) is acetylated morphine and is even more powerful and addictive as a narcotic than morphine. Although heroin use is not necessarily on the upswing, it continues as a major drug on the illegal drug market. Perhaps because heroin is available these days in a very pure state, death rates from heroin use have risen, although the actual rate of use of heroin has seemingly not. Heroin is particularly dangerous because of its depressant action on the portion of the brain governing respiration.

It has been illegal since 1942 to grow the opium poppy in the United States for any purpose. At present, opium is legally cultivated as a drug crop in India, Egypt, Iran, and the Soviet Union. It is cultivated to a lesser extent in Bulgaria, Yugoslavia, Poland, and several other countries. Illegal cultivation occurs in many countries. The opium poppy is thought to have originally been native to Mediterranean Europe. Other species of *Papaver* may or may not contain various of the opium alkaloids. However, in these other species, morphine content is seemingly low or lacking altogether, and only *P. somniferum* is banned from U.S. cultivation. The great scarlet poppy (*Papaver bracteatum*), native to the Caucasus region of the Soviet Union, is cultivated as a source of thebaine (used to manufacture codeine).

PHYSOSTIGMA VENENOSUM: Esere, Ordeal Bean, Calabar Bean (Leguminosae)

Native to West Tropical Africa, Calabar bean is a large woody vine, with three-parted leaves, pinkish or purplish, pealike flowers in pedulous, racemelike clusters, and brownish pods with rather large, dark, red-brown seeds. Certain peoples of Nigeria have believed that "the truth will out" if the Calabar bean is employed in trial by ordeal. If the accused merely vomited from consuming a prescribed quantity of a beverage made from the seed, then innocence could be pronounced. If more serious poisoning (or death) resulted, then the verdict of guilty would be applied. Use of Calabar bean in ordeal trials has been for some time forbidden under Nigerian law.

The Calabar bean is indeed very poisonous; the seeds (and not, apparently, other parts of the plant) contain several different toxic alkaloids, the best known of these being physostigmine (eserine). Physostigmine is a spinal (central nervous system) paralyzant and muscle contractant. Respiratory paralysis (and asphyxia) due to diaphragm contraction may be the final outcome of poisoning by these seeds. Ingestion of only a few beans can have fatal results, if significant vomiting does not occur. Large dosage may result in paralysis of cardiac muscle and stoppage of the heart.

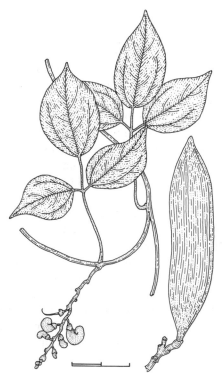

Figure 13–12 *Physostigma venenosum.* Calabar bean

Such exotic and toxic tropical plants have occasionally proved to have some medicinal value, and this is clearly the case with ordeal bean. The fact that physostigmine causes constriction or contraction of involuntary muscles has significant medical implications. Similar to pilocarpine (see *Pilocarpus*), the major use of physostigmine has been in ophthalmology in which the drug has been employed to achieve protracted pupillary contraction and to treat cases of glaucoma through pressure reduction in the eyeball (although physostigmine is more likely to cause irritation of the eye than is pilocarpine). Physostigmine has also been prescribed to treat the atony occurring with myasthenia gravis by increasing facial and neck muscle contraction, as well as that of the intestines (increasing peristalsis). In both glaucoma and myasthenia gravis, a synthetic analog (neostigmine or prostigmine) is now often preferred, but this molecule is based on the structure of physostigmine. In addition to the preceding, physostigmine has found significant use in postoperative situations in relieving the buildup of gas in the abdomen. An innovative use of physostigmine is to counteract the effect of drugs or poisons having an opposite effect, that is, those that are extreme muscle relaxants, such as atropine and curare; it has been used as an antidote to strong spinal stimulants such as strychnine. It is interesting how one type of poison may prove antidotal to the effect of another type of poison.

PILOCARPUS PENNATIFOLIUS: Jaborandi (Rutaceae)

A brief account should be given of *Pilocarpus pennatifolius* and *P. jaborandi*, species of shrubs or small trees (belonging to the citrus family) with alternate, pinnately compound leaves (showing translucent dots when held to the light) and numerous white or purplish flowers in elongated racemes or spikes.

Leaves of these species are rich in the simple alkaloid pilocarpine, a compound receiving considerable use in ophthalmology at the present time. Through parasympathetic nerves, pilocarpine (a cholinergic or myotic drug, that is, one mimicking the action of acetylcholine) acts to constrict the pupil of the eye (myosis) by stimulating contraction of sphincter muscle fibers in the iris; concomitantly, the lens of the eye is widened (through contraction of the ciliary muscle, attached by a thin ligament to the lens), and near-vision focus is improved.

Pilocarpine is a primary drug prescribed for the disease of the eye known as glaucoma, in which vision may become indistinct or ultimately lost; pilocarpine is perhaps now more commonly utilized in treating glaucoma than is physostigmine (see *Physostigma*). In glaucoma, it is thought that adrenaline surges (arising from sympathetic nerve stimulation) may contribute to excess fluid secretion and pressure buildup in the aqueous humor of the eye. The effect of pilocarpine is counter to that of adrenaline, and its use typically results in decreased intraocular pressure. Administration of pilocarpine (as eyedrops or ointment) not only potentially relieves pressure in the eyeball, but, as mentioned, vision is sharpened in the near range.

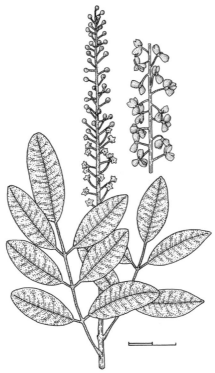

Figure 13–13 *Pilocarpus pennatifolius.*
Jaborandi

RAUWOLFIA SERPENTINA: Snakeroot, Serpentwood (Apocynaceae)

Rauwolfia serpentina, a member of the dogbane family, is a shrub or subshrub with simple, typically whorled leaves and terminal or axillary, stalked clusters of tubular, pink-white or green-white flowers. The plant has a cylindrical, tapering and often twisted taproot; it is the taproot that is of commercial value; the bark of the root is considered more valuable than the wood.

Powdered taproots have for centuries been used medicinally in India for the treatment of what is interpretable as "moon disease," or lunacy, and also for the treatment of snakebites (hence the common names) and insect stings. However, it was not until the early 1950s that American medicine adopted the use of this plant. It is estimated that as many as 50 alkaloids have now been isolated from roots of serpentwood. The most famous of these is certainly reserpine (deserpidine and rescinnamine are also well known). Reserpine was first employed in U.S. medicine in the treatment of the mental disorder known as schizophrenia. The sedative action of reserpine allowed many patients suffering from this condition to lead seminormal lives. An indole alkaloid, reserpine bears a chemical similarity to the neurotransmitter molecule serotonin (and as well to LSD), a fact in all probability related to the effectiveness of reserpine in the central nervous system.

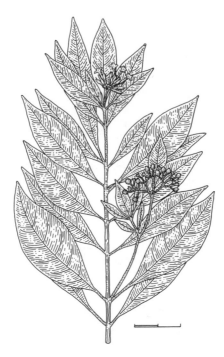

Figure 13–14 *Rauwolfia serpentina.* Snakeroot, serpentwood

A side effect discovered during its use on mental patients was that reserpine was hypotensive (that is, could lower blood pressure); as a consequence of this discovery, reserpine found an even greater use in the treatment of high blood pressure (often in combination with other drugs) than of schizophrenia. The use of reserpine in hypertension therapy is based on the action of the drug in dilating blood vessels and thereby reducing pressure. Reserpine reduces blood pressure gradually, and if faster action is sought, other drugs are employed instead. However, reserpine may well be the drug of choice in controlling chronic, nonacute hypertension.

Rauwolfia serpentina is native to northern India, eastern Pakistan, and parts of Malaysia. Other species of *Rauwolfia* that have been employed commercially (for their reserpine alkaloid content) include *R. tetraphylla* (American serpentwood), native to Central America and the Caribbean, and *R. vomitoria* (African serpentwood), native to central Africa. In some countries, including the United States, the medical use of *R. vomitoria* may now exceed that of *R. serpentina*.

STROPHANTHUS GRATUS: Sawai or Smooth Strophanthus (Apocynaceae)

A member of the dogbane family, sawai is a rather large vine with opposite, simple, evergreen leaves and showy, funnellike, purple- to pink-white flowers exuding nocturnal fragrance. The paired follicles, about twice longer than broad, release a number of brown, twisted seeds. Seldom formally cultivated, sawai is native to portions of western tropical Africa.

By certain native peoples of Africa, seeds of *Strophanthus gratus* were mashed into a thick fluid into which tips of arrows were dipped. As an arrow poison, this dip from sawai seeds is considered to be among the most rapidly acting toxins, even on large animals; in lethal dose it leads quickly to cardiac arrest. Perhaps as elliptical as connections can be, the valuable glycoside ouabain (G-strophanthin) was isolated from seeds of sawai, the effort being based on knowledge of the apparent action of the arrow poison on the heart. Ouabain today retains a place in the International Pharmacopoeia and the Pharmacopoeia of the United States. It is indeed official for use in certain cases of heart failure. Whereas digitalis may be the drug selected in treatment of gradual, congestive heart failure, ouabain might well be the cardiac glycoside relied on as a heart stimulant in a situation of rapid or acute cardiac failure (if not due to myocardial infarction). Although having a digitalislike effect on the heart (not necessarily a digitalislike effect on the peripheral blood vessels), the action of ouabain is much more rapid and drastic; however, the effect is not as long-lasting. Ouabain is typically applied intravenously or intramuscularly. Contrary to digitalis, ouabain is not considered predictable as an oral medication, since it is poorly absorbed from the digestive tract into the bloodstream. Digitalis and ouabain cannot be administered together to the same patient.

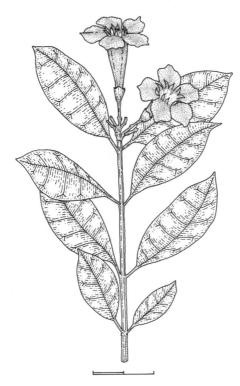

Figure 13–15 *Strophanthus gratus.*
Sawai

CONCLUSION

So, the preceding and perhaps a few more plants have made a major contribution
to medicine of the mid- to latter twentieth century. But are there more? Is this
the end of the story? It would be well to conclude this chapter, and hence this
book, by coming full circle and retouching on a topic entered into in the introductory chapter of the book. As Tyler (see selected references) points out, the
recent success story of plants useful in formal medicine has not been especially
great. As an example, Tyler alludes to the fact that 25 years of testing of some
40,000 species of plants by the National Cancer Institute failed to yield "a single
agent of general use in the treatment of human cancer." As a consequence, a
pessimistic attitude developed among scientists concerning the future of plants
in medicine. However, as Tyler mentions, there are mitigating circumstances,
including a lack of interdisciplinary communication among scientists, an unfa-
vorable federal regulatory atmosphere, and the fact that everything these days
must be cost-effective.

In a dramatic turnaround statement, Tyler asserts, and I concur, that there
is in fact every reason to be optimistic about the future of plant drug development. He cites a number of recent breakthroughs in other countries in the
development of plant drugs, not presently available in the United States (including, among a variety of examples, successful antiviral creams prepared from
plants). And Tyler believes that it is very likely that new plant drug discoveries
will eventually develop in the United States in consort with: additional tropical
exploration for plants, new methods of drug analysis and development, new
bioassays for drugs, refined methods of plant tissue culture in which quantities
of rare plant material can be produced cheaply, and last, but not least, a
resurgence of interest in (and demand for) green medicine by segments of the
public at large.

In actuality, some discoveries, perhaps seemingly commonplace, are on the
scene already, as in the new skin (especially acne) creams containing vitamin A
or other retinoids (for example, Retin-A), based ultimately on beta-carotene from
plants (see Graedon and Graedon, selected references). Although use of retinoids
is controversial, the message of the Graedons and others is to become involved in
understanding pharmaceuticals and their potentials. After all, future health is
everybody's business. The first part of the twenty-first century is projected to be
the time interval in the United States in which various factors will conspire to
produce a new boom in the development of additional natural drugs (and their
derivatives) from plants that will have once again a major impact in formal
medicine. The early twenty-first century is the time that, given all the ages of
humankind, may be the most exciting and meaningful to be a plant biologist. It
is hoped that this book will contribute to public awareness of the benefit of the
pursuit of plant science and the study of medical botany in particular.

SELECTED REFERENCES

CHIEJ, ROBERTO. 1982 (English translation, 1984, by Sylvia Mulcahy). *The Macdonald Encyclopedia of Medicinal Plants*. Macdonald & Co. Ltd., London. This is an extensive and beautifully color photo illustrated, yet virtually pocket sized, account of major and minor medicinal plants for the field-oriented student of the subject. Giving as it does rather precise chemical information, the book will be of special interest to those intrigued by the topic of phytotherapy.

DUKE, JAMES A. 1985. *Handbook of Medicinal Herbs*. CRC Press, Boca Raton, Fla. Although the present chapter dealt primarily with plants used in formal medicine, a wealth of information also exists on the use of plants in folk medicine. The reader is referred specifically to Duke's encyclopedic and scrupulously scientific coverage of herbology.

GRAEDON, JOE, AND TERESA GRAEDON. 1985. *Joe Graedon's The New People's Pharmacy—Drug Breakthroughs of the 80's*. Bantam Books, Toronto and New York. Although not a great many obvious plant products are to be found between its covers, this book, among others, is important in signaling a growing public demand for knowledge of pharmacy and medicine; Chapter 10, "A Practical Guide to Drugs of the 1980s," is very interesting; see within the chapter especially "A Revolution in Acne Treatment," pp. 350–352, and pages immediately following, for a discussion of new plant-based products in dermatology.

LEWIS, WALTER H., AND MEMORY P. F. ELVIN-LEWIS. 1977. *Medical Botany—Plants Affecting Man's Health*. Wiley-Interscience, New York. The current standard text on medical botany; excellent coverage, presented basically in a human organ system format; well-organized tabular summaries, rich in information, occur at numerous points in the book.

MORTON, JULIA F. 1977. *Major Medicinal Plants: Botany, Culture and Uses*. Charles C Thomas, Springfield, Ill. Scholarly descriptive coverage of the plants that have had the most significant impact in formal medicine; an indispensable reference.

OLIVER-BEVER, BEP. 1986. *Medicinal Plants in Tropical West Africa*. Cambridge University Press, Cambridge, England. A straightforward, pharmacological approach to the study of West African medical plants; good accounts of *Strophanthus* and *Physostigma*, among others.

SWAIN, TONY (ed.). 1972. *Plants in the Development of Modern Medicine*. Harvard University Press, Cambridge, Mass. A series of well-referenced articles on a variety of medicinal botany topics; particularly interesting is "The Ordeal Bean of Old Calabar," by Bo Holmstedt.

TAYLOR, NORMAN. 1965. *Plant Drugs That Changed the World*. Dodd, Mead & Company, New York. The various chapters are very readable essays on the discovery, history, and human impact of major medicines from plants.

TYLER, VARRO E. 1986. Plant Drugs in the Twenty-first Century. *Economic Botany* 40(3): 279–288. Must reading in terms of the future possibilities of plant drug development.

WAGNER, H., HIROSHI HIKINO, AND NORMAN R. FARNSWORTH. 1985. *Economic and Medicinal Plant Research*, Volume 1. Academic Press, Inc., New York. Provides insight into current and possible future research in plant drug development.

Glossary

Accessory fruit: A fruit in which floral (or rarely other) parts in addition to the ovary make a contribution to mature fruit structure; for example, a pome.

Achene: A type of small, dry, indehiscent fruit; in an achene, the seed is not fused with the internal surface of the fruit wall or pericarp (as in a grain), but rather is more or less free from it; for example, a sunflower seed.

Actinomorphic: Refers to flowers that have regular and evenly spaced parts (petals, and the like), that is, flowers that are radially symmetrical.

Aerobic: Conditions in which oxygen is present.

Aggregate fruit: A compound fruit derived from a number of separate, simple pistils (ovaries) originating within a single flower; for example, a blackberry.

Aglycone: The nonsugar component molecule of a glycoside (see definition).

Alkaloid: A major category of secondary compounds; alkaloids are generally basic in reaction and often bitter in taste; their molecules typically contain nitrogen as a component of a ringlike configuration. See Chapter 3 for details and for an account of different types of alkaloids.

Allelochemic: Nonnutritional chemical effects of one organism upon another; for example, certain plant alkaloids, such as nicotine, may act as insecticides.

Allergen: An agent (for example, types of pollen or spores) triggering an allergic response or reaction.

Allergy: Unusual sensitivity to a substance or substances considered ordinarily harmless.

Allopathy: The regular or standard medical practice at any given time period; that provided by the formal and official medical establishment. In nineteenth-century America, allopathy was associated in some cases with heroic medication (see definition), including treatment by bleeding, blistering, and the use of mineral toxins.

Alternate leaves: One leaf per node; alternate leaves frequently describe a spiral around the stem when all nodes are considered.

Amines: In comparison to peptides and proteins, amines are generally the smallest of the proteinaceous compounds; they are derived from single amino acids by decarboxylation (loss of the organic acid group) and perhaps other chemical modifications.

Amino acids: Molecules that constitute the building blocks, or subunits, of proteins. Amino acids are acidic on one end of the molecule and basic in reaction on the other; hence, they tend to join together in chains or polymers (acid end of one amino acid to base end of another).

Anaerobic: Conditions in which oxygen is absent; the term is usually used in connection with types of bacteria (such as the botulism bacillus) that grow in the absence of oxygen, or anaerobically.

Analgesic: Substance reducing sensitivity to pain.

Analogs: Molecules that are chemically similar.

Anemophilous: Wind pollinated.

Angiosperms: The great plant group known as the flowering plants; among others features, fruit development is a characteristic distinguishing feature of flowering plants.

Annual plant: Plant living no more than one year, and generally dependent on successful seed production for survival.

Anodyne: Relieves pain; relaxant.

Anorexia: Nervous loss of appetite.

Anther: The terminal, usually dilated, pollen-producing portion of a stamen.

Anthesis: The opening or blooming of a flower.

Antibodies: Protein (glycoprotein) molecules produced by the body's immune system (specifically, by a type of lymphocyte) in response to the introduction of certain kinds of antigen (such as bacterial or viral, or even plant, protein).

Antidote: Counteracts poison.

Antigen: Foreign substance, often proteinaceous, stimulating some type of immune response in the body (such as the production of antibodies or cell-mediated hypersensitivity).

Antirheumatic: Relieves rheumatism or rheumatic infection.

Antiseptic: Helps prevent infection.

Antispasmodic: Counteracts muscle spasms or rigidity.

Antitussive: Cough suppressant.

Aphrodisiac: Increases sexual desire.

Aril: An appendage or covering (often fleshy) present on certain seeds; for example, seeds of *Euonymus*.

Aromatic: Fragrant (perhaps spicy fragrant); also refers to chemicals containing or patterned after benzene rings.

Arrhythmia: Disturbance of heart rhythm (heartbeat).

Astringent: Shrinks swollen tissues.

Ataxia: Muscular incoordination; sometimes also implying a state of confusion.

Atherosclerosis: A form of hardening of the arteries (arteriosclerosis) that involves accumulation of lipids (fats), carbohydrates, calcium, and other deposits in the arteries.

Atony: The absence of usual or normal muscle tone.

Atopic individual: Individual with a predisposition to a particular allergy.

Autonomic nervous system: The components of the nervous system involved in the control of involuntary activities or body functions. The autonomic nervous system is subdivided into the sympathetic and parasympathetic systems (see separate definitions).

Axillary: Refers to the upper angle where leaf joins stem; branch buds, or sometimes flowers, occur in leaf axils and may be referred to as axillary.

Bacteremia: Illness due to bacterial infection.

Berry: A simple, fleshy fruit (fleshy throughout its diameter); for example, a grape or a tomato.

Biennial plant: One living two years (that is, living through two but only two growing seasons); for example, mullein.

Bilabiate: Refers to certain zygomorphic corollas that are two-lipped (that is, the corolla lobes are arranged into an upper and lower lip); for example, members of the mint family.

Bilious: Relates to bile and/or to gallbladder or liver functions or dysfunctions.

Binomial method: The two-name method of classification of plants or, more generally, of organisms; for example, *Conium maculatum*, for poison hemlock. The first name is the genus (generic) name, and the second is the species (specific) epithet.

Bitters: A bitter flavoring agent, used to increase appetite.

Blade: The flat, expanded, sheetlike portion of a leaf; the lamina.

Bract: Modified leaves associated with inflorescences or even with individual flowers, but not a part of the floral whorls per se.

Bradycardia: A slow rate of heartbeat.

Bronchi: Main air passages leading to the lungs (from the windpipe).

Calyx: A collective term for the sepals of a flower.

Capitulum: See *head.*

Capsule: A dry, dehiscent fruit derived from a single compound pistil; usually dividing up into two or more valves at maturity to release the seeds; for example, a buckeye fruit.

Carbohydrates: Compounds of carbon, hydrogen, and oxygen, in which the ratio of hydrogen to oxygen is 2 : 1. Common carbohydrate polymer (polysaccharide) reserve foods include starch (plants) and glycogen (animals and fungi); carbohydrate polymers also serve as structural materials of cell walls (for example, cellulose in plants and chitin in fungi). Sugars (monosaccharides) such as glucose represent simple-state, immediately available, food sources.

Carcinogen: A substance potentially inducing cancer or malignancy.

Cardenolides: A major category of cardiac glycosides; the terms are sometimes used interchangeably.

Cardiac (cardiovascular): Referring to the heart or the heart and blood vessels.

Cardiac glycoside: A type of steroidal glycoside with cardioactivity. The somewhat similar saponin glycosides do not possess such activity.

Carminative: Relieves or reduces intestinal gas (flatulence).

Carpel: The longitudinal, somewhat leaflike units of which compound pistils are composed; a carpel is the equivalent of one simple pistil.

Caryopsis or grain: A small, dry, indehiscent fruit in which the seed is joined uniformly to the inner surface of the pericarp to form a unit structure; for example, a grain of corn or wheat.

Catechol: A general type of phenolic molecule found, for example, in certain members of the sumac family (for example, urushiol from *Rhus radicans*); technically, catechols are dihydroxy derivatives of benzene.

Cathartic: A purgative or bowel stimulant.

Cauline Leaves: Leaves borne on aboveground (flowering) stems.

Cell-mediated hypersensitivity: An immune response involving types of white blood cells, but not antibodies; poison ivy dermatitis is an example of such a delayed hypersensitivity response.

Cellulose: Structural carbohydrate material occurring as a primary ingredient of plant cell walls. Like starch, cellulose is a glucose (residue) polymer; however, the molecular bonding pattern of one glucose residue to another is different than in starch.

Central nervous system: The brain and spinal cord.

Centrifugal inflorescence: See *determinate inflorescence*.

Centripetal inflorescence: See *indeterminate inflorescence*.

Chitin: A polysaccharide substance, chemically related to cellulose, contributing to the cell wall structure of a number of fungi and the external skeleton of various invertebrate animals.

Cholinergic: Simulating the action of the neurotransmitter molecule acetylcholine. Most typically, a substance that stimulates parasympathetic nerves and resultant responses.

Cirrhosis: Chronic liver disease characterized by increased development of connective tissue, parenchymal cell degeneration, and possible reduced blood flow through the liver.

Cocarcinogen: A substance inducing tumors that are nonmalignant; for example, substances isolated from the milky latex of certain members of the spurge family of flowering plants. A cocarcinogen may also enhance the effect of a true carcinogen.

Collagen: A common, fibrous, proteinaceous substance characteristic of connective tissue (including bone and cartilage).

Complement system: Proteins carried in blood plasma required for the destruction of foreign cells in immunological based defenses.

Compound fruit: A fruit originating from more than one pistil (that is, more than one ovary); usually a number of at least initially distinct ovaries are involved in one compound fruit. Compound fruits are generally subdivided into aggregate fruits and multiple fruits (see definitions).

Compound leaf: A leaf in which the blade is divided into separate leaflets; to qualify as a compound leaf (versus a simple leaf), the division into separate leaflets must be essentially complete.

Compound pistil: A pistil that is composed of two or more longitudinally fused units, that is, two or more carpels.

Conifers: The conifers or coniferous (cone-bearing) trees constitute the major category of gymnosperms; they are characterized by the possession of both pollen cones and seed cones, and by often slender, needlelike or scalelike foliage; for example, pines, spruces, firs, and cedars.

Corm: Erect or vertical underground stem, resembling a bulb; a corm has more stem tissue than a bulb (which is mostly leaf tissue).

Corolla: A collective term for the petals of a flower.

Corolla lobes: If petal fusion (anatomical union) exists in a corolla, the lobes of the corolla constitute the free or unfused portion of the corolla, that is, the portion distal to the corolla tube.

Corolla tube: If the petals of a flower are fused through part of their length, the term corolla tube refers to the fused portion; the corolla tube would be proximal to the corolla lobes.

Crenate: Leaf margin with obtuse or rounded teeth; not as sharply toothed as when serrate (see definition).

Crude drugs: Drugs (typically of botanical origin) of uncertain or at least unspecified chemical content; raw extracts.

Cutaneous: Relating to the skin.

Cyathium: Small, cuplike inflorescence unit characteristic of *Euphorbia*, a member of the spurge family; a number of cyathia may be borne on a single plant.

Cyme: A type of determinate inflorescence; cymes usually exhibit opposite branching.

Cytotoxic: Poisonous to cells; that is, toxic at the cell level.

Decoction: A liquid plant extract prepared by boiling.

Decompound leaf: A leaf that is more than once compound.

Decussate: Opposite leaves in which the leaf pairs at a given node are rotated 90 degrees with respect to those pairs immediately above and below.

Dehiscent: Opening or splitting open naturally, as in the case of certain types of dry fruits at maturity; for example, a capsule.

Demulcent: A soothing agent, perhaps applied to irritated skin.

Dermatitis: Skin rash or inflammation, including allergic skin irritations.

Determinate inflorescence (centrifugal inflorescence): A general designation for an inflorescence in which the central or terminal flower is the first flower to open (see also *indeterminate inflorescence*), and the direction of anthesis (order of bloom) thus is from the inside outward.

Diaphoretic: Stimulates perspiration.

Diarrhea: Frequent and watery stool.

Dichasium: Basically, a cymelike inflorescence (see *cyme*).

Dicots (dicotyledons): Dicotyledonous plants constitute one of the two great groups of angiosperms (flowering plants); dicots are characterized by the presence of two seed leaves (cotyledons) per embryo (in the seed) and correlated characteristics of flower, leaf, and stem, distinguishing them as a group from the monocots (see Chapter 8 for a fuller explanation).

Dioecious: Refers to plants with unisexual flowers, the male flowers being borne on one plant and the female flowers on another.

Disc flower (disc floret): A type of usually small, radially symmetrical flower often found in the headlike inflorescences of members of the sunflower family.

Dissemination: Term referring to the dispersal of seeds, fruits, and even vegetative parts of plants and the various mechanisms pertaining thereto.

Diuretic: Increases urination (urine production).

Dropsy: Congestive heart failure, resulting in fluid accumulation (especially in the extremities).

Drupe: A type of simple, fleshy fruit in which the inner fruit wall (endocarp) constitutes a hard stone containing the seed or seeds; for example, a peach (the pit of the peach is the stone or hardened inner pericarp).

Dyspepsia: Indigestion, heartburn.

Dyspnea: Labored breathing or respiration.

Eclectic medicine: A largely plant centered medical movement of the mid- to late nineteenth century focusing on drug variety and eventually on methods of drug extraction and purification.

Eczema: Skin inflammation often due to nerve irritation; more generally, a rash.

Edema: Swelling due to fluid accumulation.

Emetic: Promotes vomiting.

Emmenagogue: Effects menstrual flow.

Emollient: A soothing agent, that is, a demulcent.

Endocarp: An inner, often hardened part of the pericarp (fruit wall) of certain types of fruits (drupes); the stone or pit of a peach is the indurated (boney) endocarp.

Enervate: To eliminate the nerve supply to a body organ or part (such as muscles) either chemically or by nerve removal.

Enteritis: See *gastroenteritis.*

Entire: A leaf margin (or other structure) that is smooth and even, not toothed or lobed.

Entomophilous: Insect pollinated.

Enzymes: Proteins that act as catalysts for biochemical reactions (reactions taking place within the living cell).

Epigynous flower: A flower with an inferior or apparently inferior ovary; for example, the flower of a wild carrot.

Ergotism: Poisoning due to the ergot fungus, resulting in a possible variety of symptoms (including hallucinations and gangrene).

Erythrocytes: Red blood cells.

Essential oils: Typically, rather simple terpenoid (see definition) compounds, found for example in a number of members of the mint family.

Eukaryotic cells: Those of plants, animals, and fungi. Cells that have definitive, organized nuclei (contrast prokaryotic cells).

Even-pinnate: Said of a pinnately compound leaf possessing an even number of leaflets (6, 8, 12, and so on); such a leaf would often not possess a clearly terminal leaflet.

Excretion: Elimination of waste substances from cells or from the body.

Exocarp: In certain fleshy fruits (for example, the peach) the outermost portion of the pericarp or fruit wall is differentiated as a skin or covering; this skin is the exocarp.

Expectorant: Promotes ejection of phlegm or mucus from the chest (respiratory passages).

Fairy ring: Arrangement of mushrooms of the same species in a circle. The fruiting bodies (spore-producing organs) appear at the edge of an underground, radially growing mycelium (see definition).

Febrifuge: Aids in the reduction of fever.

Fertilization: Generally, the union of sex cells. In angiosperms (flowering plants), double fertilization occurs in which one sperm from a pollen grain eventually fuses with the plant egg cell (in the ovule) and another sperm fuses with an additional cell (possibly resulting in endosperm development). The phenomenon of double fertilization is unique to angiosperms.

Filament: The slender, stalklike portion of a stamen; the anther of a stamen is characteristically attached to the distal end of the filament.

Flaccid: Limp, soft, and weak. Not firm or turgid.

Flatulence: Intestinal gas.

Flora: Descriptive treatment of the plants of a particular area or region.

Floral: Relating to flowers or flower parts.

Floral cup or tube: See *hypanthium*.

Floret: Term for the flowers (and associated small bracts) of members of the grass family and of the sunflower family.

Flower: The sexual (technically, sporogenous) reproductive organ of flowering plants (angiosperms). Flowers contain spore-producing structures (stamens and pistil) and usually also accessory, sterile structures (petals and sepals); they may be interpreted as specially modified branches, bearing appendages interpretable as modified leaves.

Follicle: A type of dry, dehiscent fruit derived from a simple pistil; in contrast to legumes, follicles dehisce along one side only; for example, the fruit of milkweeds.

Fruit: A ripened ovary, or in some cases a group of ripened ovaries collectively, plus any associated structures that may be present.

Gastroenteritis: Inflammation of the stomach and intestines.

Gastrointestinal: Pertaining to the digestive tract, especially the stomach and intestines.

Genin: Aglycone.

Gestation: The interval of pregnancy.

Glabrous: Lacking hairs or trichomes; bald.

Glaucoma: Condition resulting in increased fluid pressure within the eyeball.

Glycogen: The typical polysaccharide storage product in animals and fungi; chemically similar to starch, glycogen is sometimes referred to as animal starch.

Glycoside: A two-parted (compound) molecule in which a potentially physiologically active molecule (or molecules), the aglycone (the nonsugar component), variable as to type, is attached to a sugar molecule (or molecules). A number of categories of glycosides exist, including steroidal glycosides such as cardiac glycosides and saponins.

Grain: See *caryopsis*.

Gram stain: A method of differentially staining the cell walls or cell coats of bacteria for purposes of classification (that is, gram positive versus gram negative bacteria).

Gymnosperms: The nonflowering seed plants; gymnosperms do not produce fruit (in contrast to angiosperms); conifers (cone-bearing trees) constitute a significant group of gymnosperms.

Hallucinogen: Substance capable of inducing visual (or in some cases auditory) distortions; that is, sensory perceptions that do not exist.

Hay fever: Respiratory allergy, frequently due to plant substances or microstructures such as pollen.

Head: A cluster of small, sessile flowers, the whole sometimes resembling a larger, single flower; heads (or capitula) are characteristic inflorescences of members of the sunflower family.

Hemagglutination: The sticking together or clumping of red blood cells; this may be induced by certain types of plant proteins known as lectins (see definition).

Hemolytic: Agent causing a rupturing of blood cells.

Hemorrhoid: Dilated and often protruding blood vessels around the anus.

Hemostatic: Cable of stopping bleeding.

Hepatic: Refers to the liver.

Herbaceous: Refers to plants that are relatively soft (and usually relatively small) and nonwoody.

Herbology: The use of plants in the treatment of disease and discomfort, especially in folk medicine.

Heroic medicine: Often extreme medications and practices utilized by allopathic physicians (see definition) in former centuries, such as bleeding, blistering, and the use of strong mineral toxins.

Heterotrophs: Organisms that obtain nutrition from ingestion or absorption of food and that are incapable of making their own food, as are plants (autotrophs).

Homeopathy: A medical practice (medical movement) of the nineteenth and early twentieth centuries focusing on plants or plant products or extracts; homeopathic physicians believed that a small dose of a given substance would cure symptoms (or illness) similar to those induced in a healthy person by a much larger dose of that same substance.

Humors: Body fluids.

Hydrazine: A corrosive, ammonium-containing base.

Hydrogogue: An agent effective in eliminating excess internal water (fluid) accumulation from the body.

Hypanthium: A cuplike or tubelike structure, also called a floral cup or floral tube, found subtending or surrounding the ovary of certain types of flowers (for example, perigynous flowers, such as those of cherry trees).

Hypertensive: Increases blood pressure.

Hypha (plural, hyphae): The filamentous, often branched, growth unit of a fungus.

Hypogynous flower: Flower in which the ovary is superior; that is, the other floral parts (sepals, petals, and stamens) attach to the receptacle of the flower below the point of attachment of the ovary base; for example, tomato flowers, flowers of St. John's wort.

Hypotensive: Reduces blood pressure.

Immune response: The reaction of the body, through the activity of types of white blood cells (including lymphocytes) and/or by means of antibody production, to the introduction of foreign substances (antigens, especially proteins). This constitutes the basis of disease resistance.

Immunoadjuvant: A compound that enhances antibody production without acting as an antigen itself.

Indehiscent: Not splitting open; said of fruits that have no special anatomical mechanism by which to open at maturity.

Indeterminate inflorescence (centripetal inflorescence): A general designation for an inflorescence in which the central or terminal flower is the last to open and, consequently, the direction of anthesis (order of bloom) is from the outside inward (or from the bottom up); in general, indeterminate inflorescences are capable of more elongation than determinate inflorescences (see definition).

Inferior ovary: Condition in which other floral parts (sepals, petals, and stamens) are or appear to be attached to or near the top of the ovary of a flower (as opposed to below the ovary); for example, flowers of wild carrot and of apple trees.

Inflorescence: The arrangement or grouping pattern of flowers on a plant (or on a branch); the collective pattern of all the flowers.

Ingestion: The intake of substances or materials (usually food) orally; that is, eating.

Innervation: The nerve supply of (nerve terminations in) a body component, such as musculature; also, nerve stimulation of body components, as of various muscles.

Lacrimatory: Pertaining to the secretion and shedding of tears.

Lamina: The flattened, expanded, sheetlike portion of a leaf; the blade.

Lathyrism: Lameness, skeletal deformity, possible paralysis, and perhaps other symptoms resulting from ingestion of seeds of various species of the plant genus *Lathyrus*, a member of the legume family.

Lavage: The therapeutic washing out or cleansing of a cavity (as in gastric lavage) to remove unwanted substances, such as toxins.

Laxative: Relieves constipation.

Lectins: Certain plant proteins (often from seeds) capable of causing agglutination (clumping) of red blood cells. Some lectins are also capable of stimulating types of white blood cells to divide; that is, they act as mitogens (see definition).

Legume: A type of dry, dehiscent fruit, arising from a simple pistil, in which the lines of dehiscence (opening) occur on two opposite margins of the fruit; legume fruit is characteristic of the pea (or legume) family. Members of this family are often called legumes.

Leucocytes: White blood cells.

Lipids: Substances classified generally as fats or oils; also sterols.

Lobes: Indentations along the margin of a leaf or other structure that are deeper (larger) than teeth (the distinction between lobes and teeth is subjective).

Lymphocytes: A category of nongranular leucocytes (white blood cells); lymphocytes are present in lymphatic vessels, in the bloodstream, and in connective tissue; types of lymphocytes (B and T cells) are highly significant in immunity.

Lyrate: Lyre shaped; more specifically, said of a leaf that is pinnately lobed, the lower lobes small, but with a larger rounded terminal portion (rounded terminal lobe).

Lysis: Rupturing or bursting, as of blood cells under certain conditions.

Meiosis: A specific type of cell division in which the chromosome number is reduced by one-half, usually resulting in sex cells or spores.

Mesocarp: In certain fleshy fruits (for example, peach), the pericarp (fruit wall) may be subdivided into an outer skin, a middle portion or flesh, and an inner hardened part, the stone. The mesocarp or mid-wall constitutes the fleshy portion.

Metabolism: The sum of all the biochemical (and biophysical) processes that occur in an organism; metabolism may be broadly subdivided into assimilative processes (anabolism) and disintegrative processes (catabolism). Another convenient though clearly imperfect way of subdividing metabolism is into those processes that are life sustaining (primary metabolism) versus those that seemingly are not (secondary metabolism).

Metabolites: Products of metabolism; however, in general usage the term metabolite has come to pertain to any product, entrant, or component molecule involved in any type of metabolic process.

Mithridate: An antidote.

Mitogen: An agent promoting mitosis or mitotic activity; certain plant lectins (see definition) may act in this fashion, as upon types of white blood cells.

Mitosis (mitotic activity): Division of the cell's nucleus; in mitosis (typical somatic or vegetative cell division), in contrast to meiosis, the full chromosome number of an organism is maintained in each cell.

Mold: General term for rapidly growing hyphal fungi that produce proliferous, wooly-appearing growth on and in substrates.

Monocots (monocotyledons): Monocotyledonous plants constitute the group of angiosperms (flowering plants) other than dicots or dicotyledonous plants (see definition). Monocot seed embryos possess a single cotyledon; additionally, a number of correlated characteristics distinguish monocots from dicots (see Chapter 8).

Monoecious: Plants with unisexual flowers; however, male and female flowers occur on the same plant (variously widely separated, as on different branches, or close together).

Multiple fruit: A compound fruit derived from the ovaries of a number of different flowers; for example, mulberry fruit.

Mutagenic: Inducing genetic mutations, that is, change or changes in the genetic code; some mutagenic agents result in birth defects (see teratogen).

Mycelium: An assemblage of hyphae (see definition) visible to the unaided eye. The mycelium growing underground is what gives rise to the fruiting body (spore-producing organ) of a fungus, such as a mushroom.

Mycetismus: Poisoning from eating fleshy fungi, such as types of toxic mushrooms.

Mycotoxicosis: Poisoning from consumption of food contaminated with toxic fungi or their toxic metabolites, as that contaminated with certain types of molds that produce toxins.

Mydriatic: Causes the pupil of the eye to dilate.

Myotic: Causes the pupil of the eye to contract.

Narcotic: Pain relieving and sleep inducing through depressant activity on central nervous system; sedative.

Natural product drugs: Those coming directly from plants (or animals), unaltered except by extraction procedures.

Necrotic: Refers to tissues that are dead.

Neoplasm: New and unwanted or abnormal growth of tissue, as in cancerous tumors.

Nephrotoxin: A substance that damages the kidney, the kidney being the major site of its toxic action.

Nervine: Agent that calms a nervous condition; a relaxant.

Node: Position on the stem from which leaves arise; the term node is also used in connection with certain structures in the nervous system and lymphatic system of an animal or a human being.

Odd-pinnate: Said of a pinnately compound leaf possessing an odd number of leaflets (7, 9, 13, and so on); such a leaf would typically possess a terminal leaflet.

Opposite leaves: Two leaves per node, the point of origin of one leaf of the pair being 180 degrees around the stem circumference with respect to the other.

Ovary: The lower, often enlarged portion of a pistil; the ovary, containing structures (ovules) that form seeds, will typically develop into a fruit.

Ovule: Immature (unfertilized) seeds, contained within the ovary; the egg cell develops inside the ovule.

Oxytocic: Promoting or accelerating childbirth.

Palmately compound: A compound leaf in which the leaflets arise from the end of the petiole like the fingers of a hand; also called digitately compound.

Panacea: A cure-all; an agent allegedly useful in treating virtually any sort of illness or disease.

Panicle: A branched (usually alternately branched), typically elongated, pyramidal, indeterminate inflorescence.

Paramunity: Temporary defense against disease effected by stimulation of the body's immune system.

Parasympathetic system. Part of the autonomic nervous system (see definition); among other functions, stimulation of parasympathetic nerves generally results in slowing of the heartbeat (and lowering of blood pressure) as well as contraction of the pupil of the eye; for contrast, see *sympathetic system*.

Paroxism: A sudden, intense recurrence of disease symptoms; for example, periodic malarial fevers.

Parturition: Childbirth.

Pedicel: The stalk of an individual flower.

Peduncle: A common flowering stalk; that is, one from which two or more flowers (pedicels) arise.

Peptide bond: The carbon to nitrogen bond formed when one amino acid joins to another (acid end to base end), as in the formation of polypeptides and proteins.

Perennial: Said of plants that live an indefinite number of years (but more than two) due to the presence of overwintering stems and buds. If the overwintering stem is underground (for example, a rhizome) and the aboveground stems are relatively small and soft, the plant would be termed a herbaceous perennial, as opposed to a woody perennial.

Perianth: A collective term for the calyx and corolla of a flower or for either if the other is missing.

Pericarp: The fruit wall; the ripened ovary wall.

Perigynous flower: Flower with a superior ovary, as in a hypogynous flower; however, in a perigynous flower the ovary is subtended by, and sometimes surrounded by (but not attached to), a hypanthium or floral tube to which the other floral parts (sepals, petals, and stamens) are in turn attached.

Petal: Of the four basic parts (or whorls) of a typical flower (sepals, petals, stamens, and pistil) attached to the receptacle, the petals are next to outermost or lowermost (the sepals being outermost or lowermost); the petals, like the sepals, are leaflike; however, the petals are often more colorful and attractive, and perhaps more ephemeral, and are frequently involved in the attraction of insects during pollination.

Petiole: The stalk of a leaf.

Pharmacognosy: The study of natural or natural product drugs and their properties; plant drugs constitute the major category of natural drugs.

Pharmacology: The study of drugs (natural and synthetic) and their actions and effects on living organisms.

Pharmacy: The methods and technology of formal and legal drug dispensing.

Phenolics: Aromatic alcohols; more technically, substances the molecules of which are characterized by hydroxylated, aromatic (benzene) ring structure; a number of plant resins or resinoids are phenolic types of molecules; for example, urushiol from poison ivy.

Phlebotomy: Bleeding practices; the practice of extracting blood (sometimes in sizable quantities) to "remove" disease.

Photodermatitis: Skin inflammation resulting from an increased sensitivity to sunlight; often plant induced.

Phytotoxin: Generally, any toxin from a plant could be called a phytotoxin. However, the term was traditionally applied more specifically to toxic plant proteins.

Pinnately compound: A compound leaf in which the leaflets are more or less evenly placed along both sides of the stalk of the leaf (the stalk beyond the end of the petiole being called the rachis); that is, feather-compound, the origin points of the leaflets resembling the branching pattern of a feather.

Pistil: The female part of the flower; typically composed of the stigma, style, and ovary; in strictly technical terms, the pistil is a spore-producing rather than a sex-cell-producing structure.

Placebo: An inert or inactive substance that, if taken as medicine, provides psychological relief, that is, is believed by the patient to be of benefit.

Placenta: The part or parts of the interior wall of a flower's ovary where the ovules (immature seeds) are borne.

Plankton: Floating microorganisms (types of algae, protozoa, and the like) in bodies of water such as lakes or oceans.

Pollen: Produced in anthers of flowers of angiosperms and comparable structures of cone-bearing trees, pollen grains are cells containing sperm which may eventually fertilize the plant egg cell. Pollen of certain species of plants, for example, ragweeds, is significantly involved in the development of respiratory allergy (hay fever).

Pollen rain: Significant quantities of pollen present in the air at certain times of the year, for example, late summer.

Pollination: The transfer of pollen from the anther of the stamen to the stigma of the pistil; pollination is commonly accomplished by wind or by various animal vectors (especially insects). Pollination and fertilization are not the same thing (see *fertilization*). Pollination is, in fact, prerequisite to fertilization.

Polymer: A compound composed of many repeating units, that is, of many, usually similar, smaller molecules joined together.

Polypeptides: Similar to proteins, but smaller molecules. Polypeptides are commonly composed of between five and ten amino acids per molecule, not hundreds or thousands, as are proteins. Cyclic polypeptides (cyclopeptides) are significant toxic compounds produced by certain types of fungi.

Polysaccharides: Carbohydrate polymers composed usually of many simple sugars (or, more technically, their residues after elimination of water), such as glucose, joined together; for example, starch, cellulose, and glycogen.

Pome: A type of simple, fleshy fruit in which a structure other than the ovary wall (in this case the hypanthium) makes a substantial contribution to the fleshy structure of the mature fruit; for example, an apple. Because of the largely nonovary origin of the flesh of an apple, it constitutes an example of an accessory fruit (see definition).

Prokaryotic cells: Those of bacteria. Cells that do not possess definite organized nuclei.

Proteinaceous substances: Types of molecules composed of or derived from amino acids. Categories of proteinaceous molecules include proteins, polypeptides, and amines.

Proteins: Macromolecules composed of hundreds or thousands of individual amino acids.

Proteolytic: Causes the degradation or breakdown of proteins.

Psychoactive: Mind altering.

Pubescent: Hairy. Technically, hairs of plants are called trichomes.

Purgative: A cathartic or strong laxative.

Raceme: An elongated, unbranched inflorescence, the pediceled flowers being borne, usually alternately, along the one main axis.

Rachis: The portion of the leafstalk of a pinnately compound leaf beyond the end of the petiole.

Raphides: Sharp, needlelike crystals of calcium oxalate (the calcium salt of oxalic acid), present, for example, in leaf tissue of dumbcane (*Dieffenbachia*).

Ray flower (ray floret): A type of bilaterally symmetrical flower often found in headlike inflorescences of various members of the sunflower family.

Receptacle: Small, thimblelike structure to which the various parts (appendages) of a flower attach. If the flower has a stalk (pedicel), the receptacle may be construed as the distal, expanded tip of the stalk.

Regular: Said of flowers that are actinomorphic or radially symmetrical (see *actinomorphic*).

Renal: Refers to the kidney or to kidney function.

Resins: A catchall term for a variety of amorphous, sometimes semisolid, perhaps gummy substances from plants. A number of significant resinous plant substances are in actuality types of phenolic molecules (for example, resin from the marijuana plant and from poison ivy).

Respiratory: Refers to the lungs, bronchial passages, and nasal passages, that is, to the respiratory system.

Rhinitis: Inflammation of the nasal passages.

Rhizome: A horizontally elongated, underground stem; rhizomes, or other types of smallish, overwintering, underground stems, are common features of herbaceous perennial plants.

Rodenticide: A rodent poison or, more specifically, a rat poison.

Ruminant: Cloven-hoofed, cud-chewing herbivorous mammals, such as cattle; ruminants characteristically possess four-chambered stomachs, the first chamber being known as the rumen.

Salverform: Trumpet shaped.

Samara: An indehiscent, dry, winged fruit; for example, the samaras of ash trees.

Sapogenin: The steroidal aglycone of a saponin glycoside.

Saponin (sapogenic glycoside): A type of steroidal glycoside, in this case not possessive of special cardioactivity; thus, a category of steroid glycosides other than cardiac glycosides.

Scape: A leafless flowering stalk of certain herbaceous flowering plants (for example, bloodroot) arising at ground level.

Scoliosis: Skeletal (spinal) deformity.

Secondary compounds: Natural product chemicals (often produced by plants) that are not considered essential to typical life-sustaining metabolism, that is, to primary metabolism (of a plant or animal). Several categories of secondary compounds, for example, alkaloids, are significant for their physiological activity when introduced into an animal system (that is, into an animal's primary metabolism).

Secretion: A substance produced by the body of an animal or plant for use in the body; secretions are generally associated with glandular organs or structures.

Sedative: A relaxing or perhaps sleep-inducing agent.

Seed: A ripened or matured ovule; consists of a covering (seed coat), an embryo (the immature plant), and in some cases endosperm or nutritive tissue.

Sepal: The outermost (lowermost) and usually most apparently leaflike of the four basic types of parts or appendages of a flower (see *petal*); sepals are usually smallish structures and, as opposed to petals, are typically green or greenish.

Serrate: Leaf margin with pointed or acute teeth (saw-toothed).

Sessile: Said of a structure (for example, flower or leaf) that is not stalked.

Simple fruit: One derived from a single pistil or, more specifically, a single ovary; the ovary (pistil) itself may be simple or compound.

Simple leaf: One in which the blade is not divided into separate leaflets; the blade may nonetheless be toothed or lobed.

Simple pistil: One composed of but a single carpel.

Spadix: Fleshy, spikelike inflorescence of aroids.

Spathe: Hoodlike bract surrounding the spadix in aroids.

Species: A species is difficult to define; however, it may generally be regarded as an interbreeding population group.

Specific drugs: Drugs of known (specified) chemical contents; that is, those with precise ingredients; refined natural product drugs.

Specific epithet: The second half of the name of a species; the epithet follows the genus name in completing the species name. For example in the scientific species name for poison ivy, *Rhus radicans*, *Rhus* is the genus name and *radicans* is the epithet.

Spike: Elongated, often unbranched, indeterminate inflorescence in which the flowers are sessile upon the main axis.

Spore: Unicellular or few-celled structure functioning in the dispersal and reproduction of an organism; fungi produce many different types of spores, such as ascospores, basidiospores, and conidia.

Stamen: The male part of a flower; a stamen typically consists of an anther and a filament; technically, a stamen is a spore-producing (rather than sex-cell-producing) organ.

Starch: The typical carbohydrate reserve food of plants; starch is composed of many polymerized glucose molecule residues.

Steroids: Steroids are triterpenoid derivatives. Technically, all have a characteristic sterane (four-ringed) structure. Steroids encompass a variety of compounds, including sex (and other) hormones, D vitamins, and certain molecules in plants such as the aglycones of cardiac glycosides and saponins.

Stigma: The pollen-receptive surface of a pistil; typically, the stigma is the somewhat expanded tip of the style.

Stipules: Small, leaflike flaps of tissue sometimes present at the point of union between the leaf base (petiole base) and the stem.

Stomachic: A substance that, when ingested, improves the condition of the stomach, making it stronger and improving digestion.

Style: The usually slender, necklike portion of a pistil; the style forms a connection between stigma and ovary.

Styptic: Useful in the control of bleeding; astringent.

Superior ovary: Situation in a flower in which the ovary is the uppermost structure (attachment-wise) on the receptacle; that is, the other floral parts (stamens, petals, sepals) attach, one way or another, to the receptacle below the point of attachment of the ovary base.

Sympathetic system: Part of the autonomic nervous system; in contrast to the parasympathetic system (see definition), stimulation of sympathetic nerves generally results (among other effects) in an acceleration of the heartbeat (and a concomitant rise in blood pressure), along with dilation of the pupil of the eye.

Syndrome: A group of symptoms that, collectively, characterizes a particular abnormal condition or illness.

Synthetic drugs: Chemically altered or composed drugs; that is, those generated in the laboratory (manufactured).

Tachycardia: A fast rate of heartbeat.

Taenifuge: A compound that causes worms to flee a system (see *vermifuge*).

Taxon: A taxonomic category of any rank; for example, a species, genus, or family.

Taxonomic key: A series of written statements providing clues to the identification of organisms.

Taxonomy: The science of classification.

Teeth: Small, often regular indentations in the leaf margin. The ultimate distinction between teeth and lobes is subjective.

Tendrils: Slender, twining or clasping, modified branchlets or foliar structures that contribute to the climbing capabilities of certain vines or vinelike plants.

Teratogen: A substance (chemical agent) inducing potentially severe, anatomical birth defects; teratogenic agents are one category of mutagenic agents, that is, those inducing deformity in the fetus.

Ternately compound: Said of a leaf that is divided into three leaflets or a multiple thereof.

Terpenoids: Chemically, terpenoids are derivatives of a molecule known as isoprene (that is, composed of a varying number of isoprene subunits). Included under terpenoids are a wide variety of substances, ranging from simple (mono-terpenoid) molecules, such as the essential oils of mints, to complex triterpenoid derivatives, such as steroids.

Thomsonian medicine: A system of medicine originated in the early nineteenth century (by Samuel Thomson) based on the alleged cure-all plant *Lobelia*.

Tonic: A stimulant or substance that is invigorating if consumed.

Toxemia: Poisoning due to products of bacterial metabolism.

Toxicosis: A condition of illness or disease developed as a consequence of poisoning.

Toxigenic: Capable of producing a toxic material; the toxic substance may be within a plant or fungus or released by the organism into a substrate.

Trichomes: Plant hairs. Unlike animal hairs (which are composed of strands of dead protein), plant hairs commonly are living, cellular structures.

Umbel: An inflorescence in which the flower pedicels are of generally similar length and arise from the peduncle at approximately the same point; such an inflorescence may indeed have an umbrellalike contour; umbels or compound umbels are a characteristic feature of the carrot family.

Vasoactive: Substances active on the cardiovascular system; particularly substances that dilate or contract blood vessels, thereby altering blood pressure.

Vermifuge: A worm medicine.

Vesicant: Causes blistering of the skin.

Whorl: Three or more parts arranged in a circle; for example, three or more leaves occurring at (spaced around) one stem node.

Wort: Word of Anglo-Saxon origin meaning the equivalent of herbaceous plant.

Zygomorphic: Term for a flower that is not regular or actinomorphic (see definition), that is, not radially symmetrical. Bilateral symmetry is the most common category of zygomorphy; in bilateral symmetry, only one projected plane divides the flower into equal halves.

Index